Other Books by Carole Hyatt

The Woman's Selling Game
Women and Work: Honest Answers to Real Questions
When Smart People Fail (with coauthor Linda Gottlieb)

How to Master Career Change and Find the Work That's Right for You

SIMON AND SCHUSTER
New York London Toronto
Sydney Tokyo Singapore

SHIFTING GEARS

Carole Hyatt

Simon and Schuster
Simon & Schuster Building
Rockefeller Center
1230 Avenue of the Americas
New York, New York 10020

Designed by Nina D'Amario/Levavi & Levavi
Manufactured in the United States of America

10 9 8 7 6 5 4 3 2 1

Library of Congress Cataloging in Publication Data
Hyatt, Carole.
Shifting gears / Carole Hyatt.
p. cm.
Includes index.
1. Career changes. 2. Employees—Interviews. I. Title.
HF5384.H93 1990 90-38063
650.14—dc20 CIP

ISBN 0-671-67311-4

To Ariel Hyatt
As she shifts gears from high school teenager
to young woman in college.

For her assistance, creativity, and professionalism in the preparation of this book, I want to thank my collaborator, Connie deSwaan.

For moving fearlessly through the life and times of this book and for his editorial insights, many thanks to my agent, Al Lowman.

To Barbara Caplan, Randy Sher, and Susan Bloxsom for their assistance in preparatory research and arranging focus group sessions.

To my mother, Shirley Schwartz, for her eagle eye and expert newspaper clipping service.

To my check-in support group who get me going: my husband Gordon, who heads the group; Elaina Zuker, Sonya Hamlin, Robert Meola, Wendy Synder, Charles Schwartz, Dory Previn, Beverly Kievman, Judy Katz, Rhoda Lerman, and Virginia Kiser.

My appreciation goes to the hundreds of people across the country who generously shared their lives and experiences, many of them during tumultuous times. Without their contributions this book would not be possible. Many have permitted the use of their names; for others who so requested it, their names, identifying characteristics, and location have been changed to protect their privacy. Although such personally identifying details may have been altered, the hearts of the stories about career change are *all* authentic.

Security is mostly superstition. It does not exist in nature nor do children of men as a whole experience it. Avoiding danger is no safer in the long run than outright exposure. Life is either a daring adventure, or nothing.

Helen Keller

CONTENTS

INTRODUCTION **11**

1 THE GLOBAL VILLAGE: The Urge to Merge and Why You're Shifting Gears **21**

2 UNDERSTANDING YOUR STYLE: What's Your M.O.? **46**

3 ANATOMY OF CHANGE: The Trigger **79**

4 ANATOMY OF CHANGE: Caught in a Downtrend—Seven Reasons Why You Get Stuck **106**

5 A CRASH COURSE IN CHANGE **145**

6 SORTING OUT I: Following Your Own Star **159**

7 SORTING OUT II: Seven Ways to Define a Career Path **187**

8 STARTING OVER AND SELLING YOURSELF **211**

9 OPPORTUNITIES AND ENTREPRENEURSHIP **231**

EPILOGUE **254**

APPENDIX **259**

INDEX **264**

INTRODUCTION

Welcome to America's *fastest growing* club: The Club for Shifting Gears.

Each day, an astonishing 80,000 new members are admitted to The Club—and you may be among them. You don't need connections to join, and if you're already in transition between jobs, you have already paid your dues.

Joining this club is either involuntary or a matter of choice. Since the *average* member joins five or six times over a lifetime, many members are not surprised to find themselves *once again* on its rolls. Others who once believed faithfully in continuity, loyalty, and an ongoing career, are shocked to find themselves card-carrying members of The Club, in spite of their convictions. In the past, more women than men joined The Club, but men are now shifting gears more frequently and in larger numbers.

If you are not already in transition between jobs, but are *considering a change,* congratulations—you too are a member of The Club. Wherever you may be standing, career change is now a predominant issue in your life. How do I know?

If you have picked up this book, it's not an accident. The title said something meaningful to you about your own life at this point. You may be *shifting gears* and the following is happening to you:

- You are caught somewhere between frustration and anger because you don't know *how* to take the first step toward making a wise career decision.
- You are a casualty of reorganization—a merger, expansion or diversification, relocation or financial setback—and you are in that sensitive, vulnerable stage of transition between jobs.
- You've been in one profession for a long time, but now you have a compelling reason to pursue another career, but you feel *stuck*—wavering in your confidence. You're unsure about taking the first step down a new "path with a heart."
- You've never been quite sure of what you really want to do. Intuitively you know you should make the effort to define yourself, but you don't know where to look for information or guidance and what questions to ask. In some cases, you were never really required to test yourself fully.
- You have an excellent stockpile of *skills,* but you have lost your passion for the work you're in now. Or, you want to figure out how to utilize these skills to cross over into a new field.

When you are a member of The Club for Shifting Gears, you have experienced one or all of these problems at some time in your career. If you look back, you will recall how some shifts went smoothly—like a well-tuned engine that turned over instantly, even defying the cold. Then there were the disappointments—the transitions between jobs when the gears stuck, the engine rattled and sputtered, and you ran out of gas.

Shifting Gears is about getting back in that stalled car and making it run again—better than ever. It's about how members of The Club, through instinct or outside guidance, found their way through the difficult transition periods. *Shifting Gears* is also about helping *you* reignite a passion for the work you choose.

I hope *Shifting Gears* will make the vulnerable transition periods easier for you.

I know these feelings firsthand.

I've also been a member of The Club.

DEMYSTIFYING CAREER CHANGE

I ran a company several years ago with a partner who good-naturedly described us as "women who could get from here to there." Whatever else, we followed through. In 1982, we projected a "good" year for us—a million dollars in volume. This was the sum we divined would magically put our market research company on a higher plane and redefine success for us. We made our million, but since economics are deceiving, our million served the opposite of our intentions.

What happened? Our collective experience in the business world should have accounted for more, but apparently we proved Edmund Burke's cryptic warning that "you can never plan the future by the past." The neat line of profit-loss balances sagged under the weight of overlooked details: overhead and taxes. To our surprise, success was not only fleet footed, it leaped into the unknown. We watched it go. We weren't ahead at all, our accountant told us, but behind.

To reach our million-dollar volume and do business effectively we required larger office space, additional employeès, a better but more complicated telephone system, plus all the usual incidentals of running an office. We listened to the figures; our million was actually worth half that! To reach our original goal, we were advised to think *two* million dollars.

My own experience in business points to a number of issues affecting all of us now: *Things rarely turn out as expected,* even with the most credible professional goals. In a changing world, there are a fickle economy and the realities of the marketplace. For me and my partner, that million-dollar "magic number" was meant to solve a few problems, but life doesn't conform to one's dreams. The "magic number" proved we could expand successfully, but it also taught us that the outcome of goals may shift unexpectedly.

One thing you can count on: The future you're certain of is often uncertain.

We still had a successful business, our skills, and our passion for what we were doing. But a few factors had to change to achieve the continued success we planned for: the *definition* of our goal and the *adaptive action* we would need to take to suit the demands of the time.

If you are reading this book, you are probably dealing with similar surprise events or ongoing anxiety about either (1) what to do about your future, or (2) how to summon the courage to face it.

Change, not an easy companion to travel with, has a lot to teach us along the way. Dealing with it is not a simple matter, and you are not alone in puzzling it through. Whether you quit or are fired—or suffer a setback in your own business as I did—some of you will be closing out options while others will be meeting unexpected opportunities.

CAREER SHIFTS: UNCOVERING THE COMMON LINKS

For most of us, intricately overlapping layers of skill, self-esteem, emotion, and a measure of power make up the work day. When you are in a state of transition, these layers dislodge and pull apart—like subterranean rock shelves during an earthquake—and you are set temporarily off balance. Your equilibrium is upset, in part, by the tremors of self-doubt and the "unanswerable" questions that commonly haunt many members of The Club:

- You wake up in the middle of the night, panicky. You wonder, What's next? What if you are due another loss, not a blessed change? You fear that this period will signal the start of a downward trend.
- You worry all day about ever fitting in to a company other than the "perfect" one you've just left. Then you decide a priori that the search for another perfect company/partner/job is futile, so you might as well give up any ambitions for starting over. Or should you give up?
- You have flash anxiety attacks walking down the street: What

if you never have a passion for any kind of work again? What if you just evolve into someone for whom having lunch is a reason for living? What new kind of work could you do?

• You fear you made a foolish decision by quitting/making the move that got you fired/selling your company thereby clipping the "golden threads"—a paycheck, a place to go to, and health benefits. Why didn't you have the wisdom and foresight to hang on?

I know what answering these questions is like firsthand. Many years ago, I played things safe. It sounds almost paradoxical to me now, since over these years of great growth and change for me I've shifted six times to six different careers. Early on, the transition periods between at least four of these careers were fairly painless. I segued from a brief career in the theatre into teaching, to entering the corporate world, to cofounding the above-mentioned market and social behavior research firm.

In those days, I sought *structure* and its partner, security. Before I moved from one career to the next, it had to exist in ponderable form—there was an absolute title, a job description that allowed some flexibility, coworkers, an operational address, a salary, perks. I let go of one career when the safety net of another was cast in concrete.

For more than eighteen of these years I ran the market research company with a partner, June Esserman. It was set up to mirror the order and predictability that is inherent in most mainstream businesses. In 1983, following June's sudden death, I decided to sell the company, and the form of my life changed dramatically.

I suddenly shifted from defined structure to *no* structure. And I was lost. There was no "next"—just space.

I had a sense of what I wanted, but how these wants would combine to take the shape of another career, I did not know. What I *did* want made sense to me: I wanted the freedom to pursue my many interests on a free-lance basis. I was interested in consulting, working on books, leading seminars around the world, continuing with my market research projects.

Free-lancing on a foundation of the very loosest structure was a frightening prospect to me—I had no experience improvising or living entirely by my wits. The safety net was always part of the picture for me. This forced a dilemma. I needed to establish some form, some accountability for myself. I started by replacing structure with *guidelines.* These guidelines *authenticated* my projects and set certain ground rules for helping me choose what to do next and how to proceed, such as: I would seek short-term projects that had a clear beginning, middle, and end; I would work with a partner, a team, but never alone; I didn't want to burden myself again with payrolls, employees, and office maintenance, but I could hire a part-time assistant/secretary who could work out of my apartment.

My struggle to create a *loosely structured* but smoothly running "organization" took *five years* to set up. It took many of those years to give myself permission to even run a business in such an unconventional style and another few years to come up with the idea that I could have many projects going at the same time.

It was painful building through such emotional and economic change, but each change sharpened my survival skills.

My primary goal is to uncover how *you* feel about shifting gears and to provide some of the answers that are demanded of you in this time of great change. This book will scrutinize and clarify the steps that successful people take, both internally and externally, in making a career transition decision.

WHAT THIS BOOK WILL REVEAL TO YOU

Shifting Gears speaks with the combined force of over 300 voices who have *been where you are now.* Their stories are models for you to learn from. Whether it is dealing with inevitable change or sorting out the possibilities, you will see solutions emerge for you.

Shifting Gears is not a how-to career guide, but an excursion into what people do to master transitions. You'll discover what language they use to describe decision making, how they react to the triggers that bring on change, and what motivates them to stay creative.

All the people I interviewed have gone through a notable career change. Their ages range from twenty-two to seventy-two; among them are extraordinary men and women who work in corporations or own them; they're displaced stockbrokers or onetime masters of Silicon Valley; they're performers and world-class athletes, politicians, doctors, and civil service employees; they're entrepreneurs who defied early failures or cultural dictates and built successful enterprises. They work in banks, bake cookies, make films, counsel others, work as designers, teach school, rebuild old ships, and compose popular songs.

I conducted the interviews in many cities in a number of ways: I spoke to people on a one-to-one basis by phone or in person, or they participated in one of my focused discussion groups. These groups were formed with one or two qualifiers—the common ground was general age range and general interest, rather than gender (although I led some groups of men or women only). As a curious aside, most women preferred to be interviewed by phone while most men preferred to be interviewed in their office.

A wide range of professionals generously contributed valued insights and important perspectives about the social, psychological, and practical impact of career change. The professionals I spoke to one-to-one or in focus groups were social behaviorists, psychologists and psychiatrists, human resource and outplacement specialists, career counselors practicing a variety of traditional or "new age" techniques, trend analysts, economists, futurists, computer specialists, and even one parole officer.

I tried to get a sense of the shape of things in all parts of the country, and found people who openly shared their stories with me from urban, suburban, and rural areas; economically, most were middle and upper-middle class. Racially, they included a predominance of whites with representative Asians, Blacks, and Hispanics; a few were new immigrants to America.

Everyone who was generous enough to attend these groups not only analyzed his/her personal experiences in the business world, but helped contribute a *language of change* that I developed into an "anatomy of change." This anatomy describes the key stages of transition from one point in your career to another—and it is this anatomy and how people deal with it that form this book.

The anatomy is generally made up of eight key points taking you from where you are to where you will be, or can be. It begins with:

• how the *marketplace and its various trends affect you* and why you must keep up with the world. This may lead to . . .

• the *trigger,* an event or internal resolution that kicks off the process of change for you. When this happens, you will need to . . .

• reappraise your skills and what you want from life, or *understand your style,* or modus operandi, in the marketplace. You may, at this point . . .

• *get caught in a downtrend and get struck*—you hit a point where confusion reigns and you seem unable to pull out of a funk or make what seems like a reasonable decision. Here, you can examine what you are going through in a . . .

• *crash course in change,* where I'll take a reassuring close-up look at how change affects you. Once you understand the changes taking place, you can begin to . . .

• *sort things out*—that is, define your career path, either by following your own star or seeking the assistance of counselors, mentors, or other experts. Once you know where you're going, you can more easily . . .

• *start over.* To gain confidence, I provide a number of ways to effectively sell yourself and achieve the success you most want, and to . . .

• be bolder about *pursuing opportunities,* and, if it suits you, going into your own business.

What is fascinating about the anatomy of change is that I've presented it in a linear or step form, but in real life, *change* itself is never so orderly. Instead, change is a slowly revolving spiral—looking a lot like a strand of DNA. Points representing the stages of change occur along the spiral, but they may not necessarily occur in sequence. Rather, you may skip some stages or bounce back to one point because of one accident of fate or another. Change, for you, may look like this:

Trigger
Sorting Out
Stuck

Trigger
Modus Operandi

Marketplace Information

Following Your Own Star

If you are typical, you'll go through the anatomy of change relating to work six to eight times, and each time it will be different. You'll learn more about the process as you read through the book. You'll see how others defuse preconditioned psychological responses—the ones that get you stuck in self-defeating patterns. You'll also discover how to apply effective problem-solving techniques to help break those patterns. My chief goal in this book is for you to learn from their combined experiences and share the knowledge that will inspire you in your own quest.

An especially rewarding outcome in writing this book is how the research benefited the participants in the groups I worked with. Until these groups, many people had not openly discussed their opinions or concerns about career change and had felt isolated or confused about their shaky journey through unfamiliar territory. The interaction with others who were going through similar anatomies of change was, in many cases, *liberating.*

Of the people you'll meet in these pages, the majority spoke candidly and personally about career change and the *soul of working.* Work not only means salary, security, or stability, but soul. For some, the "soul" was opportunity for creative challenge; many sought risk and growth when choosing another career while, for others, fulfillment and achievement was the answer.

No matter what their goal, they *all* told of the anxiety attached to finding the "right fit" in a career change.

We all seek security and this makes good sense. What traps us, though, is a limited view of change. Buddha said that the principal cause of human suffering is a belief in permanence. *Everything changes.* Ongoing change is inevitable, whether it's within your profession or within your soul. And paradoxically, change is the one constant in this world. It's not necessarily loss, but an onset of miraculous growth. Change can bring out the best in us.

Through crises of confidence, periods of confusion or vagueness, faltering steps forward, and finally sorting things out, nearly every person interviewed came through challenging times, shifted gears, and thrived. They moved through the demands of change with adaptability, flexibility, and a sense of humor.

Each person I spoke to added strongly to my feeling that each of us has a right to pleasure in work and deserves the opportunity to pursue it. *Doing the work you are passionately committed to is a gift.*

Doing the work you are passionately committed to is also the definition of a *career.*

A FINAL NOTE

You *must change* to keep up with a rapidly changing world. The world is no longer a matter of young and old or rich and poor. It is a world shaped by those who *adapt* to change and those who don't. As members of The Club, knowledge of this simple fact can alter your destiny.

The past tells us where we've been and what we've accomplished. Change will always derive from the past, but intentions, growth, and courage arise from a respect for the future. If any theme came up in the course of this study, it is that *everything ends,* but a belief in tomorrow restores confidence and keeps most of us going.

I believe in the basic human gifts of awareness and reason and the trenchant abilities we have to *tune into* them when change is called for. Most of all, *Shifting Gears* celebrates these gifts and offers discovery, new directions, and, hopefully, a new beginning for you.

1

THE GLOBAL VILLAGE

The Urge to Merge and Why You're Shifting Gears

This book is about the complexities of career change, but it's as much about your life and how you relate to a real and *ever-changing* world. The nature of business has been altered in the last two decades, sometimes dramatically, and it has shaken up how we define a career, even how we make decisions. Being aware of the shifts the world takes is essential if you want to keep your career on course—and get more out of life.

To shift gears now is, I believe, a healthy response—as unpredictable as the world seems to be. It's a time when the legitimacy of the work system feels like it's being put to the test. And it is doubly challenging if you are reevaluating what you want to do with your life.

Getting in touch with basic information about how the world works will help you decide the path to take. This is true if you are struggling with career dissatisfaction because of its limited growth or income potential, or if you are drawn to a new profession but are uncertain about how to proceed.

In studying *why* people shift gears, an unexpected revelation turned up: As much as we've become a *goal-oriented* society where money represents one's level of success, people are still connected to fundamental values in terms of work. They worry about the "broken promises," "job satisfaction," "belonging," and continuity as much as achievement, financial security, and the corner office.

It's a changing world, but your fundamental values need not change—you just need to understand the marketplace and how you can fit in. *Reality* and *practicality* demand you keep up with changing times and adjust your goals and game plan accordingly.

What you think about the marketplace will determine its effect on you. It's this simple. How you interpret the information, the trends, and your commitment and connection to work—and the degree to which you are willing to make adjustments rather than protect outmoded ideas—will change the course of your career.

WHO IS SHIFTING GEARS: AN OVERVIEW

Right now, 12 million people are progressively *engaged in switching* to a new career. Twelve million more are *actively planning* the change. Another 25 million are *contemplating a move* to a new profession. The Rand Corporation projects twice this number of career changes by the year 2000.

So, on the face of it, 50 million people are actively challenging the noble tradition of the single-lifetime career. By doing so, they're part of a cultural and economic movement that is redefining what it means to choose a life work—not once and for all time, but as many times as can be realistically and wisely brought about.

The way things look now, *one in five* people changes jobs *every* year—half leave involuntarily (their job was phased out or it was a performance problem) or move on voluntarily (the job was a wrong fit). Not surprisingly, the group most likely to seek job satisfaction are the "Baby Boomers," the twenty-five- to thirty-five-year-olds—in fact, they account for one-fourth to one-third of the people the Bureau of Labor Statistics found were dissatisfied with their professions.

The average person today now works at ten-and-a-half different jobs and has *three* different career changes within his/her life work. As the world changes, so does the industry style. The "old boy" networks may exist as strongly as ever, but longevity no longer makes for the most esteemed "old boy." A president of a bank once stayed for forty years, now he's in for twelve. Headhunters are currently placing CEOs for an expected *five*-year term and a bailout with a "golden parachute"—a generous retirement package. Such generally short-term thinking ripples down through the ranks. In just a decade, *six to ten* career changes over a lifetime will be a common occurrence, not a curiosity.

How we choose a career and what we have to choose from has changed enormously over the last thirty years. The 1970s and early 1980s saw a wild growth of "middle manager" positions—then *2 million* of them were fired due to restructuring of businesses rather than to performance-related problems. If you were a casualty of some degree of reorganization, you may now be shifting gears because of a merger, expansion, diversification, relocation, or financial setback. Why did this happen?

Following World War II, America realized twenty-six years of sustained productivity and prosperity until we hit a plateau in the mid-1970s. Much of the world caught up with us during this economic slowdown. As the global village grew, OPEC controls increased, American banks set up lending policies to make it easy to buy and sell businesses, global competition got fiercer, and American business began to restructure itself.

The 1970s ushered in a strong case for personal fulfillment—a period that economist Herman Kahn called "the great transition." This era was typified by changes in "social priorities, values, and tastes," Kahn said, that were *more* influential than actual resources or "gross world product in influencing productivity, growth, and supply and demand." Strong stuff.

Plumbing the "internal battles" was an acceptable aspect of management until practical survival got tougher. Self-expression on the job suddenly wasn't as critical as coping with the actual battles being waged in companies—restructuring, forced early retirement, shutdowns, and brutal competition for the plum jobs.

Then we were in the 1980s and there was the "L" word—the prospect of rumored *layoffs* hit employees hard. Billions of dollars in profits were lost, experts say, because of employee malaise and low productivity from a sense of diminishing expectations at work. People were waiting for the other shoe to drop. One survey revealed a 60 percent decrease in employee loyalty than was common five years previously.

And the bottom line prevailed.

An Employment Management Association survey revealed that about 79 percent of the companies they polled reduced their staff for *economic* reasons. Those hardest hit were in the managerial and professional ranks, even among ordinarily stable companies such as Du Pont and Eastman Kodak. More than half a million positions have been cut in a few hundred companies since 1984.

The American Management Association conducted another survey and found that 35 percent of the 398 companies they questioned had *downsized* the preceding year—*each* company eliminating an average of 150 jobs. The process would not necessarily end there: Of the companies that participated in this survey, 30 percent said they planned to cut back again.

Oklahoma executive recruiter Jean Kelly has seen a startling number of people caught in the economic ripple effect of the oil crunch downsizing who have voluntarily *downgraded* their credentials. Fired from six-figure jobs, many people, she told me, have rewritten their work histories to capture a $40,000-or-less a year job to survive in a tight market!

In response to such changes in the workplace, the number of entrepreneurs in America grew tenfold in the last twenty years. If job stability is no longer a guarantee, self-sustained business may prove to be one answer. *Intrapreneuring,* or establishing a company that is independently run but subsidized by a larger corporation—a version of a "subsidiary"—is another working arrangement.

Job titles and types of work have mushroomed to over 45,000 known listed categories, some arcane, some astonishing, some enlightening. New technology has the power to make an occupation like elevator operator nearly obsolete, but it also creates specialists to deal with growth and crises. Bruce Kraselsky, for example, is a Washington lawyer who formed the first team of *space lawyers* involved in regulatory law and counsel pertaining to space travel; the group evolved naturally out of the Challenger disaster.

Ingenuity counts.

And as America uses its resources more wisely, businesses will embrace more opportunities for women, minorities, and the elderly. Studies show that by the year 2000, *one-half* of all businesses will be owned by women. The work force will also be older by the turn of the century—"the graying of America" is already a reality. Just a decade away from the year 2000, nearly 21 percent of the American population is over fifty-five years old. Many of them will delay retirement as productivity and experience, not age, are the determining factors of who works; and of course, greater medical advances promise to prolong life. Consequently, many people are returning to the work force in post-retirement.

The World Future Society also forecasts a shorter work week—thirty-two hours will be typical. One benefit of reduced time, they predict, is that in the time you gain not working the extra hours, you will be *preparing for your next career.*

UNDERSTANDING THE MARKETPLACE

I discovered two overriding principles in my efforts to understand the marketplace. And I believe they're important to mull over as you read through this chapter:

- The word to characterize these times is "contradiction," but you need to see such contradictions as the *demands of change.*
- You are more likely to succeed if you have the dual abilities to *adapt and learn* rather than rely on the same skills transferred to a different work place.

In your career search, you'll notice that five critical factors will characterize the change in the marketplace now. While one or more will determine the career decisions you make, the factor that influences every one of them to some degree is:

• *the globalization of business* and the influences of foreign culture.

The other four are:

• the *rapidly expanding technological growth,* such as the development of sophisticated communications and information technology, like the fax machine
• *the restructuring of American business*
• *trends that bear watching,* such as work attitudes, including the "graying of America"—that is, an older work force, and
• *the wide diversity of career options* based on either the new application of existing skills or retraining and reeducation

Philosophically, work no longer need be a matter of long-term obligation from which you retire.
Let's look at each factor individually.

THE GLOBALIZATION OF BUSINESS AND THE INFLUENCES OF FOREIGN CULTURE

We're living in a global village that is shrinking—where America looks over her shoulder to see Japan and West Germany gaining speed and power, further shrinking the world as these nations claim economic territories. The "baby tigers"—the Pacific rim countries such as Korea—are also setting up economic challenges to America. In 1992, the European Common Market will undergo a significant change; Gorbachev's perestroika not only felled the Berlin Wall, but it opened up potentially vast consumer and industrial markets in Eastern European countries. All this change will have an inevitable bearing on your future in some way.

But, the omnipresent question that haunts American business now is: What is the possibility of our losing out to the Japanese? Known for their legendary productivity, the Japanese business structure reflects thousands of years of military hubris and philosophical order.

Japan mobilized from postwar devastation to world business leader in four decades and recreated itself into a formidable economic power. The Japanese people's belief in long-range planning, company loyalty, hard work, achievement, and tenacity obviously works: they leave trails of quality products, claim nine of the world's ten largest banks and concentrate on replenishing and perpetuating a skilled, educated work force. The dazzling spectacle of their buying power inspires studies on how they do it on the one hand, while Washington senators submit bills to limit foreign acquisition in America on the other.

It has also spawned the proposition that we adopt the Japanese techniques, or else be doomed to become a second-rate power by the turn of the century. How true is this?

The influence of Japanese management has wrought numerous experimental programs, ostensibly tailored for American sensibilities. "Theory Z" specifically imports from Japan the concept of "quality circles." Known in America for decades as labor management councils, quality circles are simply that—a way for labor and management to get together to discuss how to increase quality and productivity.

Japan, Germany, Great Britain, Australia, and other countries are competitors as well as *investors* in America—and employers of American labor. There are days when Sony reverberates like an emerging world power on its own.

RAPIDLY EXPANDING TECHNOLOGICAL GROWTH

If the global village is shrinking, nothing is more responsible for uniting the compound than communication and information technology. Rapidly changing technological growth and expanding global competition have probably changed American business more than any other reasons. Communications satellites, fax machines, robotics, and the simple computer chip with its astonishing memory capability that can, for example, store the *contents* of 6 million books in the Library of Congress in a five-by-seven-foot room are examples of such technology.

World markets are manipulated in what seem like random events to us. In October of 1987, a fateful computer program seemingly took control and changed Wall Street. Monetary controls are not safely contained within the borders of our fifty states, but are influenced by the global nature of finances—fluctuating one day, stable the next.

Then there are the "older" media that are stronger than ever—newspapers, radio, television. The average person sifts through ninety-four pounds of newspapers a year; the average American family watches fifty-one hours of television a week and now the Japanese are perfecting the images they will see on their exported sets: a new process fine-tunes television-picture quality to the sharpness of 35mm film. This threatens to be more than cosmetic. The Japanese process appears to be incompatible with existing American and European broadcasting equipment. This has set up another race, comparable to unraveling the mystery of the double helix in genetics, or the race for the superconductor. Unless we come up with an alternate system, the improved Japanese standard could dominate the market.

Information technology is breathtaking. Superconductors promise to change the world; supercomputers find applications in fields as diverse as aerospace and biochemistry. Engineers use them to build a better light bulb or recreate the "Big Bang" theory on the origin of the universe.

This year, business will spend nearly $100 billion on data communications services alone. As could be expected, the variety of jobs in information processing are growing rapidly. Every year, business processes 1.4 trillion pieces of paper. Computers generate mountains of data each day.

This flowering of the "Age of Information" will influence how we think, how we make choices—it will even affect our values. Strategic planner Edie Weiner describes these developments in information technology as "the locomotives of change" that are pulling us, sometimes at high speed, toward the future. The sense of power the image evokes isn't overdrawn, but an accurate one.

Technology, and particularly computer-related technology, said Secretary of Commerce C. William Verity, is expected to increase the worker's role in industry because of the *interdependence* of one job on another, and "the trend toward 'knowing' more than one job." If you have the skills, job opportunities abound in high-tech fields, from health diagnosis by computer to social science—the number of jobs in these fields is expected to increase 40 to 68 percent over the next few years.

In the Age of Information, this knowing is already evident in the numbers of people shifting gears. It also means that you should know how to get access to the kind of information you need.

THE RESTRUCTURING OF AMERICAN BUSINESS

Socioeconomic forecasters see the next decade as a time when economic freedom and political control will coexist with contrasts wide enough to jar the senses. *Forbes* magazine annually tabulates the count of American *billionaires*—and argued in 1988 that Donald Trump had *overestimated* his fortune by a billion or so—while the number of impoverished and homeless reaches shocking proportions. And there are more discrepancies as pockets of technological excellence square off against other sectors struggling along in marginal obsolescence.

Closer to home, it may be how individual company policies decide on financial strategies that determines why *you* are shifting gears today. Contradictions exist simultaneously: An emphasis on cost cutting is stressed on the one hand while an "urge to merge" buyout is poised on the other.

Some companies cut costs by selling off divisions or subsidiaries, trimming the number of employees to function with a bare-bones organizational structure, and putting some revenue back into improving product lines. Maybe your job was phased out.

At other companies, it made sense to expand and diversify rather than cut back and specialize. In some cases, that "urge to merge" pumped up stock prices but it also triggered a tidal wave of layoffs where people were shocked to find themselves caught in the jaws of a deal. Perhaps your company went under.

Corporations can file for "Chapter 11"—a declaration of bankruptcy—as one way to avoid liability suits or even break contracts with labor. The government deregulates certain businesses. Everyone feels the effects.

And each day, thousands of people gloomily debate the benefits of hanging on to a job for which they no longer have any passion, and pin down one explanation for staying in: a paycheck. Others gather momentum and take the risks to start up their own ventures.

What's the answer? What choices do you make?

There's good news amidst this seemingly impossible scale of global "schizophrenia": Inventiveness, gut instinct, the entrepreneurial spirit, and personal values are more than ever assets in a world that allows a greater range of individual choice than before.

We're not each just a "cluster of skills" out there earning a living, but people with values and goals. So many of my interviewees spoke about matching basic psychological needs to a coolly bottom-line culture. And this is another key factor in the change affecting the marketplace: the search for meaning and value in a career.

In the early 1970s, the catchphrase was that self-improvement was the curse of the single woman; but twenty years later *inattention* to personal or career growth is clearly the inevitable culprit, for anyone.

TRENDS THAT BEAR WATCHING: ATTITUDES ABOUT WORK

The marketplace as it nears the year 2000 is no high-tech version of the elves' workshop—a productive and orderly place operating out of internal loyalty, camaraderie, a good-natured skepticism about progress, "whistling while you work," and job security. This is an idealized picture of the working world, as quaint a concept as the wrist corsage, and one that doesn't quite exist in all its winsome fairness.

Change, not fairness, has always been the directional marker that business has chosen to follow. It's a hard truth to face, but it's the way it is.

Take the matter of commitment: Devoting ten, twenty, or thirty years to a career is no longer an exclusive indicator that you've made a right or wise choice. In 1958, when the average white male college graduate earned about $7,000 a year in the advertising business, such a statement about commitment would have sounded revolutionary. Consistency and continuity with an employer are still considered moral virtues, but in a world turned upside down, these qualities could become more self-limiting than commendable.

America's postwar conservatism embraced conformity, often rigorously. The standard mindset followed a neat line: either track the "one or two careers in a lifetime" path or be regarded as unstable. Job security was the motivating force and it was tied to a concept of company loyalty. If company employers upheld the unlikely conceit that they controlled the fate of their employees as well as ran a business, they also believed nothing could shake their omnipotence. Today, authoritarian management style is not as popular in private industry and now the smart manager knows how to motivate others to motivate *themselves.*

I was talking about the onetime norms of performance and behavior with Elaina Zuker, a New York management consultant and president of Success Strategies. Elaina thought that the kind of personality the corporation "asked for, acknowledged and rewarded" would have been, in most ways, "the opposite of a behavior profile of a healthy mature adult." In general, corporate heads equated leadership ability with how the person projected a sense of authority, not equanimity. To be compliant or in awe of power was built into the treads of a big wide "pyramid" called career. Rank and file populated the base, tapering to the CEO at the pinnacle. In seeking achievement, your mission was to scale the slopes. How you ascended also conformed to style. The image of climbing meant something. To succeed, you couldn't lose your footing, be tripped up, or look back. The images remain with us, but the pyramid is more or less unexcavated rubble and the "ladder" has fewer rungs, if it exists at all.

Some theorists once saw the true picture of career progression in an "egg" shape, with middle-manager ranks swelling the widest point. Now the egg is girdled in, trimmed back to an hourglass shape, reflecting the diminishing ranks of middle managers.

Edith Weiner, a topflight New York trend analyst and strategic planner, believes that the more logical shape of career development in these times is a wide, winding *spiral.* The spiral implies continuity—ongoing cycles that give it form. If a setback alters the path along the curve, you don't lose out. Rather, you get back on track—although you get on at *another point along the curve,* on another plane. "You can't unlearn what you've learned," Edie said. The sudden "consultant phenomenon" in the late 1980s illustrates how the spiral theory applies to a *real* situation.

Restructuring sent thousands of human resources and marketing people out into a business environment that could not reabsorb them. Instead, many worked as free-lance consultants. An $80,000 a year person, for example, suddenly drops to a $35,000 level, but with $80,000 expertise. They are still on the spiral, but at another point. Earnings are halved; they will have to figure out what they are willing to trade off if they have to stay at this level, or what they need to learn to get back on the spiral at another $80,000 point, or higher.

It is a matter of adapting to reality.

And corporations are trying. In the face of increasing global competition, a number of mainstream companies are incorporating counterculture programs and ideologies to stimulate employee productivity and increase profits. This transformation or "training boom," *In Search of Excellence* author Tom Peters said in an interview, is about the "madness of grasping for solutions."

But which solutions? There's a ring of urgency in seeking the answers.

For those unmoved by the aforementioned Japanese ideal of "oneness," there are many more American-made schools of thought to be called upon.

A crazy salad of "new age" approaches to business management—considered mass mind bending by its detractors—accounts for about $4 *billion* a year in corporate spending. What companies using such programs are getting for their money is open to question.

Body/mind and body/motivational programs abound. The Polaroid Company holds monthly "left brain/right brain" seminars to improve employee production and effectiveness by increasing brain function awareness. Dow Chemical, RCA, Proctor & Gamble, General Mills, Scott Paper, Boeing, and the Ford Motor Company are among a growing number of industry giants who have hired motivational gurus, or "consultants," to lead management programs.

Programs like these usually stress group cohesion and positive-thinking ideologies, and sometimes come complete with an accompanying glossary of new terms for employees.

While a large number of companies ride the trends to achieve their ultimate goals, other companies continue to search history for answers and reinvent the wheel.

YOUR OPTIONS: SHIFTING GEARS INTO A NEW PROFESSION

All these issues may set up questions for you; where are the answers? The fifth factor that influences career decisions may provide a few more clues. It is: *options,* and understanding how to use the marketplace. Let's take it step by step.

Baby boomers entered the job market in the 1970s and many are finding themselves in a career squeeze. The biggest culprit is the economic slowdown and, in some industries, even slower salary increases. As we've noted, those who are treading water in middle manager positions are competing with others of their generation for scarce promotions. People in their forties and fifties, coping with burnout or seeking a second—or sixth—career are looking for their niche in a tight, and for some, a baffling, market.

The news is not all about rising taxes and cutbacks but about *options*: there are alternatives for those who are motivated, committed, and are willing to take a risk.

Here are a few ways you can go, without going back to school:

- *choosing small business over big*
- *"extender" or service jobs*

- *intrapreneuring*
- *working at home*

CHOOSING SMALL BUSINESS OVER BIG Many experts see small businesses as the key to job creation, if not stability.

Officially, small businesses operate with less than 500 employees, still big by some standards. Most critically, small business outpaced large business by nearly 6 percent in the last few years of the 1980s. In looking for a small business in the industry of your choice, you may have to consider location. Many companies are attracted to states where costs are lower, sales opportunities are greater, tax breaks are incentives, or the area is known for a general area of specialization. For example, Silicon Valley, just south of San Francisco, is dense with computer software/hardware companies, and employment here is the fastest growing in this specialty.

In one survey, the top cities for best job growth in small business opportunities were basically in the south and southwest. Orlando, Florida, growing in tourism, finance, publishing, and agriculture has Disney World, but it is also the second most humid city in America. The other nine contenders are: Phoenix, Arizona; San Diego, California; Raleigh, North Carolina; Durham, South Carolina; Atlanta, Georgia; Las Vegas, Nevada (the *least* humid city and one that's growing in retirement communities and administrating the lowest tax bite in the United States); West Palm Beach, Florida; Austin, Texas; Washington, D.C.; and Tucson, Arizona.

Relocation is one of the most significant trends of the future. If you're shifting gears, packing may be in your schedule.

What do you need to consider about relocation? "I have a notion," Stan Bowles, a onetime advertising account executive, told me. "I sense a migration of people, like in the Depression, with hordes of people relocating across America, looking for the missed opportunities." He raised an interesting point and I asked him to explain. He said:

> My notion of the missed opportunity is that if corporate America abdicates the chance to spark people's creativity, who will? I

> know—*each of us* can. That's great if you're independent, but not if you are someone who is part of a company. They need a way to captivate a healthy mutual dependency with us. If not . . . too many of us will move on.

"Missed opportunities" in your home city, as with Stan, have led the way to phenomenal opportunities in other states for millions of people sidetracked in mid-career, many because of corporate restructuring, others because they are so inclined. Communications and technology make it possible for large corporations to spread out, often relocating key divisions to smaller cities. The migration Stan mentioned is already filling the highways.

Although the World Future Society forecasts that, by the year 2000, 52 percent of the world's population will live in urban centers, now, in America, the smaller town is growing in appeal. Drawn by a lower cost/higher standard of living, lower crime rates, and ease of "drive time" in getting to work, thousands of people are opting out of large city centers.

Relocation seriously affected married couples in this two-income culture. According to the Bureau of Labor Statistics, about 700,000 married people are living long-distance marriages. And one out of five couples turn down "intercity transfers" because one spouse couldn't find a satisfactory job while the other had a firm offer.

Where is everyone moving? States experiencing more than a 20 percent growth rate include Arizona, Colorado, Florida, Hawaii, Nevada, New Mexico, Oregon, and Wyoming.

Seattle is realizing a boom in trade and financial services growing beyond Boeing, its largest employer. The "Massachusetts economic miracle" that was Michael Dukakis's pride is still viable, but growth has slowed down. The miracle was the proliferation of high-tech companies along "America's technology highway"—Route 128 that encircles Boston. Utah is a leader, too, for research in biomedical devices—especially artificial hearts—and like Houston, has a large medical population.

"EXTENDER" OR SERVICE JOBS One dynamic phase of this age is the increase of service industries—industries involved in the nontangible but profit-making side of manufacturing and selling a product. Advertising, market research, product research, wholesaling, and retailing are such examples.

"Helping" or "extender" positions also fit another category of service jobs. These are directly related to complementing professionals like doctors, lawyers, dentists, and computer experts. The Bureau of Labor Statistics predicts that the fastest growing occupation between 1986 and 2000 will be that of *paralegal,* with four times the opportunities for them, in fact, than the lawyers they will work with.

INTRAPRENEURING The entrepreneurial spirit is alive in a "safety net."

Gifford Pinchot III, author of *Intrapreneuring,* labeled the concept of promoting entrepreneurial innovation within the corporation. Intrapreneuring keeps dynamic, valuable employees who might otherwise move on to work for the competition. As an intrapreneur, you set up a business, protected by a corporate umbrella, with the understanding that your primary loyalty is to them—although you can also take on other clients, like a conventional business. Xerox Corporation, for one, has experimented successfully with intrapreneurial enterprises.

The benefits of intrapreneuring are numerous. In your independent niche, you can realize your goals, for you, while you also raise product quality or improve the efficiency in the organization, for them.

Gifford discussed with me the approaches to being an intrapreneur, especially as a good option for shifting gears. Attitude comes first. He said:

> Intrapreneurship is a state of mind where you take responsibility for your own job within a large organization. You are no longer wholly responsible to the hierarchy, but to making your dream happen within that organization, to the benefit of the organization.
>
> Most of all, you can't see it as the company setting you up. Instead, get your idea to happen in terms of what the company wants to accomplish. Figure out how what you're doing fits in with their goals.

With *intra*preneuring, you're an entrepreneur with one major difference: You're getting some form of payment from the company. Sometimes your compensation is identical as you change roles from employee to intrapreneur; often, it is lower than the salary you would draw, but the position provides you with opportunity for gain, and a safety net. This company safety net is psychologically motivating. It's scary to throw yourself out into the world and start a company. You can go through desperate times. One of the big advantages of intrapreneuring is that even if you fail, the risk is much less. Gifford added:

> Intrapreneuring gives you a chance to learn about yourself at someone else's expense: what your talents are, to learn about business with a tremendous network at your disposal. If you don't have an idea you're willing to bet your house on, intrapreneuring could be for you.

One intrapreneur has gone the gamut from employee, to entrepreneur, to budding intrapreneur. A "child of the networks," award-winning News Producer Av Westin left an executive position at ABC-TV to go out on his own to develop programs. The fear of financial insecurity and the improvisational quality of working project to project had, he said, "a high stomach lining quotient." Even with the great success he achieved as an independent producer, the process was, for him, "torture."

The television market has changed over the last decade and the players are different from what they were then. Now with cable stations, superstations, satellites, and local stations buying programs independent of their network affiliates, along with the growth of the international market, it is a seller's market. This is how Av fits in.

Uninterested in being an employee or an entrepreneur, Av has been approached by a company who will back him. He provides his expertise in developing programs for a worldwide market and the company takes the financial risk while giving Av a share in the profits.

Intrapreneuring works on this high plane or on more modest levels. It is perfect, for example, for market research, marketing a training program, developing a product, or anything else that gets a company's vote of confidence.

WORKING AT HOME Another option for those with an entrepreneurial bent is the growing home business. In 1987, over 3 million people were working at home. From cottage industries to superautomated executive home offices, Americans are either supplementing income or building growth industries, many with the help of sophisticated computer/communications technology. Telephone "tie lines," imaginative applications of computer technologies, fax machines, copiers, and, in many areas, an abundance of available part-time employees, make the home business a relevant option.

OPTIONS: WHEN GOING BACK TO SCHOOL MAKES SENSE

With people surviving downsizing and repositioning in the era of contradictions, the question becomes: What do you need to learn? To take advantage of change, futurist Alvin Toffler wrote, you must "wake up" three capabilities: Learn how to learn; learn how to choose; learn how to relate. Learning is a process, and if you are to *adapt,* what you learn and how you apply it is one answer.

You have to be smarter to survive in these times—you need to invent, plan, be *flexible*; to close a deal, make money, and achieve. You need analytical tools. And if you're changing careers, one requirement may be returning to school. When times are harder, statistics show, more people return for degrees, new accreditation.

The question of learning poses two other questions: If you have already graduated from college or have an advanced degree, how much more education do you need to get to your next goal?

What kind of education holds the most eventual rewards?

Some opt for experiential learning, that is, getting the information you need *on the job* rather than spending the time to get conventional graduate school credentials. By approaching each project you're associated with as a learning experience—*and learning more than is required to accomplish the job you have*—your company literally serves as your "business school." With such a mindset, your approach to work as job and education will ultimately prepare you for a move up. A broad base of understanding the functions in your company can only help improve your odds in getting promoted, or acquiring the expertise you need to go out on your own.

As I see it, any book, or course, or institution, or mentor that helps you make ethical professional and growth-oriented decisions and provides for you a good idea of marketplace limitations and opportunities makes good sense. People with the broadest training are likely to be the most successful among us. Where this training is obtained matters less than *keeping up* with your field and interrelating with other fields of interest.

BASIC EDUCATION AND BUSINESS SCHOOLS: WHAT THEY CAN DO Schools teach reading, communications skills, writing, and some of them prepare you for change. There are other *competencies* we learn there to negotiate the world: information access and abstract communication, such as understanding symbolism, music, arts, and body language. However, education can't teach you everything. You'll still have to know how to make a phone call, ask for a promotion, form networks, puzzle out corporate politics, and perfect your skills.

Donna Shalala, Chancellor of the University of Wisconsin, an educator and innovator, believes strongly in getting the best education you can. Education, she insists, must "give you a sense that you are always learning." The same sense holds true for a career: You need to keep acquiring tools, and not "hang on" when you are past your growth. She offered a wise evaluation of education vis-à-vis careers. She said:

> What is vital in education is to look at job number *three,* not job number one. Think ahead. Specialization isn't important in school, but general education is. From there, take chances. If something feels good, do it. Don't overintellectualize. Don't be too shrewd and overanalyze.

> Talented people have to constantly learn new things, to be flexible, open to ideas.
>
> In a sense, the ultimate education is moving from job to job.

Education is not static—not if it's alive with a purpose. Of the richest men in America, if this is one standard to examine, the top eight have degrees from business schools. Some of the greatest changes in Wall Street were first conceived of in academia—physicists picked up the study of the mechanics of prices and rocket scientists worked out how to predict the value of an "option," that is, figuring the worth of a stock at some point in the future. Elitism and isolation of specialties and information are no longer considered relevant.

Education is not all about making money—although some schools approach education as prebusiness preparation, even forging links with big business. Others seek to humanize issues. Norman Berman, a professor of economics and Director of Executive Programs at the New York University School of Business, employs the innovative "cohort" techniques for those in an executive masters degree program in business. These cohort groups have integrated five students each with a different area of expertise—such as, accounting, foreign studies, and marketing—who all contribute a point of view, coming out of a different specialty. The groups deal with real global issues about international trade and money markets and prepare them for eventual marketplace experience. "I can't think of any business that won't be affected by global competition," he said.

His isn't just a student ideal; cohort groups and "sapiential circles"—a similar phenomenon among those with diverse but specialized knowledge—are becoming common in business. Bruce Kraselsky, the previously mentioned space lawyer, headed a "tiger team" after the Challenger disaster—a team put together with a financial expert from Wall Street, an expert in international trade and export control, and a scientist in robotics. "There was a synergy," he said, "a pooling of our expertise to learn from each other."

Ben Barber, a brilliant scholar and theorist who holds the Walt

Whitman chair in Political Science at Rutgers University, believes that education is about education for life, not just for a job. He is opposed to colleges with a structure set up as "prebusiness trainers." Instead, he believes they should create broad-based generalists who know how to use their critical faculties.

The more segmented the marketplace becomes, the greater the need for people with the "capacity to put things together and understand contexts. To be successful in the marketplace, you have to have skills of analysis and the capacity to understand the *connections between things.*" Philosophy, literature, and poetry, he believes, have their place in this rapidly changing world. He told me:

> That things are changing is true, but it's a narrow and time- and culture-bound point of view. What literature gives you is a sense of continuity and connectedness of human beings over time. Political and economic forms are changing but at a more fundamental level. If you're sensitive and alive to that more profound level, things are not so different.
>
> Maybe the word is *perspective.* People who come through hard times and even failure have perspective. They can see beyond immediate things to the long run and make some sense of them.

Remembering a passage from *Moby Dick* may one day affect a decision you make; remembering a line from a poem may bring you consolation. *Ideas* can create other ideas. And *applying* information is the real basis of adaptation in this world.

SHIFTING GEARS: TWO SUCCESS STORIES IN MARKET KNOW-HOW

Linda Gottlieb, coauthor with me of *When Smart People Fail,* is a survivor and gifted tactician in one of the most brutal marketplaces of all—film. Following the success of our book, Linda became an independent filmmaker and produced her smash hit film, *Dirty Dancing.*

Linda is, above all, a realist. As successful as she has been with one of the great hits of all time, she knows the marketplace doesn't allow for her to produce films back to back. Typically, *years* may pass before another film is ready to go. Therefore, being market sensitive, she has diversified—using her other talents as a writer, lecturer, and producer to shape her career and to earn a living.

Linda has always moved with the market. Her career began in educational films, but when government grants dried up, the funds that enabled schools to buy her work were depleted. Much of the educational film business collapsed with these cuts. Then a second change altered the business: video cassettes. Cassettes were many times cheaper than film and it restructured the economic basis of the business.

The picture was clear enough to her: she would have to change markets. But where would she go?

Linda looked around and there shone television, when it was in its "golden age" and very much a viable business. Linda reasoned that if she had a marketing sense for what worked in educational films, the same good sense could be applied to successful television. It was a wise choice. Ultimately, Linda ran the television arm of Highgate Films—a career spanning eighteen years—where she produced many award-winning shows.

Then the nature of television changed when the golden age tarnished and *cable* gained strength—her marketplace shifted once more. Before deciding which direction to take, she had to assess the facts: the networks were hard under fire, competing both with cable and with outside producers for "product." It became a tougher business than ever, with costs up. Then Linda lost her job at Highgate and she was suddenly facing a major career change bottlenecked within yet *another* shift in the industry.

Linda thought she would try producing a feature film, but by then the real activity in the film business was pretty much centered in California. Operating from her base in New York City was proving difficult. If she had wanted to work strictly with the marketplace, she'd have relocated out there, to the hub. However, her personal choice was to stay in New York. So she evaluated the marketplace, looked at her strengths, and concluded: the film business may be in California, but, she said, "I know how to work best with writers and I can do that anywhere." And so she put together *Dirty Dancing* in New York.

But even great success doesn't mean smooth transitions. She told me:

> When I made a deal to do the film in 1984, there were producer deals to be had. They gave me an office in New York and paid me a lot of money to be exclusive to them.
>
> But the industry changed *again.* Studios now tended to make deals with directors or stars or writers, but not producers. I thought, how do I support myself? Why not try television again? It's still a business.

This brings us to the present and another shift: Linda has set up a company in New York, funded by Vestron, where she is free to produce what most pleases her. Linda's strength, she thinks, comes from being a fighter . . . and a realist.

> People who can't change and change with the times will drop by the wayside. Some people nurse dreams. I'm more pragmatic. I look at the world with a degree of suspicion. I always have a bailout plan.
>
> I believe that some people are motivated and some are not. To survive you have to focus on your strengths. I feel it was the right move for me to spread my roots.

Linda is a master of *using* and *fitting in* to the marketplace. She studies its movement, sensibly consolidating economic trends with her creative abilities and personal preferences. And the solutions she came up with always work for her. Many of you who shift gears as easily as she are in tune with this phenomenon.

Others of you become familiar with a marketplace quite inadvertently. A common scenario goes like this: you stumble upon a bit of marketplace information but you're unaware that it could ever be applied to a career decision. It is just information—neutral, powerless. Then one day, a *need* is expressed. Your need. Someone else's. And the pieces fall into place. A light goes on and *you know what the information means.* Take "Dan," the guy who called in to speak to me when I was a guest on a Fort Worth, Texas, talk show.

My subject was success and failure and Dan's call was a highlight. He told how he'd pulled himself up from failure—from the "real pits." Dan was an ex-con.

He had served two years in prison for grand larceny and now, a free man, he faced a dilemma. Two options were open to him: resume his criminal career or go straight. A greater part of him wanted to change his life around, but the quandary was very real: *what could he do?*

He remembered what it was like in prison, and his memory literally served him well. He recalled what could have made life there more humane—little touches, things that were hard to get, like a good hairbrush, better quality stationery, decent underwear, a long list of paperback books and magazines that were unavailable inside. And more.

He told me, "I knew I could go back to stealing or work an area I knew was open for real opportunity. So I thought, I'm going to open a business and call it 'The Great Escape.' " Thus was born a direct marketing business offering an inventory of such grooming and "household" products to prisoners, sold via a newsletter.

This is perfect use of marketplace strategy—albeit an unconventional one. In essence, "The Great Escape" is positioned for a particular segment of the population—it is true "niche" marketing and an original marketing concept. Dan has created real and purposeful change for himself through his business.

POINTS TO REMEMBER ABOUT STAYING IN TUNE WITH THE MARKETPLACE

There are some basic rules to keep in mind when you start analyzing the marketplace in terms of signs and trends, whether the changes are in your industry or in one that interests you.

• *Ask questions.* Speak to experts. Establish contacts who can answer your questions.

• *Keep in touch* with your specialty and develop an awareness of related fields to which you can apply your expertise.

• *Keep your options open.* Ask questions and research possibilities before declining any offer.

• *Diversify.* Gain experience to "layer" your skills.

• *Analyze and apply* the information you garner creatively and productively.

• *Seize these opportunities* in disaster or crisis. When one door closes, another opens.

Planners. Analysts. Those who operate out of instinct or accident. The meticulous list makers and goal setters. The artists and the motivators. You're all part of the marketplace and involved in its changes as much as you are changed by it.

Not one of you is excluded. Life around you is going to change. The point is to *take advantage of the opportunities that are always out there.*

How you seize the opportunity is another subject.

2

UNDERSTANDING YOUR STYLE

What's Your M.O.?

If the 1980s brought us any revelations to consider, it's that work no longer has one interpretation throughout a lifetime. Work can change—and so can we.

What you work at describes you just as a detailed physical description singles you out. Work, inarguably, is one of the foremost influences on your behavior. In fact, some people change occupations believing that such a decisive shift in their lives will bring with it a decisive change in *basic personality.* It's a persuasive argument for those who view their professional lives in terms of a career rather than a job. Work enables one to have a sense of empowerment.

The distinction between *job* and *career* can be as divergent as that between motivation and fatalism. In general, it's looking a bit closer at the two chief interpretations of work. The first rendering defines work simply as a job. There's a real lack of commitment, and less passion, connected to employment; fulfillment barely extends beyond the benefits of a paycheck and a pension.

A job is simply a means to survival for those so inclined—artists, dancers, actors, and writers.

The second rendition describes those who pursue a *career.* For them, work is an object of careful thought, concern, and long-range planning.

What matters in this marketplace to gain career satisfaction?

Those who shift gears successfully learn to operate with this guiding fact of life: by being attuned to *change,* they can observe situations, figure out how to fit in, calculate the benefits and losses, adjust their behavior, and *act.*

How you act tells certain truths about you:

- if you set your economic and professional goals too high or your spiritual goals too low, or the reverse
- if you tend to focus on the projected desired results you set out with (and achieve) or if you linger over the possibility of failures and go for your goal with jerky starts and stops
- how much you trust your instincts when the going gets rough—or, knowing that risk taking is crucial to career success, how you deal with the times when you must convert fear into challenge
- being smart enough to take advantage of good things that fall in your path. Do you handle them well, or badly, or not at all; do you get bitter and take fewer chances after a setback?

If you review your past experiences with work, you'll begin to form part of the picture that makes up your style.

WHAT'S YOUR STYLE?

Work "style" is a broad picture of how you interact with others and interact with the process of *work* itself. Style tells how you visualize possibilities and act upon them; it can predict how you problem solve effectively within an organization and how your ideas and actions impact on it. "Style" reveals your emotional and mental predispositions; it shows which types of work and work conditions you seek, which you enjoy, what you would like to eliminate. It is your M.O.—modus operandi—your method of operation, your quirks, your strengths, your *patterns*.

The profiles that follow will help you clarify your style and, possibly, set you on a more realistic course to finding and reaching your long-term career objectives. Through example, you'll see how others used self-appraisal techniques to evaluate their fit in a career—and how they judged its true potential or faced the fact of having outgrown "the perfect job." Who made a change, who stayed on—or who added on? Such decisions are part of an M.O.

Styles have qualities that overlap, but in general, four distinct categories typify most of us. In researching *Shifting Gears* and listening to over 300 people describing their talents, competencies, limitations, and goals, I found that work style qualities fell into these categories:

- Lifers
- Builders
- Synthesizers
- Reinventors

THE LIFER

The Lifer feels the tremors from mergers and corporate shake-ups, but stands firm about where he or she belongs: *with one company* or in one profession, often for a lifetime. *Two* long-term jobs—or one change of profession—is about their limit. Lifers are monogamous types, people who tend to find what they need in a single relationship—with a profession, a product, a company, or a talent, such as music or art. They are committed for the long run. This "long-term marriage" may not be perfect, but its foundation is strong, the familiarity is comforting, and it provides the sense of continuity much required by a Lifer. Any threat of loss or separation rouses a fierce territorial drive to fight for his/her turf and *endure*.

If you are a classic Lifer, the adjustments you make tend to be primarily interpersonal: your key to dealing with change is about learning to work with new managers or new owners. Lifers are basically gifted diplomats. The Lifer's ability to show flexibility is also called upon when the company expands or diversifies, or products change and the individual is suddenly required to learn new information, techniques, and procedures.

Lifers are studies in optimism, with an overlay of a tough-skinned practical orientation. And no one I know is more the aggressive optimist and quintessential Lifer than H. Bud Walters, a vice president of sales for an entertainment conglomerate. Bud has not only prevailed through *four* different regimes, but he artfully convinces incoming administrations how invaluable he is to them. He is "organization man" to the core.

A forty-two-year-old New Yorker, Bud is openly hard driving and resourceful. While he embraces traditional values and lives a moderate life, in spirit Bud is modern man at his best. He accepts change *reluctantly,* but he acts with flexibility and ingenuity when it counts. He also has a remarkable talent. In his unique way, Bud understands the nuances of fitting in to a changing world, and what he must do.

When he was fired from a high five-figure sales job because of a corporate merger, Bud was shaken up. Three previous administrations had helped him make earlier transitions with relative ease. This time, he was *out.* True to his nature, he wouldn't take rejection without a stand. Bud clung to one piece of information. The man who fired him complimented him on his legendary tenacity at getting and keeping accounts.

Instead of feeling trounced, Bud analyzed as best he could the style and "conventional wisdom" of the incoming management. He made calls. Asked questions. Read anything he could find about the takeover company in business periodicals. The new management hadn't yet brought in a new man for his job; his office was still his. As he was packing his things, a plan hatched. "I had a timetable with no options," Bud said, "and forty-eight hours to win everything back." He told me:

> I've always been a stalker, and if I have to be, a predatory animal. I had to change this guy's mind about me. I was willing to lay myself on the line in any way.

> The truth is, I didn't want to work anywhere else—they have the top product, the best in the business. I wanted this job and I was going to keep it.

Bud figured out a strategy and destiny rearranged it. His first step was to get everyone he knew with influence to call the man who fired him and recommend him vigorously. Step Two—"the confrontation" with the man—required some agile reworking. When the man fell ill with the flu, Bud played the turn of events like a master. Ill, the man was vulnerable and Bud's captive audience.

A lesser tactician might have taken this twist as a setback. Instead, Bud coaxed the man's unlisted home phone number from an ally at the office, then called a deli near his house; at Bud's orders, they set up a huge pot of chicken soup and delivered portions of it at regular intervals. Such caretaking got the man's attention and Bud moved in with a final flourish—he sent a tape recorder with a sales pitch—Bud's own argument for being rehired.

He said candidly:

> I had nothing to lose and everything to gain since he didn't consider me a likely candidate *for my own job.* It was a selling situation, so I had to sell him. If it was tenacity that impressed him, I would give it to him.
>
> I was rehired.

Simple, unflinching tenacity is a very real component of the Lifer's makeup. A more reticent individual might have followed the path of least resistance, conceded defeat, and never have taken action. Instead, politically, Bud used every bit of strategy and any pressure point available to him, like the man's illness, to make things happen. Rejection was not on the menu with the soup.

People change their minds. This is one guidepost Lifers always heed. By altering his approach, Bud turned an "unchangeable" decision around in his favor.

LIFERS IN A CHANGING COMPANY Barbara Rabke is a Lifer of another sort. While Bud was committed *first* to the excellence of the product he was selling and second to the company hierarchy, no such internecine politics or a job in jeopardy affected Barbara

Rabke's decision to be a Lifer. When she started with TransArt, it was a small but growing southern-based direct sales company dealing in art and art framing, operating on a "multilevel" basis. TransArt was the kind of commitment she was seeking at the time. She'd quit her teaching job to be a full-time mother; to work part time in direct sales gave her an ongoing connection to the business world as well as an additional income.

It was a perfect match. After a year with TransArt, Barbara was their number one salesperson in residential sales. Her achievement reflected a real talent for sales and emphasized another of her strong points: she is a motivated self-starter. Barbara succeeded without any of the rallying support systems common to multilevel marketing companies—the meetings, seminars, and training sessions that are often great inspiration to those who attend them. She'd been recruited by a woman who'd then relocated from the area, leaving Barbara to function as a sole entity in New Jersey, with no support system. She was also isolated from company headquarters in Atlanta, she told me, "not knowing enough about them to feel loyalty or a sense of belonging." She said of this time in her career and of being a "Lone Ranger":

> Some women get caught up in networking in direct sales—they get filled up by support teams and *stop*. In independent sales organizations the essence of each person is variable, but an achiever always understands that 98 percent of drive comes from you and your commitment to what you're doing.
>
> To me, it's having an entrepreneurial mindset.

Then a combination of her early achievement and a recognition that she was in the midst of a great opportunity triggered a real surge of energy: TransArt was reborn as TransDesign.

Over a decade, TransArt grew from marketing art framing exclusively to selling fine art originals that attracted designers, not just the person who wanted part-time opportunities. The company made *greater* changes as their salespeople requested more direction from management and greater potential earning power. TransArt made a move to expand their product line to include accessories, furniture, fabrics, and textiles; they even issued their own credit card. TransArt became TransDesign with swatches, rugs, and chairs arranged like a mini-shop in a mobile van.

This was a test for Lifers and newcomers alike. Surprisingly, many salespeople left when the company expanded. Barbara Rabke saw the challenge and bought the van. When we spoke about the effects of radical company changes on a salesforce, Barbara said:

> Some people have a fear of change and use expansion as a test of their likes and dislikes—not a *fact* of growth. It's a way of saying, "I can't change," and an excuse to not move forward.
>
> In terms of TransDesign, I saw many women worried about changing from simply art prints to bigger stuff. To me, it means you have to be adaptable. It means learning the "whole look" of putting a room together, not just adding a single finishing touch—the art print. It means reinvestment.

She is still number one in the company, earning nearly $80,000 a year in a home-based business. After twelve years, she cherishes the power over her career that direct sales provides. She is a Lifer, one who is growing with the company. Henry Ford said that he didn't have to know how every screw turned to run a multimillion-dollar business, he just needed access to the areas he didn't know. He might have been speaking directly to Barbara. In her way, she followed this credo. She said:

> The company offers me flexibility, and I can learn what I need to know. The information is always there and I can find it. To me, the entrepreneurial spirit means creativity and growth.
>
> Most of all, I feel in control of my destiny. It wasn't an easy decision to stay in direct sales. I had to decide if I wanted to compromise my life for a good Blue Cross/Blue Shield package at a full-time job or take a chance on myself with this company.
>
> I stayed all these years because of the sense of recognition that comes with the achievement.

Barbara is a Lifer who has changed and adapted to the needs of the marketplace as her company wisely chose to do. Other motivated long-run players gain perspective on their careers and discover they've been coasting through the last few years of their careers. Bob Schwartz is one such Lifer—a man who built a finely tuned organization that grew and changed to meet marketplace demands, but who himself grew and stayed the same.

THE INNOVATIVE LIFER It was a day Bob Schwartz had not reckoned for. He was suddenly in a position to sell his unique and prestigious organization when it was still at its peak. "I had created a personal kingdom where I could do what I wanted," Bob told me. "Why would I leave?" When it became clear that his self-styled kingdom was Nirvana with an *emotional* time clock to punch, he knew it was time to go. Finding the exits to Nirvana and not looking back is a real task of the will. But Bob did it, to his own surprise.

Founder of the Tarrytown Conference Center—the progenitor of conference centers—and one of the more innovative businessmen, the dynamic Bob Schwartz started out as a journalist and publishing executive. He decided he could run a business using the same amount of energy as it took him to write an article for *Time*. "The door was open for me in journalism, but I wasn't happy inside," he said of his choice to go into business.

An ardent appreciation and interest in Eastern architecture and Asian design influenced his decision to build a motel in the Japanese style on the New York Thruway—90 percent of the financing coming from friends. It was a wise investment. The Motel on the Mountain was a great success, eventually expanding twice over. Then a number of large corporations, such as IBM, asked Bob to help them find a suitable place to hold meetings and training programs.

Bob took the opportunity to create one. He bought the Mary Biddle Duke estate in Tarrytown and it became the first conference center in the country catering entirely to business functions. When he opened its doors, it could sleep twenty-four people; when he sold it, it could accommodate 300. Over the years, between ten and twenty meetings were held there each day—everything from human potential movements, to sales meetings, to international conferences.

Bob did for the conference business what Club Med did for selling vacations: provide democratic *access* to location and information, sold with a sense of bounty. The effect he created in Tarrytown was "easy elegance," a care to details, and a "management of plenty" that told employees the company cared about them. Understandably, it was a huge success and Bob never gave a thought to letting go.

During this time, Bob formed the distinguished school for entrepreneurs—the Tarrytown 100—with leading innovative executives who shared their ideas. Bob explained their objective:

> We used the work place like a petri dish to explore how people worked together. The bottom line was fun, but it was also fun to figure out better work styles. What came out of this group were lifelong friendships, partnerships, and a shared value system about being executives.

Then a remark changed Bob's destiny.

Two years ago, he sold the center—reluctantly. He was a Lifer in his own organization. It had been twenty-four years from the day the doors opened and he founded the "kingdom" where he could do what he wanted—a goal most of us strive for. But a friend had offered another observation about Bob's holding on to the Tarrytown center. It was a confrontation that stirred a strong response in him:

> A friend said, "You think you've built a platform to make things happen in your life, but now it's just a job where you only change the light bulbs." He said, "*Sell* . . . take the money, move away, invest in something, and see the world differently. Let go."
>
> Thinking about leaving got me very distressed. I wondered what I would do and if I would be crazy to give this up after all these years. It took months of bad dreams and my unconscious saying: *Stay,* no one needs this much change.
>
> But leaving was the answer.
>
> It was time.

Currently, Bob is involved in five different projects the dimensions of which he says are "thrilling." He's working with a company that is developing new types of grains and with a scientist he met while lecturing on a different project. He said:

I believe in a right to work—finding pleasure in what you do. It's fun to make money, but you don't change the world by putting your heart on the bottom line, you change by putting your heart first in what you do, then making the bottom line real.

Now I can't believe I stayed in Tarrytown so long. I don't miss it.

LIFER PROFILE Because Lifers believe that work provides the best of all possible worlds, having to move on feels like an impossible choice. For many Lifers, an abiding sense of *connection* to work keeps them holding fast to what they have. The catch phrase for the Lifer resonates like a fugue and goes: At least I know what I have where I am.

The Lifers I've interviewed were mostly like the three people written about here: motivated, ambitious players. And for each of the three, there was a prevailing factor at the core of their being Lifers: Bud Walters analyzed his *product* and its standing in the market and knew it was foolish to give up "the best" without a fight. Barbara Rabke built *seniority* in a company that also provides flexibility and ongoing growth possibilities. It makes sense for her to stay. Bob Schwartz built a company around an *ideal,* but it was an ideal he stayed on to perpetuate although he'd outgrown it.

There is another shading to the Lifer, the bleaker side. These second-string Lifers are less likely to find pleasure in work, whether from long-term growth, enthusiasm about their products, or actuating ideals. They are people who single-mindedly focus on seniority and are essentially *stuck* at jobs that offer security first and satisfaction last. They are less likely to take a stand that will make them visible contenders in office politics, defy authority, or introduce progressive ideas. What happens when they hang in, and what they can do about moving on, is discussed in Chapter Five.

But the determined Lifers, while as security-minded as their counterparts, can be fierce competitors and scrappy fighters. They are also inclined toward peace making and establishing the status quo. In fact, their well-honed political skills allow them to function effectively with each new administration.

Lifers are cautious risk takers with a bent toward autocratic behavior, but they are the most immediately adaptive when authority changes. They need to fit right in. Once they have formed a loyalty to a company, a person, or a profession, they will accommodate themselves to the tides of change to assure their place. Of the four styles, they fight the hardest for consistency. Lifers require a sense of belonging to the future of their profession or company and identify strongly with it.

In terms of fitting into a changing marketplace, Lifers may be too dependent on the power structure to take the first steps out into the world. They tend to wait for news to come to them and pick over information for affirmation that the foundation beneath their feet has not cracked. Lifers often need the *shock* of change to dislodge them from the home front.

Lifers work best in companies where there is a presence of power—either the company or its head has the "name"—authority and continuity. Of their shortcomings, the greatest struggle for many is to work in a loosely structured situation or one that is too entrepreneurial.

THE BUILDER

Take the Lifer and introduce a *second,* or even third vocation to which he/she is passionately committed and you have the Builder. Now think *parallel lives* and you get a sense of what the Builder is all about. The Builder, like the Lifer, seeks the foundation and security of the long-term commitment, but unlike the Lifer, the Builder is not content with a single marriage. His/her tendency is an honorable bigamy—the Builder has found another true love and will not relinquish the one he/she knows best for the one newly discovered.

But this is not a frivolous dalliance. It is, after all, the strength and solidity of their first career that frees the Builders financially to pursue a second. There is never a question about which career provides what and which comes first. The trial lawyer who performs with a jazz band on a semiprofessional basis has no illusions about his/her priorities and his/her purpose over his/her passions.

Yet, to him/her, surrendering the second career would be equally as painful as failing at the first.

While the Lifer looks to his or her job as the primary source of identification, the Builder is more circumspect. The Lifer will tell you about his/her hobbies, but Builders rarely have such pastimes—they have *interests,* such as sports or the theatre, and avocations that they design as carefully as their first-choice careers. Builders are rarely dabblers or ardent dilettantes; they're either committed or not. In fact, true Builders seek satisfaction, recognition, and success from their primary *and* secondary careers.

As the name implies, Builders focus on growth, *adding on* to what they have and who they are. These additions tend to be *life* goals as well as career goals. Builders, by nature, perceive of work as pleasure—a credo they energetically transmit to those they work with. One such master Builder is Nick Kelley, a manufacturer and film producer who runs his dual businesses from his headquarters in the picturesque Massachusetts town of Great Barrington.

THE MANUFACTURER/MOVIE MAKER Nick Kelley is a fascinating study in dualities. He's a cautious risk taker, but newly in the film production business, he has entered one of the more high-risk professions. A man who is excited by the improvisational quality of the creative trades—like theatre, film, and art—he is equally as heartened by the precision and methodology of science. Comfortable with his position as chairman of the board of the large and successful company he built from the ground up, he is also openly dependent on a sound "infrastructure" of trusted advisors, secretaries, researchers, and workers to keep it going and growing. This infrastructure allows him to work full time with his film production company.

Nick's first company, in the heart of the Berkshire hills, is involved in manufacturing paper products, semiconductors, products for the aerospace and computer industries, and is "inventing new things all the time." He told me how he felt about starting a second business, "building on success, rather than rebuilding from failure":

I'm so lucky I can't believe it. First, I'm not transitioning out

> of something I hate, but expanding on something I really care about. I'm in a leadership position, but I build my foundation on the excellence of my colleagues' management skills. They're the ones who are liberating me to do the *other* things I've always wanted to try—produce films.
>
> If there's a down side to running a company and starting a second business, it's that I'll wind up doing a half-baked job at both. Yet I don't feel so limited in my abilities that I can only do one thing well. What I know is that I can't run two businesses at the same time. I have to plan time for each of them.

Twenty years ago, Nick had no real career choice in mind. What he had was energy, ambition, and a drive to create a successful future. It was 1969 and Nick had just returned from an army tour of duty to the Berkshires' town where he used to spend summers. Few men, he said, came back from the war and wanted to be in the entertainment business. And he wasn't among those few. He thought practically—he had to engineer a career, "earn a living and then build a business." He worked at a factory, learned the paper business, and soon opened his own company—now a multinational operation. Nick credits the army with teaching him the importance of setting up and maintaining an effective infrastructure—those trusted people who keep things moving without his constant surveillance.

His interest in films and acting evolved out of his working on the board of the Berkshire Theatre Festival in Stockbridge. On a business trip, he happened to meet Doug Trumbull, the special effects film artist who, among his many credits, worked on *2001* and *Close Encounters of the Third Kind.* From this meeting, Nick's interest in film grew, he said, "in a passive way" at first. He was fascinated by the process, "the most powerful medium for communication. You can tell a great story, tell the truth; it's artistic, and you can make a lot of money. You can have more impact in one film than twenty-five senators [have] in ten years."

Nick's position is unique. He has the technical business expertise of a large successful company at his disposal to support his "upstart" enterprise. It's high quality and professionally run, although he is not in the film business "Hollywood style." Nick juggles his businesses smoothly. He said of his ventures:

> The film business is high risk and often you wind up working with people you don't like or don't trust. This way, I can live in my home in the Berkshires, run my business with capable managers, and have none of the anxiety of changing careers. Financially, it's not high risk and it provides me the time to make the transition from one to the other *without* having to sell the company.
>
> I understand there will be disappointments on a regular basis—it's a given in the film business. But I try to maintain some equilibrium. I'm not totally relying on the film business to pick me up. My company is a stabilizing influence.

An able Builder, Nick believes in making transitions, but in doing them slowly and carefully. This connects to his deep sense of rootedness and a need for continuity—traits all Lifers and Builders most often talk about. Not giving up important relationships too easily in a quest for new ones reveals the Builder at his best.

While being traditionalists with the freedom and confidence to express themselves, Builders need not always be mainstream achievers. They can also have their beginnings in a field such as the art world and, as if in a mirror image of Nick Kelley's career, build a "company" of assistants and support teams in a second business venture. Such an image would suit that of the great painter, Tom Wesselman.

THE PAINTER GOES "COUNTRY" Tom Wesselman is one of the handful of history-making painters who rose to prominence in the late 1950s having helped define a powerful new force in art called "the New Realism," or "Pop Art." Along with Roy Lichtenstein, Robert Rauschenberg, and Andy Warhol, Tom Wesselman revolutionized the look of American painting. Still producing much sought-after works of art from his studio on New York's Bowery, Tom has found another passion.

In 1984, this single-minded artist who never thought he had it in him discovered a second gift—song writing. That is, song writing country and western–style. The man who is acclaimed for his "Great American Nude" series may soon be known for "Pictures on the Wall of Your Heart," words and music by Tom Wesselman. To his own surprise, he has become a Builder.

Born in Cincinnati, Tom described himself as "directionless" and lacking ambition until the army. There, the seeds of his dual careers would be planted—in art and in music. It was in the service that, like Nick Kelley, Tom discovered he had a talent for telling stories and making up "one-liners." Being a cartoonist sounded like the right answer for combining these skills. And it was there that he also had a change of heart about the music he now "gushes" with. He said:

> I grew up with the country and western music when it was considered "hillbilly." I disliked it intensely and associated it with things I didn't want to be a part of. When I was in the army, I started listening to it, and found I was intrigued with the humor, the way in which tragedy is expressed, and the story-telling quality. I'd start writing songs, then drop it. Then I'd write titles and not follow up with a song. In 1961, I got an instruction booklet and learned three basic chords and how to strum the guitar. And dropped it.

After the army, Tom went to art school on the G.I. Bill and learned to draw; he soon sold a few cartoons to a number of magazines and newspapers, like *The Wall Street Journal* and *The Saturday Evening Post.* To pay the rent, he taught school.

It was a meeting with Willem de Kooning, a major figure in American Abstract Expressionism, that influenced Tom to leave cartooning and consider painting. "Art at the time was revolutionary," he said. "It drew me in." It did more than inspire a need in him to paint, it also provoked him to discover ideas, to read . . . and "to slip into the idea of being an artist."

When gallery owner Sidney Janis gave his "New Realists" show, Tom was asked to show his work and he was discovered.

Then fate clapped a hand; in 1984, Tom was asked to participate in an "Art World" album—artists doing on record whatever they so chose for four minutes. Tom picked one of his songs to do; a friend sang it and Tom played backup with harmonica. "I was off to the races," he said. "From then on, it was like a sickness. I couldn't turn song writing off."

He recently signed a contract to get his first song published and a "demo" record made, a milestone event for a man who has written nearly 150 songs a year over the last five years. His schedule is a quirky one—he writes songs before and during breakfast, during lunch and/or dinner; he uses all "traveling time to and from appointments" to dictate his songs into a tape recorder. But most of his time is spent painting. He is first of all a visual artist, and he doesn't let song writing intrude:

> Painting is what my life is about, but music is more an outgrowth of what happens to me or what could happen. *It's not my life.* I have to paint, and I can't be rational about explaining it. It's a spiral where I get in deeper and deeper.
>
> Oddly, there is no parallel between how I paint and how I live. Whereas in music—since country music is literary and you're telling stories about yourself—I draw on the course of my life.

A true Builder, Tom acknowledges that song writing is a secondary passion, but he would happily become a professional at it. Now that one of his songs has been bought, he has the "thrill" of hearing it performed. Writing may be a "bit of an indulgence" to him, but music is an important additive in his life:

> If I had shown my songs to someone four years ago for an honest evaluation, I'd have quit if I was told I wasn't good enough. But I just kept writing and by sticking to it and pushing myself, I improved dramatically.

For a man who has written over six hundred songs and has had one bought and twelve performed live at a gallery opening, I could say that Tom, somehow, will have the odds in his favor for success. He is that sort of dedicated Builder, graced, I think, with strokes of good fortune that he takes advantage of. While his dream is to keep making art, the dream includes a background score of his better-written songs—and access to the great country and western singers and arrangers. "I know that what I'm doing and what I want in music is multiplied 100,000 times across the country," he told me. "But I still want it."

Tom has no thoughts of combining music and painting into one art form; the closest he has gotten is in finding a model–art studio assistant who also has a good "country" singing voice. "I have a built-in prejudice against being two things at the same time," he told me. "In my way, I want my 'wife' and 'mistress' in two separate relationships."

BUILDER PROFILE Builders are energetic achievers—total workaholics in the best sense. Never content with an eight-hour day, Builders assume second "identities" while Lifers are still plugging away at their primary job. Persevering—and they must be to keep all this energy going—Builders have a clear sense of themselves. Highly organized, they are deft facilitators and delegators. If anyone can rally forces behind them and charge an office—or studio—with energy and productivity, it's the Builder.

Part of the Builders' mystique is their attitude toward work: by their standards, work is play, work is spirit; to the barons of the group, work is accumulating property or money. But such money-minded Builders might endow a museum or set up a scholarship fund. Work, most of all, is rarely thought of as a problem in life. Builders, as with Tom, are often surprised when a talent or inclination is uncovered later in an established career. Their need to be accomplished is often complemented by a need for recognition.

In terms of the marketplace, Builders have a valuable ability to conceptualize ideas and bring them to fruition. Once they make a decision about a career, they will go through the steps that are necessary to create it successfully. Builders rarely back down with a weak excuse. Since they aim high, they can devise the strategies and idea-a-minute innovations to reach a goal. If they question their confidence, Builders do so silently—these people tend to act on principle, and instinct.

Intensely focused, they are likely to head companies, like Nick Kelley, or help found movements, as with Tom Wesselman.

Builders are an unusual group, though. Most of us veer toward the next type—the Synthesizer.

THE SYNTHESIZER

A majority of people who go through career transitions are in this category. The Synthesizer has some of the Builder's energy, some of the Lifer's inclinations toward security, but primarily, the Synthesizer is always alert to *opportunities.* Ever ready to hop on the next step up, a Synthesizer's career, were you to diagram it, develops the shape of an inverted pyramid, widening at the top as he/she learns more and does more.

Synthesizers have a combination of talents, skills, and work experience that increasingly makes them eminently promotable in a corporate structure or good at independent enterprises—they make successful entrepreneurs. These synthesized skills and competencies are a natural part of each person's makeup. We all have strengths, such as a flair for language, for numbers, or a good color memory. Above that, we have certain *skills* that we've acquired from job to job, such as learning how to coordinate many departments at once or managing money.

Synthesizers are constantly aware of the information around them; they have a strong sensing mechanism that informs them of the realities in the environment and the clues that signal upcoming change. Many of them operate on multi-layered backup systems—they often have two or more sources of income coming in at the same time. They usually have a way of not getting caught short . . . of not getting trapped by blind spots.

Unlike many Lifers, Synthesizers tend to accept change with greater ease and are more confident risk takers. Risk is often the *frisson* that gets them going.

Many Synthesizers are successful late bloomers, finding their niche after four or five careers and many false starts. Others find their way to achievement in spite of humble or difficult beginnings that could have programmed them for failure or mediocrity had they not heeded their own instincts. The gregarious Wally Amos is among the latter group.

AN "ORIGINAL" AND THE SECRET OF SUCCESS He brought new cachet to the chocolate chip cookie, but the compelling Wally Amos, founder of "Famous Amos" cookies, once believed that the "path of least resistance" was where he'd find his life's work. A high school dropout from Tallahassee, Wally had always been, paradoxically, a self-starter and hard worker. He got his high school equivalency degree in the Air Force, took a brief interest in "food trades"—learning to be a cook—then switched to electronics. His first job was with Saks Fifth Avenue, in the supply department. It was a menial job, he said, but he took responsibility because "I didn't want to stand around and wait for someone to tell me to do something. I've decided since that *this* is the secret of success."

Pondering a better future, he went to school at night to learn typing and office skills. He didn't yet know where these skills would take him. When he was promoted to manager of his department—it was 1961—he was earning \$85 a week and his wife was pregnant. Wally requested a \$5 raise and he was refused. He quit the store, but with a glowing recommendation.

Still unfocused and with no set career goal, Wally heard that the William Morris Agency was looking for a Black trainee who was a college graduate to work his way up from the mailroom to agent. He wanted the job. Although he didn't have the credentials, he talked his way into it and agreed to work for a salary lower than the one over which he'd left Saks.

His secretarial skills were his entree to a promotion out of the mailroom. He worked as a secretary "with just about every agent" until his energy, confidence, capabilities, and appealing personality took him to another promotion. In less than a year, he was an agent in the music division—"the rock and roll department," agenting for Simon & Garfunkel, Patti LaBelle, and the Supremes. In the late 1960s, his "entrepreneurial bent" emerged, and he moved to California—leaving his big-time clients behind—to begin a talent management company with a partner.

A Synthesizer was born in Wally Amos.

In Hollywood for seven years, Wally was a personal manager for up-and-coming performers. Work for him then was about the pursuit of "the goal of being materialistic and living to impress people. There was no inner meaning to my life." He said of those years:

> My career wasn't happening. My clients weren't making enough money, and I had to leave my office and move to another apartment. As you are progressing downward, you think how bad it

> feels, then you reach a point where it doesn't matter what anyone thinks, because you have no choice.
>
> What you do is regroup on a dime.

I asked him what brought him strength at this point, when he was facing the possibility of losing his business and having to start over.

> It's self-confidence. If you don't believe you can do it, you won't. I think people make the mistake of analyzing the future—why they should do something and what will happen—rather than looking back to figure out why things did or didn't work out.
>
> By analyzing some events in my life, I see they can look catastrophic but they're only catastrophic if I make them so. I think you have to listen to every experience. They're all directing you to what to do. If you learn to get rid of the old beliefs that hold you back, you can discern the truth for you.
>
> Now I know what change is about—it's about *taking you to something better,* I don't care how catastrophic it is. Every experience got me to where I am today.

The father of the upscale cookie met his destiny when a client brought him a batch of chocolate chip cookies, the recipe for which had been taken off the back of a package of chocolate chips. Wally liked them so much, he made them at home with a variation of the recipe and gave them away as his "calling card."

After five years, the writing was on the wall—his management business was in trouble and all signs began pointing toward change. One client was injured, another decided to leave show business, others weren't paying him; he "stopped wanting to be a big shot." He felt beaten down and he was losing his competitive drive. He sought a simpler, better life.

The greater force was somehow saying, he said, "go sell cookies." It made sense. Wally's bottom line Synthesizer's skill is his promotional ability, and with each job, he improved on that ability while learning other skills. He went from being a secretary to theatrical agents to being an agent himself representing rock musicians, to being a talent manager advancing performers' careers. So promoting a cookie as his product, with his flair for showmanship, synthesized all his skills.

The idea was actually spawned by an offhand comment in 1974—a friend suggested that Wally open a storefront and sell his own cookies. They were the right words. He borrowed the capital—about $25,000—and the original home of "Famous Amos" chocolate chip cookies opened for business. From that night on, he never looked back. "Famous Amos" cookies had meteoric national success and his trademark embroidered shirt and Panama hat would eventually be part of the Smithsonian Institution's permanent collection. Wally told me how he felt about his success:

> The thought that I could find the money to open a store and sell cookies is about following through in a positive way. My friend who made the suggestion was the conduit through which the thought came to me. I could have said: I can't do it. But somehow I knew it was right.

LAYERING FROM NONPROFIT TO PROFIT New Yorker Deborah Krulewitch made the difficult transition from the nonprofit sector to corporate administrator at Estēe Lauder. Deborah is the classic Synthesizer. Her key skills and talents—being a good organizer, a "people person," tenacious, and enthusiastic—served her well as she worked her way up to a number of prestigious administrative jobs. She began as a social worker, then moved on to health care, criminal justice, and she was on a landmark year-long commission that investigated nursing homes.

Deborah felt she was "languishing" in these jobs and decided it was time to make a change into the business world. What she wanted was as yet "undefined," and she grappled with how to make the most prudent move:

> I couldn't figure out where to go and I didn't know the language of the corporate world. I wanted another career and I was willing to accept a "bridge" job—not the ideal job, but at least a foot in the door. I told *everyone* I was looking.
>
> Then a miracle happened. Through a friend, I got a job organizing a corporate townhouse, where they held meetings and parties. I convinced them to hire me. It was the wrong job, but a perfect beginning.

This "bridging" principle was wise: Deborah learned her way around a business environment, made contacts, and gained confidence. Ultimately, she moved up to an administrative position at a Fortune 500 company before joining Estēe Lauder.

SYNTHESIZING ART AND ENTERPRISE Follow sculptor Van Craig's career and you will uncover an interesting model of the high risk–taking Synthesizer. His artistic and organizational abilities have taken him from dancer to sculptor to publisher of greeting cards, with an offbeat entrepreneurial side trip. What makes Van notable is that he approaches each new endeavor by putting himself on the line in an ongoing *pursuit* of his goals.

He studied art and stage design in college, but an abiding interest in dance took Van to England where he studied dance "intensely." He eventually had a successful career on the Broadway stage that lasted for nearly ten years, but when he reached thirty, he knew that within five years his life would change. Dancers have peak years, then stop performing as the physical demands of work and younger competition dramatically change the course of their careers. Van decided to plan his next career move before that time was up. He said:

> First there were great dance opportunities and then there were none. I didn't want to be a chorus boy to the end. Time was running out and I had to take control of the circumstances and get a clear vision of what I wanted to do next.
>
> First, I had to just work at something in the interim until I figured it out.

Van was sculpting for his own pleasure—doing papier-maché portraits and "character studies" that he gave away. His friends chided him for his casual attitude toward the value of his work and suggested he sculpt "for a living." Unsure of himself, he put the idea aside temporarily, worrying about the logistics of finding a gallery to represent him, and producing saleable work. Over a holiday visit with his family, he helped his mother clean out the garage—and a bottom-line idea was revealed: *organize* garages, closets, rooms, and life's chores for other people.

and a bottom-line idea was revealed: *organize* garages, closets, rooms, and life's chores for other people.

When he returned home, he "marketed and packaged" his idea, and called himself a "Life Systems Analyst." The business not only provided Van with an ingenious and profitable career transition, but the venture allowed him freedom and flexibility. He had the *time* to sculpt. Soon he had a body of work—ten portrait heads, ready to sell. But no place to show.

Van systematically made appointments with gallery owners, and was turned down by all of them. But one shop—a boutique—agreed to take him on. Over a year, he sold a few pieces—among them a near life-sized marionette of '40s film star Carmen Miranda. More confident as a working artist, Van once again actively sought representation at an established gallery.

In a stroke of good fortune, he was taken on by a gallery in Soho, New York's downtown art district, where he showed successfully for four years. He's been twice profiled on television magazine shows and his work has appeared in the prestigious Tiffany & Company windows. Although he phased out his Life Systems business with his increased success as an artist, he learned from it that he had a knack for business, a good sense of organization, and marketing. Van's next move shows how: His sculptures may be one of a kind, but photographs of them can make them accessible to others in another medium. With that thought in mind—still layering—Van has branched out into greeting card publishing; the first edition of them are illustrated with photos of his unique sculptures. He told me how he feels about this venture:

> I'm looking at my new business as a balance sheet of sorts. On one side is fear of failure, but on the other side it is knowing I have talent. One side tells me the greeting card market is huge, but the other side is, I have an innovative approach to it. Third, starting a business costs a lot and I don't have all the money to get it started, but I know I can come up with it. I've done it before.
>
> Any reservations are more than just business conflicts—they're personal conflicts. I know change starts on the inside.
>
> I can listen to the people who say, "You can't do it," but I know I can.

edge increases, competencies and talents are fine-tuned, and the degree of specialization and expertise grows markedly over the years.

SYNTHESIZER PROFILE Synthesizers may move from job to job or business to business, but the classic Synthesizer's career history almost reads like a recipe. Each new skill, including interpersonal abilities, is added like ingredients to make a cake. The expert Synthesizer's true gift is in finding and applying the frosting that binds the layers to make a totality.

In terms of the marketplace, Synthesizers tend to work best in established businesses, but they can manage real challenge by building start-up companies. The Synthesizer's mindset has an ingenious perspective. When they look at what a company's needs are, they ask themselves: How can I create an answer to that? It isn't surprising if the answer they come up with creates a new job for themselves.

What makes a Synthesizer? Part of it is having a certain kind of intelligence that lets him or her more easily see the *connections* between things. How does being part of an investigative team probing nursing homes eventually relate to high-level administrative duties at a cosmetic company? Synthesizers, the expert synthesizers, know the answer. They can take what looks like two or three diverse skills or interests and come up with a result that combines them into something different. Deborah Krulewitch was willing to take the transitional steps between jobs because she could see the totality of her career goals. And her organizational talent would have been an isolated ability without a future unless she thought ahead and acted.

Synthesizers are receptive to suggestion, very good at asking insightful questions, and are great catalysts. They are the most adaptive of the three categories I've discussed so far—being flexible, aware, thinking strategists and, importantly, goal oriented. Synthesizers are more likely to be risk takers than risk averters—they see what they will gain over what they may lose. Those with a broader experience in taking risks over the long haul don't wait until their specialty changes under their feet. As with Van, they are willing to jump into the fray, even though, he confessed, "there were moments when pure horror alternated with pure reason."

One kind of training makes you a city mouse; a second one makes you a country mouse. But a third makes you an *effective* mouse who can go to the city, look it over, and try it out, and if things don't work out there, relocate to the country. These are the Synthesizers. They not only survive, the stronger Synthesizers build and rebuild.

THE REINVENTOR

Your situation may be calling for a new outlook. An inner drive draws you from a long-term protective environment and you commit yourself to real, observable *change.* You shift gears dramatically in how you think about your career. Now you are the classic Reinventor.

The two most common entrances to this kind of change are: 1. you *give up* an established career for a totally *un*related one, or 2. never having declared yourself, sudden *circumstances* thrust you into being resourceful. You not only make a momentous decision, you learn how adaptable you can be.

A POLITICAL MOVE Complete change can be "shocking, a bit scary, and frustrating because you're not up to speed," says former New York City councilwoman Carol Bellamy, whose toughest career transition was from government to industry. She joined an investment banking firm after having lost a mayoral race—which happened in her thirteenth year in government. She said:

> When I ran for mayor, it was either up or *out.* If I didn't win the election, I couldn't fall back on where I was before. There is no returning. I'd have to go out there. This was part of the choice I made. I saw colleagues stay a term or two too long and I thought, better to put myself on the line now than be afraid to do it later.

When she had to make a choice of what to do next after "living in a political fish bowl," Carol had several options—practice law, go into real estate, or banking. She chose banking because she "had to learn a new set of skills and a whole new profession." Many of the skills she acquired in perpetuating a mostly successful long career in government would easily carry over to a different industry, too.

Challenge is a great part of Carol's makeup. As a high-powered woman who almost never gets stuck, she is a motivated self-starter and risk taker, someone who never gets "too comfortable." She's not without support systems, though, to help her through the low points and to celebrate the highs.

"I've been lucky," she says from her office.

It's luck with a lot of energy, effort, and common sense.

THE END OF AN ERA As with Carol Bellamy, former television producer Phyllis Bosworth confronted the finality of one career and the difficult search for another. Phyllis, however, had not expected a "natural end" to her career until it was time to retire. She was fired from CBS, rehired, then fired again. Being twice burnt brought Phyllis a unique understanding of change. Because of it, she is a classic model of a successful Reinventor.

With blond tousled hair and a radiant smile, Phyllis transformed both her life and her look within six months of leaving CBS the second time. She reached her goal winningly, strategically, and realistically, but it was not without difficulties. Looking back now, she recalls:

> CBS was my identity. It wasn't just work, it was a way of life, my father, my friend. It meant an interesting job, security, a pension. Most of my social life revolved around work and I thought it was the best place to be. Suddenly, I was out, fired—a "lifer" with no place to go.

Phyllis Bosworth, "grateful for the job," first took her desk at CBS as a secretary twenty-two years ago when television was a "fat" industry, growing up through its golden age. A self-proclaimed "good listener," Phyllis was the first woman in the early 1970s to be promoted to researcher, then associate producer. Eventually, her credits included those of producer of the CBS news, newsworthy features such as the "Bicentennial Minute," and various daytime magazine shows. The position gave her credibility and ready access to the world.

In 1985, a precipitous budget cut at the network put Phyllis out of work for the first time in her life. "I was, in effect, a money target—a high-salaried producer—and the logical cutback," she explained. Understanding the state of affairs didn't make things easier for her; leaving CBS reverberated through all parts of her life. She told me what happened:

> I couldn't believe it could happen to me. I was at a point in my career where I thought things would pretty much stay the same until it was time for me to retire. Change was unimaginable. What could I do now? It was frightening.
>
> One fact gave me *some* comfort, though. I had a contract with CBS and my agent assured me they would rehire me, rather than buy me out. That was all right with me: I just wanted to go back.

Though still in shock, Phyllis made the effort to find a producing job that was equivalent to the one she'd left. Job offers eventually began to come her way, but at lower salaries; then CBS called her and she returned "home." But home was no longer the formidable communications complex, a monolith of power and prosperity. "Black Rock" was chipped and parts of it were tumbling. Coming home, she was to discover, had mixed blessings.

Work was different now; some heart had gone out of it. Her job demanded nearly twice the labor; she was working in a dual capacity because of employee cutbacks. Perks, too, were trimmed. The network was torn by management crises and financial problems. Then in March of 1987, she was fired again.

Phyllis knew television as an industry had "matured" and would never be the same again. More important to her now, her place was taken by others—it could never be recaptured. This revelation brought her face to face with some truths about her life and what to do next. Phyllis understood the fragility of a staff job like the one she'd held at CBS; in the communications business, such jobs are more easily sacrificed.

She had to figure out (1) which skills would be translatable to an industry that was still in its *prime,* and (2) where she could find some long-range security. To hit both targets, Phyllis had to think strategically. She analyzed her skills and what she wanted, in detail. Her conclusion made good sense: while achievement and security would have to be generated from her own efforts, she would not be beholden entirely to one industry or one boss—she would become an entrepreneur. But of what?

Going to law school was an appealing prospect, but unrealistic in terms of the time it would take for a degree. She found her future serendipitously. A friend was selling commercial real estate and doing well. It struck her as a prospect. She said:

> It felt like a weird idea at first, but the more I listened to her and to other people I met in the business, the more a career in real estate made sense. I thought to myself, if I could sell people on getting up at six in the morning to bare their souls on television, I could get them interested in a property and sell *that.*

Phyllis talked over her plans with a lawyer friend, her mentor. He thought the move a smart one; he even recommended a small company for her to apply to, one with great growth potential. She signed on. Her career changed, and so did her style. At CBS she could live in jeans. In real estate, she had to look the part of a real estate broker dealing with multimillion-dollar properties. That meant making a number of personal changes, including a twenty-pound weight loss and a total restyling. In all, she's happy about her decision:

> Putting a real estate deal together is not much different from producing a TV show—it's a matter of getting the facts and figuring out what goes together. In one year in the business, my first sale was a multimillion-dollar property. I see I can survive. The world isn't scary anymore. I get up in the morning and I'm learning.

In her way, Phyllis represents millions of people who have lost jobs and must look outside one profession they know for a new career. In another way, Phyllis is unique. She was given a second chance to discover that there is no going back—that to romanticize television would be living among the ruins. It was a fortunate grace period for her. It allowed her to develop an objectivity about the business, but it was painful for her to let go; she loved it so.

Resolutely, though, she looked at the truths and acted upon them—the industry had peaked and the economics of it were obvious: she could not retrieve or replicate what was lost, and it was time to move ahead with her life. She was not the only one to be fired from CBS. What made Phyllis remarkable among them is that she recognized the reality while many did not. They are still at the outplacement offices, yearning for the glory days, going nowhere.

WHO IS THE MAN IN THE MIRROR? As Phyllis Bosworth changed careers purposefully within a short time, so has Dr. William Greenspon gradually inched away from his medical practice toward his earliest love, art. Ten years ago, very few professionals—doctors, lawyers, judges—left these careers at the height of their power, unless the reasons involved ill health or retirement. They were anomalies, like Somerset Maugham, Anton Chekov, William Carlos Williams, and Michael Crichton—all medical doctors who decided to follow another star.

Essentially entrepreneurs, doctors are part of a new wave of specially educated professionals who are giving up practices because of economics, particularly mounting insurance costs. Others, as Bill Greenspon, have completed this part of their lives—medicine no longer holds their interest as a life's work. They have done it. Even with the sense of completion, separating away from a practice isn't easy. There are important issues to contend with, as Bill Greenspon's story reveals.

Physically, he doesn't fit the preconceived picture of how a psychiatrist specializing in the treatment of autistic children would look. Tall, shambling, and with unruly hair, Dr. Greenspon is closer to one's picture of the classic preoccupied artist in old sweat pants and teeshirt.

Dr. Greenspon has been easing into his recently acquired occupation of art dealer over the last twenty years. The turning point came from him, coincidentally enough, when *The New York Times* did a decorating feature on his apartment and the exceptional art and antiques collection he has assembled. He said:

> I was having a good enough life. My practice was going better than okay. I was working like a dog. I had a stately apartment, my wife was at home, and my kids were going to the right school. My friends were mostly doctors, conventional men, more interested in getting through life without making any mistakes than anything else.
>
> Then I opened up the paper and looked at myself on that page. I saw myself as some wiseass doctor, twenty pounds overweight and smug, sitting there, showing off my possessions. I thought: Is this me? Is this what happened to me? Do I *really* look like this . . . a bore, some guy who's lost his juice, someone you wouldn't want to spend time with?

Bill Greenspon was raised to fulfill his parents' expectations. An only child, he respected his optometrist father's wishes and went to medical school, although his earliest inclination was to be an artist. "How does a boy from Bluefield, West Virginia, become an artist?" he asked. "When I was younger, I didn't have the ego to do what I wanted." Instead, Bill went to medical school, interned, and found his way into psychiatry when the army sent him to Korea.

Eventually, he married, fathered two children, and built his career. He ran a private practice as well as taking on the medical directorship of a Brooklyn psychiatric center. "I was doing what I was supposed to be doing. I didn't *feel.* I just *did.*" All the while, he was collecting paintings, meeting painters, building a unique collection of antiques and period objects.

Then the *Times* feature appeared.

It took the death of his father two years later before he acted on his dream. "*I am not quick to change,*" he said, but when his father died, he was stunned. What Bill felt is something other men I interviewed vouched for too—that moment when you know you are face to face with your mortality. One day, an event glaringly points it up and you are finally moved to act. He said:

> I not only saw my own mortality, but I was shocked by the fact that I was still just going through the motions. Like anyone else, you only go around once and I was not living. My social life was a bore, full of people who didn't take chances, either. Work was

> plugging along. My marriage was wooden. I was forty-five years old and . . . now what?

Bill gave up the directorship of the clinic in Brooklyn, trading it for a part-time consultancy there, and separated from his wife. His income was limited, but with his impeccable eye, he bought "significant pieces." A mentor and friend changed him "from a dilettante to a professional." Within a year, he had a plan.

The next step was to rent a booth at an upcoming antique show, where, to his "amazement," he sold a few things. Later, he sold objects from his home. Although dealing in antiques was actually harder than he thought it would be, he wasn't discouraged. He knew this was the direction he would take.

For Dr. Greenspon, the transition from being a medical doctor working twelve hours a day to being a full-time antiques dealer and working artist mostly took place over the last five years. There were no sudden and startling changes in his life, but he didn't want to worry about money during the transition. He told me candidly:

> I know dealing art isn't "safe," but as it turns out, being a practicing psychiatrist isn't that safe either. Patients come and go, directorships may not last. This is how it is. I'm trying to do something with my life, and art has a certain significance. I didn't actually fulfill my father's dream, although I tried to for twenty-five years.

Most of his medical colleagues don't understand the transformed Dr. Greenspon. They think he's "nuts" for giving up a medical practice. They don't understand how he dresses or behaves. Such opinions don't matter much to him now. And except for two special patients, he has given up psychiatry. "Why hold on?" he says. "I've done it. I want to go on and make art."

REINVENTOR PROFILE Those who are willing to put themselves on the line and seriously change professions are a fascinating study in courage, self-understanding, and *will.* It's not easy to give up one life for another, or to put oneself in a situation where others decide your fate, as with Carol Bellamy's running for elective office.

Those who turn around have a particular M.O. that demonstrates their personal strength and conviction. They are committed to what they work at and do it well, until they know it is time to give it up for something different. They have three qualities that the Lifer, for example, does not exercise very liberally or at all: Reinventors have a high tolerance for ambiguity and deal brilliantly with sudden crises or quick-change priorities. They prefer a looser kind of control, although they may work in very structured environments, even bureaucracies.

Reinventor personalities like visibility and many like being first—they are action-oriented people and can think on their feet. They're experts at evaluating information and they often operate on hunches albeit using their analytical ability. And like Carol Bellamy, Reinventors are motivated by complex and challenging situations and approach them with measured daring.

Many Reinventors who make successful transitions are reformed realists. They share with Synthesizers and Lifers strong attachments to the "secure" environment but, unlike their counterparts, when they finally make up their minds, are more adventurously willing to let go.

Some Reinventors, before they make a complete change, will struggle to duplicate the market that is phasing them out; then they become super realists and let go. Phyllis Bosworth finally knew that no amount of effort would breathe life into past glory; no matter how much she wanted it to be so, there was no going back.

Enthusiastic and insightful with a need to express themselves, as is true with Synthesizers, Reinventors are ultimately higher risk takers, but don't fool themselves about what works and doesn't work for them.

GETTING TO THE NEXT STEP

All four styles of M.O. are not mutually exclusive. You can, in fact, cross the line from one to another at different points in your life. It's something that happens often.

As a former Lifer, you may have thought your entire career

was going to be in one place. Then something changed and you became a visionary who no longer had to tough it out. You became a Synthesizer, in spite of the mythology you held about yourself.

Not all predictions and plans come true.

As a Synthesizer, the thought of commitment to a profession and an avocation *at the same time* once seemed impossible, but you found a second passion and can't give it up. Now a Builder, you probably never expected to achieve what you have.

As a Reinventor, shifting from one seemingly unrelated profession to another, you then choose a profession that bridged your past experiences and became a Synthesizer. With all the wildly divergent things you can do, it is not surprising. In many cases, the shift happens accidentally—you could not have strategically planned this kind of successful layering.

But whatever your style, it is a long-term commitment to a goal that matters.

Each of the people I spoke to in this chapter had a moment when they knew that change had been set in motion, and that they would *recommit.* Where that commitment would lead them many did not know at once. They did know there was no stopping it.

Change, set in motion, transforms you. How?

Change, metaphysically, has an anatomy, and it goes through many shapes before it actually affects the action *you* take. Before you feel its first jolt—the *trigger,* the external event or inner revelation that tells you your life will never be the same—change can take on a life and shape of its own. Chapter Three examines the anatomy of change.

3

ANATOMY OF CHANGE

The Trigger

For each of us there is a moment of truth when things will never be the same again. You're fired from a job. A twist of fate presents you with an unanticipated windfall. A big promotion has your name on it. A business hunch you pursued in the face of adversity finally pays off and your life is set irrevocably on a different path. A sudden spiritual awakening beckons you down another path, this time with a real direction toward a mission, a new purpose.

This moment of truth is the *trigger*.

The click of a trigger has a single function: *to usher in inevitable change*. It's the catalyst that signals the *end* of one aspect of your life and the *beginning* of another. It puts you back behind the wheel—in a position to shift gears.

TRIGGERS: UNDERSTANDING WHAT THEY ARE

Triggers are not created equal. Some are like pebbles dropped in a pond—they create minor ripples, a by-product of inevitable change; others create major jolts that are immediately life changing. It's sudden success, the death of a close friend, or quitting a job to go into business for yourself. The more your emotional investment in a relationship or a venture, the greater the feeling of loss *or* gain and the deeper the flood of feelings when your life is shaken up.

Brenda Goodman, an innovative New York career counselor who specializes in guiding people through the vulnerable transition periods between jobs, describes the trigger stage vividly: "It's the moment you have to let go of the trapeze you're swinging on and reach for the one coming at you. You may look down at that abyss below—the unknown—and think you're not going to make it, but you do."

Triggers have no predictable form. They overlap, occur in sequences, or originate from a feeling *or* an event. Fate has been known to be relentless as one trigger after another catapults your life out of balance. The "abyss" widens, all too accommodating. Then, in a snap, another trigger puts it all back in order.

When you're lucky, life tenders momentous events one at a time and at manageable intervals, giving you time to recover between them. But whether they take their place as dramatic milestones or anecdotal curiosities, we tend to remember triggers and how they changed the course of our lives.

INCIDENTS THAT TRIGGER CHANGE

Life is shaped by daily incidents that define its structure—but *very few of these incidents actually trigger change.* Something else has to happen: the "x" factor. No formula exists to divine what this factor is or how you will feel when change occurs. In looking for "moments of truth" and what may account for them in shaping a career, I found the following responses to have a universal kinship. Triggers, people told me, are:

- "Too many little indignities at work that add up until it turns to 'murder,' " said an insurance investigator who was being forced out of her job because of a merger. It took months of fighting for her job before she could accept the fact that it was the end of an era. "I *had to quit* or lose all my dignity," she said.

• "The breaking point. You've had enough!" said one advertising art director in his late forties who quit over an "oil and water" personality clash with his boss. "When you work for a man who undervalues you and all your efforts, you've got to leave to save yourself."

• "How money changes everything," said a curatorial assistant in a large auction gallery. "If there isn't enough or suddenly you have more than you need, your life changes around it."

• "Humiliation. It's running on empty and thinking *everyone* knows. You even feel shame with your kids. You fear they think you're a loser," this, from a Boston therapist whose wife left him after twenty years, the shock of which caused him to let his practice slide precariously downhill for over a year.

• "Age. Mortality. The number itself—reaching twenty-one, thirty-five, forty, fifty, sixty-two years or older—has some magic attached to it. You give yourself an absolute amount of time to accomplish your goals," said a New York filmmaker who has himself set a time frame for "making it."

• "Family events. It's not just the death of a parent, but how it changes your *role* ever after," said a young Chicago man who decided to enter business school soon after his father died. "I was suddenly 'the man in the family,' the new 'caretaker.' It gave me a reason to straighten out and grow up."

Spiritual transformation triggers change; so can knowledge, relocation, accidents of fate, or sudden physical incapacitation. New friendships or a love relationship—as with all other triggers—can not only spark a different career decision but affect other aspects of your life, too.

WHO RESPONDS TO TRIGGERS? HOW AND WHEN DO THEY RESPOND?

Philosophers as well as scientists have examined the phenomenon of stimulus and response. The questions they raise ask what moves people to take action; what their perceptions are of the outside world; why habits are chosen and formed; how personality develops. Big issues. In experiments with laboratory animals, behaviorists can track responses in a *controlled* environment and understand more clearly what motivates animals to run a maze for a reward and stop running when they have learned that there is no reward to be had. Makes sense.

People are more complex. In life's "mazes," our perceptions, habits, and pursuit of pleasure and rewards die hard. Even when a reward is guaranteed at the end of a "run," a number of people will choose *not* to pursue it. If the reward is withdrawn, still others will continue to run the same ground, knowing the only payoff is *no* payoff. Yet others insist there's a trick involved. They'll reformulate the game and run an individual *concept* of a maze to suit themselves.

Human motivation may vary widely, but it is always a key ingredient in the value judgments we make. A trigger is only the stimulus that sets off a response, and the *same* trigger can trigger different things for different people. I learned of an interesting contrast of responses with two women I interviewed, one in Miami and the other in Atlanta. Both were in their mid-thirties, both were workaholics and career strategists, and both were coming out of an illness.

When I met them, Karen and Thea had pretty much recovered from Epstein-Barr Syndrome, a long-term, enervating disorder much like mononucleosis. Karen, an anthropologist, decided to curtail her usual mad pace of overwork, writing scholarly papers, running thirty miles a week, and sacrificing personal relationships. Her choice, coming out of an illness, was to cultivate her personal life and cut back fifteen hours on a sixty-five-hour work week.

Thea, an advertising account executive who lived on diet sodas, take-out food, and unfiltered cigarettes, was her polar opposite. With the same trigger of the same disease, Thea found a new channel for her ambition: she increased her work load by starting a *new* career, at first trying it out on weekends. Now her catering business, based on vegetarian menus she'd devised for herself during her illness, has taken off.

There's irony in hearing people report that "illness was the best thing that happened to them"—something that even cancer survivors have been known to confirm. Life is fragile and illness makes you aware of your mortality. Time is all you have to make opportunity your own.

Some people know this instinctively and are *aware of* and respond to triggers at a faster pace than others. The *speed* with which a person responds to a trigger, I found, is as much a component of personality as temperament.

New York real estate broker Gloria Sokolin is the classic paradigm of the quick trigger responder. Elegant in style and highly effective, Gloria started the first of her two successful careers with no experience and an unexpected surge of self-confidence, "always with the faith that tomorrow something wonderful will happen." It began many years ago when, out of curiosity, Gloria and a friend took an introductory course in interior decorating.

At the same time, Gloria had hired a decorator to do her own apartment, but as things turned out, most of the design input was hers.

One day, an acquaintance of hers, who'd been to her apartment and liked what she saw, called and asked Gloria to decorate her place. "She assumed I'd designed it all myself," Gloria said. Rather than apologize for lack of experience and back down, Gloria knew she could do the job and seized the chance. A decorating business ultimately evolved from this first job, and she soon joined forces with partner Judy Woodfin, an alliance that lasted ten years.

When she decided to switch careers to real estate sales, Gloria hired a staff to run the design business, although she still works with them as a consultant. The denouement is this: twenty-five years later, the friend who took an introductory class with Gloria is *still* taking decorating classes, and every other kind of course, and turning down jobs, feeling she doesn't know enough.

One woman sees her future in an unexpected phone call while another builds her future on not being ready. What is operating internally? What motivates one person to respond decisively *in the snap of a finger,* believing, as Gloria did, that "you have to put yourself on the line and if you're wrong, you're wrong," while another woman cannot make a decision because she is invested in never being right *or* wrong?

Nella Barkley, director of the Crystal-Barkley Center, a landmark consulting organization for counseling people on "life service designs"—a process of decision making in career planning—explains one reason for this behavior:

> When emotions and self-esteem are involved, motivations for not responding to a trigger are subtle. Some people are not aware of what they're doing. They literally don't pay attention to what's going on around them.
>
> For some reason, they lose energy, decide something looks more attractive, and become unfocused. There's a lot of activity in the subconscious that stops people from following through.

The issue of *readiness* can be a real obstacle. Jack Riley, a high school history teacher frustrated by twelve years at his job, complained bitterly to me about his situation: "I've got to get out of this career and learn a new skill," he said, earnestly. "Every year is the same; things will never get better." Complaint consumes all the energy Jack has put into the process of changing for the last four years.

Life is pushing him along, as others like him. What are the consequences of Jack's seeming boredom? He may stabilize for a while, then a trigger will detonate a recurring event in his life—extreme discipline problems in the classroom, a student harasses him, he's asked to take on extracurricular assignments beyond his interest or patience. One morning Jack will walk into his classroom and think he can't bear the same routine one more day. He may leave, but more likely, Jack may have to be fired to get on with his life; this man, simply, does not have the wherewithal to change on his own.

For the decorating student finishing up her quarter-century's worth of preparation for a career and the dissatisfied teacher, a trigger prompts not action but a deep-seated response: *fear.* For these two people, there is tremendous panic associated with embarking on any new situation that will enable them to change. The trigger need not always be of major importance; rather, the way they see it, *not* facing the fear is always less consequential than confronting the possibility of change.

Nella Barkley added a thought about this:

> Even if the trigger is big enough, I think it is *the size of the fear, not the trigger.* This is the very familiar, "I'm more comfortable in my misery than in something I don't know about."
>
> Someone who embarks on a program to take control of his or her life and then doesn't do it won't have as much to blame it on. It's a matter of taking responsibility.

New York psychologist Dr. David Yarosh believes that sometimes a response to a trigger depends on "how stubborn you are and how often you need God to kick you in the rear." Some people literally will not do anything until that "kick"—an extreme situation or series of troubling events—becomes so punishing that not fighting back seems like madness. He said:

> On occasion, such "punishments" work very nicely to make a change. If the structure of your life cracks, you are likely to take action to rebuild in some form. In this way, negative reinforcement forces a response. But, some people don't take action even though they are "kicked" again and again. They may even get used to the abuse and never take any action.

Tom Peters, author of *A Search for Excellence,* came to a similar conclusion in an interview about what makes corporations change. He remarked that "the impetus to change doesn't come until you've been knocked in the face." Hardship may trigger positive responses in a percentage of the population, but it will sink others.

IDENTIFYING TRIGGERS: INTERNAL VS. EXTERNAL "PUSHES"

Responses are individual, but the basis of response springs from either an *event* or *nonevent,* the exact line of distinction between the two blurring on occasion.

An *event* is an obvious circumstance to which we tend to put a value of positive or negative. Getting fired or winning a lottery drawing are two such clear-cut events. A single jolt can set up an opportunity to examine your life and reshape its direction at the most fundamental level.

Alfred Nobel is a vivid example of one unanticipated life story enlightened by such a jolt: he came upon his own obituary in a Swedish newspaper. It was his brother who had died, but the paper mistakenly ran the wrong man's notice. Nobel, a scientist esteemed at the time for the discovery of dynamite—and made rich by it—read what the paper had to say about him. And it disturbed him.

Among its uses, dynamite was used for easily and inexpensively manufactured weaponry. The obituary suggested that Nobel had provided the means for nations to arm themselves and threaten world survival. His legacy, *as he understood it* now, was as the man who made annihilation available at affordable prices.

Nobel was lucky. He was given a chance to come back to earth, so to speak, without the inconvenience of having had to leave it and reassess how his life affected others. More significantly, this "journey" triggered a decision he may not have predicted for himself had the paper buried the right man. Rather than dwell on the blunder and feel misunderstood, Nobel responded with a newfound purpose: to change his legacy for the benefit of others. He established what would soon be regarded as the world's most prestigious reward for professional accomplishment and contributions for the good of humanity, the Nobel Prize.

And then, there is the *nonevent*—a trigger that's much subtler, but just as powerful a motivator: you use your intuition or tune in to your "sense" of things or "gut feelings" to provide the information you need to make a decision. You can, for example, heed a strong feeling that tells you to *act* on something even though "real life" discourages you with evidence to the contrary. A nonevent is how you interpret an event.

NONEVENT TRIGGERS: THE INTERNAL SEARCH

Scott Larson is a forty-year-old New Englander with a quarterback's burliness softened around the edges. Intense and intelligent, he is as excited by ideas as he is spiritual by nature. A former minister, Scott is now a management consultant with a large international organization. His career change hinged on a moment of inner clarity. The paths to the ministry and then into business—the surprise in his career—were taken with equal conviction. He said:

> There are things that speak to your soul, these "flash points." Inside, you get a profound awareness of a connection to something . . . and you may not know why. But the *feeling* is this enormous sigh of relief that says: This is okay, this is the right thing to do.

This connectedness is something we all search for. Most of life, though, is less connection and more *activity.*

Events and *nonevents* can mount up, sometimes creating a domino effect. In a short period of time, your career is short-circuited, an important relationship deflates, a parent becomes ill, a crank sues you for a million for denting his bumper when you stopped short at a light. Too many circumstances demanding too many decisions to deal with all at once beget a rush of conflicting feelings and mounting stress. This is understandable.

Such stress can reach a point that physicists call "critical mass"—a point where an object cannot absorb any more shock and it detonates. People have described this feeling of being fragmented, "blown apart" from the chaos of many unresolved feelings and events. Others are flooded with sensations and reach a *saturation point.*

During these stress periods, typical reactions are withdrawal, acting out, indulgence in alcohol or drugs, or overeating. Enervated by stress and with limited inner resources, you may single out only one domain of your life for care and management; other areas suffer. Or, like Bob Lawson, a self-styled "invulnerable street kid," you temporarily collapse under the strain. With all these triggers, *there is no real life change*—there is just reaction.

But if the connections are right, a deluge can trigger *freedom.* This happened to Marjorie Harding.

A successful consumer advocate who began her career in her late thirties, Marjorie's is the classic story of a woman who followed tradition, married young, and, as she says, "lived by rote for twelve years." During this time, Marjorie unsuccessfully fought her husband's ultra-conservative ideas about marriage: Women don't work and so she wouldn't.

"Intellectual starvation, boredom, and a terrifying sense of aimlessness" motivated her to take the first step against her husband's wishes. She was hired by a small environmental agency where she worked part time. Eventually, she was promoted and made a name for herself locally. But Marjorie's husband begrudged her this success and began a campaign to undermine her achievements.

For two years he chipped away at her confidence. Then he pushed one time too many: he demanded she cancel an out-of-town trip to a conference where she was to be the key speaker—and she complied. Marjorie suddenly saw where her future was going. It was the trigger she needed. A week later, Marjorie took her daughters and, in a rented van, left Ohio. She told me:

> I wanted to work . . . I needed something for myself. I had all those years of being told I wasn't important, of being treated like a child. The turmoil got unbearable.
>
> I said to myself: Why am I here? Why take this constant humiliation? It was stay and perish or leave and get another chance.
>
> I must have had a belief in myself that things would work out. I know if I'd really stopped to think about breaking away when I did and what it meant, I'd have gotten myself too scared to do it.

Boris Rand, a onetime professor of international politics now director of a not-for-profit organization, shared this "now or never" trigger that sprang from a saturation point. A sophisticated European with a luminous intelligence, Boris left academia after twenty-five years to enter corporate life. His last five years at the university were momentous. He "sensed a tremendous reservoir of energy" in himself that was "being fired into the wrong area, year after year." Teaching in college was simply more limited than his range of interests or passions.

When his children went off to school and his marriage ended, the decision to leave his professorship was somehow made easier. On his own, his family obligations taken care of, Boris, with a history of total faith in institutions, jumped into the fray.

Within three years, he was fired from two consecutive corporate jobs.

He spoke candidly to me about his "failure":

> I decided that the Lord did not want me to be a businessman. I was told twice that I wasn't very good, and in looking at how I handled some transactions, I knew they were right.
>
> I literally crashed, sure I had "lost it." I paced like a panther in a cage, trying to mobilize and figure out what to do.

It took a month or so before Boris could separate his feelings of having "lost it" from the simple facts of the situation: he might have been a star in academia, but he had a lot to learn about the business world. Inexperience had flattened him, not incompetence. He'd been dropped into two high-power positions before he was ready.

Boris is a great believer in fate, as much as he is a practical man. He reassessed his losses and his feelings about what had transpired.

> I remember looking in the mirror and thinking: Who is this man who doesn't even stand up straight? Then it came to me. I knew I'd merely lost my *confidence* for a brief period because of circumstances, but I still had self-*respect.* Self-confidence is one thing and self-respect is another.
>
> It was soon clear that I was wrong for *their* business, not wrong for business.

If life is peaks and valleys, Boris made a clear *internal* decision right then to make it back up to the top. Not right for the tough, bottom-line corporation, Boris found his niche in the safer "middle ground." He soon joined a not-for-profit organization with a number of ties to academia—a more realistic direction for a man like him to take.

TRIGGERS: AREAS IN YOUR LIFE WHERE THEY MOST LIKELY OCCUR

Although the scope of event and nonevent triggers is vast, the three broadest and most characteristic areas are:

- managing loss
- the test of a belief system
- the pursuit and fulfillment of a mission or dream

MANAGING LOSS

Happy endings tend to captivate the imagination if only because they're beginnings in disguise. But *real* endings, such as being fired, losing control of a usually orderly life, or the dissolution of a marriage, tend to be viewed as catastrophes.

When the structure of your life is suddenly disabled by loss of a job, maintaining a clear-headed expectancy about the future is not the simplest of tasks. You worry about dealing with the pressures of getting a job equal to or better than the one you lost. Money, which is suddenly short, takes on added importance.

If your nature is to be the unflappable and persevering optimist, you're ahead of the game. Optimists tend to invest little time in mourning what has been lost. For them, *action* is not only part of the healing process, it is life affirming. Catastrophe teaches the optimist what *doesn't* work while it provides enough motivation to begin again. Episodes of "failure," loss, and bankruptcy are turned around and *advantage* is pried from the wreckage.

For the rest of us, loss is always shocking, even when we see it coming. We lose perspective on its meaning. Blame shifts back and forth between players as a way to deflect pain from a bruised ego. Disproportionate value is placed on the meaning of a job. The greater your identification with it, the harder it is to separate the boundaries of work and soul and the deeper the wound when it's lost.

Of course, there is loss beyond your control. It's not your fault that the merger went through, the stock market crashed, the boss died, you reached retirement age, or an industry hit a downtrend. This loss is natural—it is simply unavoidable *change.* Then there is the kind of loss you bring on yourself: You botched the job or your behavior clashed with management.

CAREER CRISIS: WHEN IT'S "PERSONAL" The career choice you make will always affect your personal life. When you make a career choice, you tend to weigh what's good or right for *you* as an individual with a particular set of skills applied to a specific job. And if that job is lost, your ego will be bruised by the hammers of adversity—but you tend to recover faster than you expected. Without a job, you still have your *self.* The most successful people are not those with fewer problems, but those who've learned to work them through.

There are also those for whom "threat"—or putting yourself on the line or *in the line of fire*—is less important than the *opportunities* that may come from taking risks. If any trigger is life changing, it is getting your name on a ballot for a high public office. Geraldine Ferraro, the first woman to be nominated for U.S. vice president, endured the intense public scrutiny common to public officials when she accepted the nomination. But she was also "subjected to bitter personal attacks" (for one, accusations regarding her husband's business and some of his associates) and these were more difficult to deal with.

When she looks back at the campaign and how people "focused on the negatives," she doesn't brood about defeat and what might have been, but *honor.* She recalled the Democratic National Convention and told me:

> I thought: This is the center of leadership in the free world. And I was so taken by the institution itself and by the fact that this kid from Queens was a part of it.
>
> I was honored to be nominated for the ticket. Thousands of people said, this woman could be vice president. Running for office was terrific. It's not what happens to you personally, but it's what you're doing.

A self-proclaimed "practical woman," Geraldine has evaluated the "options that remain" for resuming her career in law. Other than her involvement in a number of political associations for the advancement of democracy, and writing a second book, she has had to deal with consequences of being a public and controversial figure. She is so visible a personality that a return to trial work, she feels, is impossible. The "reality" of the courtroom says something different:

> . . . If I defended someone, there would be a jury of twelve, some of whom love Geraldine Ferraro madly and some who don't, but virtually everyone in New York knows me. And those who didn't like me might take it out on the fate of my client.
>
> I lost the vice presidential election, but I had to step down from my congressional chair, too. This was difficult for me. But I can't worry about this stuff anymore. I don't put myself in situations where I look at the Capitol at night and get depressed over what might have been. I have just moved on.

What are the alternatives? How could she use her experience as a politician and her vocation in law and come up with a new career direction? She told me:

> You have to be realistic and learn how to deal with life. When I was in Congress, I did some trade work and I have an ability to deal with foreign clients. I've been admitted to the court of international trade, working with foreign clients.
>
> It will be a challenge.

What inner resource allows Geraldine Ferraro to put herself out there, to fight and rally, while others would be triggered to back off?

New York psychiatrist Dr. Yvette Obadia believes that people who are *not* in a crisis are "carried by the flow of, '*Yes, I can.*' " It's a vivid and dramatic analogy. When there's a flow, the fuel you use to accomplish something is not the flooding fuel that stalls progress. If you're healthy, energy is released and "transformed into strength, thought and breath." Then if there's a trigger, things will make sense and you can accept the premise of the situation and see its range of possibilities. You can act.

THE COST OF ARROGANCE Loss is shocking if you ardently believe in your competence, your style, and your intelligence—and no entries on your résumé suggest mediocrity, never mind admitting actual failure. John Stevenson fit this profile, the man who always won. Although it belied a fragile ego, John's *attitude* was one of arrogance and entitlement. He was photogenic and quotable and his attitude won him fleeting wealth and success.

And doomed him to getting fired.

Achievement triggered in John an out-of-control sense of power; then when he lost, it was a calamity for him.

In retrospect, he sees how he twisted a great opportunity into a tangle of power games and a losing battle of personalities. William Morin, chairman of Drake Beame Morin, the largest outplacement company in America, noted in an interview that "chemistry is responsible for 80 percent of all terminations. . . ." It's an indisputable point in the difference between those who survive in an organization and those who falter.

A dynamic Californian in his mid-forties, John once thought his future was secure, if not blessed. Ten years ago, he was hired as a founding employee of what became a hugely successful computer company. He was a great salesman, hired solely on that basis. The company gave him money and freedom "because I was a talented guy," he said. But John didn't fit in.

> I'm not a team player and I didn't like being part of an organization. Instead I operated on the premise "I can do it better my way." I had no vision, no motivation except *this will be a great ride for John Stevenson.*
>
> I had the fantasy that I was some sort of prince and operated as if life would go on forever. It was the opportunity of a lifetime and I screwed it up.

From his lofty perch, John lost perspective about his place in the company. He did his job brilliantly, but what pleased him more was the high five-figure weekly salary, the limo at his disposal, and other perks. Inaccessible as an administrator, he held himself as separately from the others as possible.

The man who paid for all of this, John's employer, was physically his opposite. John was tall, patrician, and well educated; his boss was stocky, gruff, and a flashy dresser who spoke street English. John pegged him his "inferior."

An uncompromising snob, John was soon left with nothing but his contempt for others—he was fired.

Stuck in an inflated image of his own making, John set up a world where he expected gratitude from his employer for the privilege of having hired him. For years he'd gotten away with promoting this image of himself, until it burst, overextended—a deflated fantasy. John came up against a man who wasn't willing to pay his price to keep his ego pumped. A side effect of arrogance is estrangement from the reality of a situation—*you don't know what you don't know.* John explained:

> You don't know the purpose of the organization, you don't listen to what management wants to accomplish, you don't find out how you can contribute and go on from there.
>
> You don't know how to have a conversation with a boss you need to insult. You don't even know to be appropriately respectful to the man who is providing you with a terrific lifestyle.
>
> When you *think* you know everything, you can't assess anything correctly, least of all what is in your own best interest.

John managed to get a second plum job in the industry, but he was soon fired again, for the same reason: attitude. It was the loss of his second job within three years and the coincident breakup of his marriage that triggered his going into therapy.

This was one of those rare times in his life when John felt disoriented. He didn't know how to handle such unfamiliar pain and disorder. He had always been in control.

> I wanted to be the world's expert, the greatest, the best. The *facts* now said something different. I had to change the conversations I had with myself and start answering the real questions: How do I deal what's here with who I am? The only way up from this point was to literally declare myself incompetent and find the appropriate help.

John was a little afraid of his employers. He feared showing that he might not know the right questions or blurt an answer that would prove wrong. It was simply immaturity. John also diverted private characterizations about one boss's style into general truths about business. Being arrogant, he assumed these assessments were not only important, but the only opinion of value. With enlightenment and maturity, John's perspective is different. He said, "If the guy's flashy, what does that mean? Is this evidence that I can't trust him?"

More importantly now, his values have shifted. If he were ever offered something as good as what he first lost, he'd look at why he'd been invited into a unique opportunity and not do "anything detrimental" to undermine it.

BETRAYAL AND EMPTY PROMISES Arrogance can be one trigger that costs you a career, but its opposite, self-destructive resignation, can also propel you down a bumpy road. Dan Feria, a former art director at a large New York advertising agency, was fired when he precipitated the fight that brought on his own termination. Oddly enough, it was at a time when he feared being out of work.

"It wasn't about any issue, but knowing that the job had come to its end," he said. For Dan, the end really *was* about issues. There were too many empty promises and too many unwritten deals that didn't pay off for him. Staying at his job would only perpetuate more disappointment; he had to be free of it. Leaving his job with a show of strength salvaged an ego bruised by ten years of false hope, but such fortitude didn't last long.

Dan wanted to change careers, but he had no idea of where to turn once he decided *not* to pursue another position in advertising. "I see my life now as a downward spiral," he told me in somber tones. Dan cossets bitter memories over few rewards from a lifetime of work, feeling his best years are behind him.

Dan is suffering from common reactions to loss—feelings of ineptitude accompanied by a sense of loneliness, disconnection, confusion, and the fear that what has been lost is not only irretrievable but irreplaceable. Rosalind Grant, an Atlanta psychiatric social worker, shared such reaction when her pilot husband of fifteen years left her for another woman. A petite blonde with a vulnerable "Alice in Wonderland" style, Rosalind would soon discover that beneath the girlish innocence lived a woman filled with conviction. She said:

> I believed in love and that's all I needed for all those years. When Charlie left, I had no love, no husband, no money, no skills inside me to help pay the rent and no confidence in my ability to

> deal with the world. I cried for three months, scared out of my mind.

Unlike Bob, a breakthrough trigger event turned Rosalind's life around: a long forgotten memory resurfaced during an especially vulnerable moment. The message contained in the memory helped her put bitterness to one side. She could stop mourning the dissolution of her marriage and direct her energies toward finding work and rebuilding a life for herself.

The memory: Her mother had brought it up at a family dinner just the year before. It was an incident that happened to Rosalind when she was three years old. She had been in the front seat of the family car when her mother was trying to park. Suddenly, another driver shot into her spot. Rosalind said:

> My mother was furious at the guy, but *I* leaned out the window and yelled with real conviction, "Son of a bitch!" I'd once heard my father say it when the same thing happened to him.
>
> That memory of my young self, *fighting back,* gave me a glimmer that there *was* someone in there, something that would make it possible for me to get through. I found myself in the chaos.

It was the trigger Rosalind needed to gain back her confidence.

Fritz Perls, the founder of Gestalt therapy, describes a stage of extreme emotional frailty as "the impasse." An impasse occurs when outside support is withdrawn and you mistakenly believe there are no *internal* supports—that your inner strength has been stripped from you, too.

The delusion of being without internal or external resources is a powerful one. Give it too much credence, and it can bring disorder to your life. Often hinging on a complete identification with your possessions, your position, or your role, the loss of a relationship or loss of a job registers internally as a loss of self. In this way, it is a way of objectifying oneself, too.

There is the matter of getting through the impasse, the journey through which exacts a number of psychological symptoms—moments of whirling confusion or a sense of disorientation, panic, indecisiveness in the simplest matters. But, psychologists agree, if you work through the impasse without drugs or alcohol to mask the truth or distort consciousness, you can come through and find your real strength.

THE TEST OF A BELIEF SYSTEM

Often we move on assumptions about ourselves that aren't necessarily true. Or we function according to expectations. Or we aren't clear about what we believe until an issue presents itself to us and we must choose. We have many belief systems that guide our actions and thoughts about ourselves and others, but unless there is an *immediacy* to changing them, we don't consider changing at all.

To trigger a change in a belief system, experts agree, an ideology must interface with its test.

The idea raises a universal question: *How great a test can your belief system withstand?* What circumstance is required to trigger your conversion? Would sudden and extreme money problems, for one, be the trigger for you to change your values? If you've always thought of yourself as an honest person with a sense of fairness, would you "sell out" a colleague to get ahead? What *would* you sell? Can the views of another person influence your life and determine what path you will take? Or will a test of faith merely affirm your beliefs and strengthen them?

With the trigger of loss, something you cared about is irretrievable. You feel grief, confusion, even self-pity. The test of your belief system, however, reaches closer to the core of *why* you feel the way you do.

There is something in human beings that demands consistency; most of us don't anticipate situations where our fundamental belief system is put on the line. But it is, in fact, tested daily, especially in business where competition and the struggle for achievement are not often won with grace and the language of sincerity.

Ironically, a belief system can be challenged just when you most need consistency, and sometimes that consistency is hard to maintain; something has to give. Perhaps you act one way and *feel* another; you work with people whose standards offend you. Others in your life may not support a sudden shift in your thinking; now you're "different." If they have a great investment in your staying the same, they'll feel betrayed when you walk into unknown territory. They are used to you one way and fear they will lose you to a new belief.

Inconsistencies can be painful. For some people, deep conflicts are hard to maintain without substance abuse to blur the lines of demarcation.

LOYALTY AND CONFLICTING ETHICS Loyalty was once the issue at work: You stayed with a company for life, worked hard, and the company provided. There was a "contract," usually unwritten, between employer and employee of mutual responsibility to each other, within limits. You gave your time, your efforts, your skills, and the company gave you a salary, a pat on the back, and a pension. You fit in.

Times have changed; the contract is more loosely written and easily broken, not only by employees but by employers. One stock broker caught in the October 1987 stock market crash commented on what he sees as the prevailing trend: "People are always in movement, looking to advance their career—and they'll find whoever will give it to them, no matter where. There's no allegiance. The issue of loyalty has been challenged."

A young woman banker who was asked for a long-time commitment to a company had great misgivings about complying: "I worked a short time with a Japanese bank. The Japanese immediately plan your career with them—they expect loyalty for a lifetime. They mapped my career for me at a meeting—three years here, five there. They told me what I'd be doing in ten years. Finally, I said, "Thank you very much, but please take the intravenous needle out of my arm. I want to make some choices. I don't want to depend on you for the rest of my life."

Anne Anselmo, a woman in her late twenties, suffered when she was caught in a tangle of intercompany politics. It changed her philosophy forever after on how to plan her career. She'd been working at a prestigious auction house for four years when, through a contact, she was offered a better job at a rival gallery.

"The gallery I wanted to work for called my employer for a reference without my consent," Anne told me. "Instead of recommending me, my boss fired me! They were furious that I'd want to leave, especially when they found out for *which* gallery. They gave me two weeks' notice, saying they didn't owe me anything more than that even though I made a lot of money for them over the years. Then the other house decided they wouldn't 'cross-hire' and chose someone else. I guess they worried that my company would raid *them* for someone better. Suddenly I was out of *two* jobs!"

The lesson Anne drew from her double loss was a refocusing of values. Should she uphold her sense of fairness when her employer, and possibly all potential employers, protect their own interests "unfairly"? Anne decided, "I'd better watch out for myself and play the game better than they do from now on. I wasn't leaving my job out of disloyalty—I was simply going to a much better position. I felt they were disloyal to me, holding back my career, then punishing me by letting me go so easily. Four years should have meant something more to them."

PLAYING FAIR OR PLAYING THE GAME Loyalty and ethics triggered a change for an in-house lawyer who worked for a large West Coast multinational company. Feeling dissatisfied when two vice presidents brought in with new management introduced a political system that disturbed him, Steve Schultz, a thirty-eight-year-old scholarly looking ex-Midwesterner was at a loss at what to do. "Simply," he said, "these guys were operating in ways I thought were plain unethical. I was almost certain there were payoffs for putting deals together, but I didn't know what to do about it."

With no real hard evidence of corruption, Steve had no defense. Then he feared for his job. These two vice presidents stood between him and top management, and it was they who could determine his future with the company. He found himself being pushed into less important roles and given assignments normally handled by his subordinates—the classic steps employers take when they want to force someone out.

Politically handicapped and hurt by how he was being treated, Steve felt an unaccustomed sense of powerlessness and it confused him. "I'm someone who always functioned in a company according to expectations," he said. "I was always comfortable with that and then I wasn't comfortable anymore. I didn't know what to do. Everything had become a muddle."

Then he was excluded from a key organizational meeting, and it triggered a fateful change. It was a match to straw. Before this exclusion, Steve had been unable to act on the strength of his principles and report his suspicions. Neither could he just summon the courage to quit. The vice presidents clearly wanted him out. Now he felt he had *nothing to lose* by taking action—and he had an inspiration.

Steven thought about what he wanted from this company; before the new management came in he'd been with the company five years and liked them and what they produced. How could he stay with them? He evaluated his assets and his goals: "I'm a good negotiator and I believe strongly in *fairness*. . . . I prefer to work within an ethical framework," he said, "and I had to figure out what I could do to get it."

A week after the meeting, Steve went to the chairman of the company with an original proposal. Its purpose was to institute a corporate compliance system that would give all the company's subsidiaries the standards for appropriate and ethical behavior in all negotiations. In a move that would soon prove to be the ultimate "creative revenge," Steve was promoted to corporate headquarters. There now, he runs the system that will entrap his nemeses, the two corrupt vice presidents.

Although he didn't think of himself as political enough to confront the issue of corruption directly, Steve found how to deal with it in a much more far-reaching way.

PURSUIT OF A MISSION

He was known for geodesic domes, innovative solutions to housing problems, and his prefabricated shelters, but at one time, the brilliant engineer R. Buckminster Fuller believed his future doomed. A personal tragedy triggered an astonishing turnaround in thinking.

He was a young man then, married and living in marginal

poverty in a cold tenement apartment when his infant daughter died of pneumonia. Already feeling like a failure when his business went bankrupt, the guilt over his child's death drove Fuller into a period of deep anguish. One day, thinking he would end his life in the river, he faced a "jump or change" decision. In a flash of inspiration, he knew his life was worth something and what he could do. He vowed then to dedicate himself to serving others by finding a solution to accessible, affordable housing on a global and humanitarian scale.

The death of his daughter in an unheated apartment triggered a path that had taken Fuller on a lifetime commitment. In a way, it was his mission.

Finding a mission and making it your life's work bespeaks of a special kind of person. When you have a mission, you are more inclined to develop an *ideology that will change the lives of others.* The foundation of a mission is an idea that is both larger than life and, for you, transcends selfish motives.

If circumstance triggers a *purpose* in your life, then you may choose to be the one to convert others—act as a missionary—if you aren't the one who creates the mission itself.

People with a mission usually have one thing in common: a vision of accomplishment that usually goes beyond acquiring money. The pledge and obligation to a mission may trigger a desire for money—but it is money that's put in service to carry out the mission.

Any idea can set it off: early health food proponents Jethro Kloss, J.I. Rodale, and Adelle Davis, each in his/her own fashion, sought to change eating habits and educate people to the concept of good nutrition. Betty Friedan's *Feminine Mystique,* and later, Germaine Greer's *The Female Eunuch* sought to examine the course of women's lives and change the way women thought about themselves and their place in the world. People with a mission are ideologues, people with commitment and grit.

FIGHTING FOR A CANCER CURE Le Trombetta's mission was triggered by meeting Dr. Stanislaw Burzynski, a medical doctor and biochemist in Houston who has developed a revolutionary, nontoxic cancer treatment that Le is helping to get approved by the F.D.A. Her faith in Dr. Burzynski's commitment to finding a cancer cure and her fervent belief in his treatment inspired Le to pull up roots and move to Texas.

An elegant woman with a soft Georgia accent, Le, a classic Reinventor, studied theories of alternative medicine but she was unsure of how to channel her interest in the field. Instead, she held onto a number of creative jobs in Atlanta, finding them frivolous and unsatisfying. Ultimately, she wrote and produced a popular children's television show, then she became a special projects director for a large shopping mall. Then her father's illness triggered the move that put her on the path she'd always been seeking.

"My father was critically ill with cancer, and he was getting better with Dr. Burzynski's treatment," Le told me. "Then when I met Dr. Burzynski and saw his dedication and fully understood *his* purpose, I knew I had to work with him." She moved from Atlanta to Houston to become his public affairs director, screening patients and lobbying to get his treatment approved.

> There is a feeling you get when you help others that is not like any other. Once you see the results, once you help someone get well, you can never go back to organizing "Jell-O Jumps" or promoting merchandise in a mall.
>
> When I visualize returning to Atlanta and my former life, I know I can't do it. It would be emptiness. I don't believe there is a clear line of demarcation between your principles, your work, and your life. For me, everything has changed with this experience.

A worthy commitment to assisting others can extend to those in the prime of their strength and vitality, as in the following circumstance.

KATHERINE SWITZER AND WOMEN IN SPORTS Today, the idea of prohibiting champion women runners like Greta Waitz or Rosa Mora from competing in marathons is beyond our comprehension. But twenty years ago, marathoning was something women didn't do.

In the mid-1960s, female athletes were still regarded in as reactionary a way as they were in the 1930s and 1940s, when Babe Didrickson Zaharias was striving to change the image of women in sports—and open opportunities for them to compete. Katherine Switzer had a talent for running and was "confident enough to be attractive and an athlete" when she made a daring move to enter the 1967 Boston Marathon. The race would soon trigger for Katherine a mission to educate the world about women's health, fitness, and their capabilities as talented athletes worthy of public support.

Working toward a journalism degree in college, she trained unofficially with the men's track team since no team existed for women. "I was always accepted as an athlete," Katherine said in her naturally exuberant style. Then in 1966, she met an ex-marathoner who encouraged her to run long distances. She had real talent for it and entered her first marathon the next year, using the name K.B. Switzer. The officials thought she was a man.

Boston was freezing cold that day in 1967 when Katherine stood at her first starting line with hundreds of other runners; she was wearing a heavy sweatshirt. As she warmed up at the four-mile mark, the shirt came off. The press truck drove by, saw her, and the reporters were excited to discover a woman running with an official racing number. But the codirector of the race was in the truck too and "lost his temper," Katherine explained.

> He jumped off the truck and ran after me, trying to rip my numbers off and get me out of the race! He thought I was making a mockery of it, but I was perfectly serious. I wasn't violating any rule, since there *were* no rules about women not being eligible for the marathon.
>
> The truth was, I started out in this race a little smug, ready to strut my stuff, then an official tried to humiliate me and stop me only because I'm a woman. Then things changed.
>
> I started the race a naive kid and ended it a grown-up.

In the course of those long twenty-six miles, Katherine went through a gamut of emotions—anger, embarrassment, even paranoia, and then a philosophical picking apart. She wondered why there weren't other women in the Boston Marathon, why there weren't more women in sports, why there wasn't a women's marathon event in the Olympics.

If ideology is the soul of a mission, then Katherine Switzer's spirit has always been touched by how others suffer from negative reinforcement. What vexed her all her life was the kind of human nature that tries to thwart the efforts of others and begrudge them their triumphs. This race was the first time she'd been treated badly as a woman athlete. She realized how lucky she'd been. "People had always been behind me," she said. Other women deserved an opportunity too and I decided right there that my mission would be to help give it to them."

Over the following years, Katherine raced internationally and held a number of executive positions in sports-related public relations, including a pilot series of races sponsored by Avon. These races ignited a worldwide excitement for women's running and continued over eight years to grow in popularity.

Ultimately, Katherine's involvement with the Olympic Committee finalized her mission: Women's marathoning was first included in the games in 1980. "It was a truly overwhelming experience for me," she said. "In 1967, I was nearly kicked out of a race and then I led the drive that got the women's marathon event into the Olympics thirteen years later."

For Katherine Switzer, a Lifer with real grit and spirit, her mission came from an unflagging belief that she was doing the right thing and that "nobody could fault women's sports," she concluded. "I'm getting an enormous return from this effort. We're creating positive social change and giving women a chance to express themselves."

THE INEVITABLE The pace of life is swift and some triggers bring change without your consent. Even cloistered lives have an unexpected fragility and are not exempt from the flow. In the autumn of 1988, five "rebels" in an order of contemplative nuns barricaded themselves in their New Jersey convent. Having taken vows to renounce the secular world, they defied church orders to disband when a new mother superior dared to introduce progress to the convent: a television and VCR.

When withdrawal from the world is a true and spiritual vocation, the suggestion of a Disney movie is a fundamental threat to the "way things were and are supposed to be." For those of us living in this world, though, the triggers that shake up life may feel equally as portentous as insinuating video equipment.

TRIGGERS: WHERE YOU ARE TODAY

If you look back at your own experiences and put together a history of your life that makes sense to you, you'll see how triggers shaped where you are now. Loss, a challenge to a belief system, and a mission touch on most lives—and I've found that the responses to them have common bonds.

Surprisingly, *loss* is the easiest trigger for some people to handle. With loss, the deed is done, the door is closed. And while mourning is appropriate, there is no going back. This knowledge of *finality* makes it simpler to go on.

Acting on a challenge to your *belief system* requires a different set of strengths than dealing with loss—but still calls for courage. To change a belief system, *you* must instigate action, *you* are in control. And because you are in control it takes more self-discipline.

A mission develops from a deep commitment—a passion—to an idea that will change others' lives. It is passion for the idea and its rightness that pulls you through adversity to achievement. It is the depth of the commitment that will reveal whether it is a true mission or a momentary "good idea" gone wrong.

George Bernard Shaw wrote in *Man and Superman* that the "true joy in life" is when your being is "used for a purpose recognized by yourself as a mighty one." It's a powerful statement, but it's also a *reachable* goal. Work is a mighty part of your life, and it's often a trigger that puts you in touch with that might.

Sometimes, however, a trigger brings you face to face with what you least expect or resist the most—a weak spot potent enough to get you *stuck.* What happens when a basically *normal* flow of events set off by a trigger hits the cool gray wall?

4

ANATOMY OF CHANGE

Caught in a Downtrend—Seven Reasons Why You Get Stuck

Free will. Creativity. Passion. Goal setting. Decision making. They're qualities that define positive action—capabilities all of us have within us. One day, the universe is providing for us nicely and we're in control of our careers, financially secure, and reasonably happy. We're capable, competent *adults.* The next day, life tests us another way: a trigger goes off and we're faced with the possibility not only of *change* but loss. We're redundant. Obsolete. And some of us are off to see the outplacement counselor.

When a career is derailed or rerouted, we discover the factor that most influences the next choice we make: our intellects or our emotions. We can respond by absorbing the blow, not dwelling on hurt feelings, analyzing the facts, projecting a plan, and then taking action. *Getting on with our lives after a short-run setback.* But what happens if emotions take control, making positive action difficult over the short run . . . What happens if we get stuck?

A mild or serious state where *feelings* keep you from functioning effectively, being stuck means a trigger has hit a nerve. You're immobilized in some way. Usually, it's a temporary state, but you don't hurt any less until you've gone through it. Getting stuck cuts a very wide swath.

If you're in a downward trend because of a blow to your ego, you can temporarily lose faith in yourself—or in the institution of business. Thousands of people have found themselves in this predicament—stuck *between* jobs and temporarily unable to make the changes their lives require.

Others are stuck *at* jobs they've outgrown or have come to see are the *wrong fit.* When work was once the "root of all order," as it was described to me by a disillusioned young lawyer, how do you cope with a new and unsettling kind of "enlightenment"—feeling alienated from your job and the people you counted on? It's never easy to deal with.

Being stuck is rather like traveling through a state of limbo—your footing is unsure on ground that feels precarious. Horizons tend to be obscured. Your life is turned upside down and you're uncharacteristically hesitant, indecisive, even overly shy. All your energy goes into coping and getting through this low point in your career.

The human mind can process and store ten new bits of information per second—some of it critical to survival. But the mind is also a bank of perceptions and behaviors that may sometimes play tricks on your understanding of what has happened.

This is the most sensitive of all reasons why people get stuck.

Reality is always uncalculatingly real. It makes no judgments. What matters is your *perception* of reality and how you respond. Whether you think and act or act *without* thinking helps determine if you get stuck or not.

GETTING STUCK: IDENTIFYING THE FEELINGS AND WHAT THEY MEAN

Understanding the feelings involved with being stuck can prepare you to deal with them more effectively. The faster you cope with a setback—and being stuck is an attenuated version of it—the quicker you can eliminate behavior that impedes your progress and the better you can think productively to get on with your life.

Here is a checklist of the most common reactions to being stuck. They range from minor and manageable worries to more intense and self-destructive attitudes that can prolong the feeling of being immobilized.

A *sense of confusion*: Schedules, familiar faces, tasks, and a certain predictability of day-to-day work you know well are suddenly removed. It resembles the delusional thinking of the "phantom limb"—for a time, you don't accept what is gone and believe it is still a functioning part of you. Without this part, you may feel lost, aimless, or ungrounded.

A *sense of fear*: You fear that your "security" is lost for good. Without a job, or a business if you're an entrepreneur, you project crises into the future. There's the upset over having enough money, about proving yourself, about fitting in at a new job, about *belonging*, and about making a decision. The longer you're unattached to a company, the more you fear that your life won't start again. You fear that people won't remember who you are.

A *sense of diminishing self-esteem*: An over-identification with work you do is equated with who you *are*. When you lose your job, this single self-concept operates against your best interest. When self-worth becomes interchangeable with self-assessment, a false standard will keep you stuck.

A *sense of misplaced skills*: When you're stuck and lose a measure of self-confidence, with it goes the more accurate assessment of your skills. Often, you fear that over time—even weeks—you'll forget them. On other occasions, you diminish your abilities or see the world as the single and final arbiter of your fate. If you are temporarily swept away by such misjudgments, you may come to believe you're professionally inadequate, even though your career history *really* tells you differently.

A *sense of numbness*: You've lost your job and can't seem to accept this fact—the pain of loss is too great to cope with for the time being. Instead, you may go through a period of disbelief or outright denial out of which can grow a feeling of *numbness*. You choose to feel nothing. This ensuing numbness acts like a temporary balm to protect you from the pain, or even to stop you from expressing the anger you feel. These "defense mechanisms," as Freud called them, help you survive in a crisis.

Later, when time allows and your psyche is stronger, real feelings connected to the event may emerge. Paradoxically, while you protect yourself from deeper feelings, you obsess over unanswered questions: Why should they have fired *you*? Why did the company go bankrupt/merge/get new management *now*?

A sense of powerlessness: You feel you have no control over your life. You make efforts to get unstuck and get work, but you make no headway. You reach a state of inertia. This "nothingness" seems to absorb all your energy and offer no real returns or rewards—just more of the same frustration.

REALITY CHECKS

Is there a method of keeping these feelings in perspective so they don't overwhelm you?

A *reality check* is one answer.

The purpose of such a check is to examine a belief about yourself to see *if it's true* or why it's holding you back. A simple and effective *reality check* grounds you in the truth of the present. *How* are you stuck? *What* are you feeling?

Reality checks deal with *facts* of the situation, not your *feelings* about them. This is the main distinction. As you progress through the chapter, take the reality checks for each reason you may be stuck.

THE SEVEN MOST COMMON REASONS WHY PEOPLE GET STUCK

When people talked to me about this time in their lives, I noticed a commonality of stress points and a pattern emerging. These seven reasons came up most often:

1. living on the wings of "if only"
2. reliving childhood refrains
3. self-defeating attitudes
4. avoiding risks
5. getting caught up in credentials
6. staying on
7. conflict between personal life and career

LIVING ON THE WINGS OF "IF ONLY"

If you analyze all the stories people tell you about getting stuck, what you'll hear most often is the "if only" refrain. What they're really saying is, "If I could go back in history and remake it, my life would be better now," or "If only things would work out *this* way, *then* I'd be happy."

The concept that it is somehow possible to remake an ideal past from flawed personal history is a faulty one; all it serves to do is keep you living in an expired universe with the illusions you bring to it from your present discontent. What happens when you are stuck reliving childhood refrains is discussed fully in the next section. For now, let's concentrate on how misplaced reasoning complicates the future.

When you project yourself into an ungiving or unrealistic future, you are also disconnecting from the present and the satisfaction of meeting goals. Living in a future time frame tempts you with dreams based on, "*what if* . . ." such as, "Someday, I'll be in the right place at the right time and the right things will finally happen to me, if I wait long enough." Or equally as unproductive, "If I dream it, I won't actually have to do it."

These *mistaken concepts of time* proffer trouble for many people. When you live in the wrong time frame, you get stuck with a half-hearted commitment to yourself now. The present has little meaning, compared to an idealized past or future. Sherri George is one such a case.

Sherri is a very imaginative woman who keeps a number of small balls in the air—ongoing projects that have the sound of authenticity. I recently had occasion to meet with her about a business deal. With infectious enthusiasm, Sherri mapped out her idea, described how she would implement it, and how much money she would need. I discovered three weeks later that she considered her job done. To her, our meeting was tantamount to actually forming a partnership. She saw her pitch as a fait accompli. The detailed fantasy, in her mind, substituted for actually carrying out the project. Sherri had no interest in present-moment follow-through.

Arthur, a recently deposed executive at a midwestern insurance company, remains stuck in the future by clinging to a more fearsome aspect of "what if . . ." than Sherri does. Rather than picture a pleasant outcome to an event, the future looms for him as a proving ground for unfounded fears: the fear of further loss; the fear of being disliked, preventing him from getting an equal or better job; and the grimmest fear of all, the ponderous fear of failure.

Yearning for the past or living in the future sets up a misguided sense of the present. You feel stuck between two worlds, both unavailable. By overly indulging in fantasy, you can't take care of practical issues and behave in ways that are relevant to the present. And images of a negative future serve no purpose.

However, when you set up a *positive* combination of future and present, it can work to create something new. This question—"what if. . . ?"—is the source of all invention and innovation: it's the future with a goal. When you project "what if. . . ?" and combine it with resources and abilities in the present, you get a productive outcome.

If you still measure your steps with old guidelines, and search the past or project into the future for all your answers, you're cheating yourself of a full and meaningful present.

REALITY CHECK Living in the wrong time frame causes anxiety about things that have not happened yet. You have a choice of conjuring up an unchanged future or images of yourself *mastering* events. To change your life, you *must* be able to see yourself living productively in the future while simultaneously living in the present. Without this positive image of yourself to strive for, you perpetuate the same limiting behavior.

To be sure you are tuned in to your present needs, ask yourself:

- How many times have I started a sentence today with the words, "what if . . ." or "if only I . . ."?
- If I do poorly at a job interview or mess up at work, do I blame my lack of preparedness on how others treated me in the past?
- Do I spend too much time each day fantasizing about being in power positions, yet expend very little effort in actually working my way up?
- Do I have a reasonable sense of my skills, limitations, and goals so I can *focus* on finding a job or occupation that best suits me?

RELIVING CHILDHOOD REFRAINS

A second litany heard more often than not by those who are stuck in the wrong time frame is one of *blaming personal history*: "This happens to me because as a child I . . ." is a common excuse for inaction now.

Psychological theory holds that when you're stuck in your current life, unresolved feelings from the past are keeping you off balance. When past and present are suddenly linked by a trigger event, such as losing a prestigious job and the delusion of losing others' approval with it, one's own past "mythology" is at its most potent. Old feelings from childhood may be latent, but when aroused, they can flood you with images and fears that still operate as effectively as when you first felt them.

You function as you *were,* not as you are.

Thus results the temporary state of inertia.

The adult mind can process challenges, troubleshoot, make commitments, and solve problems. It can be called upon to demonstrate reason and protectiveness, especially in a crisis. But when you relive an experience through the *child's* sensibility in you, the story is very different. Once again, you're vulnerable in the same way—as if you're that child again.

Fortunately, many emotional problems wrought in childhood can be understood and defused so that they no longer have power over you.

On occasion, a childhood incident may become your "demon," as New York psychiatrist Dr. Daniel Kuhn described it, and you are stuck traveling through life with the force in control. The reasons most people go into therapy is to identify these "demons" and unburden them. Memory is fickle and can get overdrawn through the years. Therapists can help you put perspective on an event and help you see why you are holding on to it now.

Among the many possible influences from the past, the following three have been cited most among the people I interviewed: (1) recreating a key event from the past, (2) making the wrong choice from a sense of obligation, and (3) having an unrealistic fear that an event *will* recur.

RECREATING A KEY EVENT FROM THE PAST If it's true that "what has to *rerun* has to run," it's never more evident than with songwriter, performer, and author Dory Previn, who, until recently, lived with a burden from the past. I spoke with Dory on a snowy afternoon in the Berkshires. Looking sophisticated and girlish at the same time, Dory's unique stylishness is set off by a halo of curly red hair and wire-rimmed granny glasses.

Dory's wrenching ballads about loss of love or "being locked in and breaking out" brought her great popularity in the 1970s. Dory learned as a child that life was confining and fearful—and this is what she wrote about and how she lived. How this happened begins with her father.

Shell-shocked from the first World War, he suffered from extreme psychological problems. When Dory was ten years old, a recurring paranoid fantasy challenged his sanity and he literally shut out the world. Dory described this life-changing episode:

> My father nailed boards over the dining room windows, then blocked the door to the hall. My mother, sister, and I were entombed with him in this room for three months. I was allowed to

> leave for school through the swinging door into the kitchen. I feared that if I left the room at any other time, my father would kill me.

This "entombment" left an indelible imprint on Dory. Over the years, she became increasingly hypersensitive to criticism, especially about her work. For nearly twenty years, she couldn't tolerate the confinement of planes or trains, and traveled as infrequently as possible. Since she was a performer, it affected the number of appearances she made.

In many ways, her father's delusion kept Dory symbolically locked in until a "bad career move that was right spiritually" finally freed her.

In 1987, a club owner persuaded her to perform at his supper club/after-hours bistro. Although she protested that her material was not right for him, he assured her she would be a smash. Somehow unconvinced, Dory nevertheless signed the contract.

Within a day or two, Dory knew that her instincts were on the right track: her material didn't suit the club, and the late-night crowds were sometimes small. Other undercurrents began to disturb her. The owner openly showed his disappointment in her drawing power and withheld her checks for three weeks. Above all, the "room" made her uncomfortable.

Then Dory's husband, Joby, asked her *what was holding her there* and why she didn't just quit, adding, "This guy's boxing you in!" Dory has an associative mind, and this was the moment: Something clicked. Like a detective piecing together the solution to a mystery, three elements fell into place in a sudden uncalculated plot to free her.

First, the club itself was designed like "a dark but homey dining room." Second, the owner's name—and his eponymous club—was the same as her father's. And third, the manner in which she was treated by the owner was alternately loving—he was a fan of hers—controlling, and "entrapping." Dory explained the "epiphany":

> I didn't see it for the first few weeks, then it was clear. I was back in my father's dining room. I take responsibility for being

attracted to this club and going in there voluntarily, but this time, I thought, if I knuckle under to this man, I'm a dead woman! I had to confront the guy—to be treated fairly, like an adult and a professional and get paid as we'd agreed.

I wanted to walk out of there a free woman. I said, "I'm finishing my contract and never getting trapped in my father's room again."

I changed into a strong, resolved woman and I played out my contract, doing great work.

Becoming unstuck by reliving a childhood experience *as an adult in control* has changed Dory's life in notable ways. Most importantly, she interacts with the world on a healthier level. "New opportunities are everywhere. I can walk through any door and know doors don't mean being locked up."

MAKING THE WRONG CHOICE FROM A SENSE OF OBLIGATION

While Dory wrestled with the ongoing impact of her father's mental illness on her, Al and Alice Santini faced a different kind of family crisis: how people can get stuck through a false sense of duty.

Al and his brother Carl inherited their late father's resort hotel on the condition that Al take charge. At the time, Carl was working with his father while Al was a stockbroker riding a crest before the market crash in 1987.

Tall and sinewy, Al exudes the kind of energy common to fast-trackers. While he's the more managerial and risk taking of the brothers, Carl is his opposite—a good "front man," who is quietly envious of Al's abilities.

Neither Al nor his wife, Alice, were ready for a change in location and career, and told Carl how they felt. Carl persisted, working on Al's weak spot: pleasing their father, and now pleasing him when he was dead, too. In a moment of weakness tripped by his brother's manipulative urgings, Al gave in "to save the family business."

Al was soon stuck in a partnership he basically resented in a business that never really interested him. Al wound up taking on most of the responsibility, becoming more embittered as Carl sailed on the winds of Al's efforts.

After two years, they were just breaking even. Al wanted out. The resort business was the *wrong fit* for him and Alice. "The answer was to sell outright, have Carl buy me out, or find him a new partner," Al said. "Then I went crazy. How would I tell him?"

The solution might have been simple if Al wasn't run by a false sense of obligation. As the adult he is, Al could have communicated to Carl in a straightforward manner and set up a "buy out" transaction or found his brother another partner. Instead, reduced by a childhood dynamic, he rehearsed his "telling Carl off" speeches with Alice. Al recalled feeling "paralyzed" and unable to confront Carl. He said:

> I'd look Carl in the eye and panic about wanting out and panic over the money we weren't making. I'd keep seeing my father's face and I'd wind up talking about something else, my hands shaking.

Were Carl anyone else, Al could have taken care of business coolly. But guilt about abandoning his brother added a profound weight to what should have been an uncomplicated transaction: cutting his losses and getting out. Instead, he froze. The unresolved element of needing to please his father was now kicked off in the relationship with his brother. Al was taught that independent action implied family rejection, so to prove his love, Al was asked to make the sacrifices.

Entangled in the web of obligation, Al is still bound up in a self-defeating childhood role. But there's more to the story. It involves Alice.

AN UNREALISTIC FEAR THAT AN EVENT WILL RECUR The second part of Al's story deals with his wife, Alice, whose own fearsome childhood demon was triggered by Al's inability to leave the family business.

Alice's emotional investment in her husband's business transcends her wifely affection for him. Al always represented to her a man who would be an unfailingly reliable source of security. *More than anything, Alice fears poverty.* She is always worried about "having enough" money and no amount is great enough to soothe her. This is another obstacle born somewhere in childhood that gets people stuck later in life—an unrealistic fear of poverty or the "Bag Lady Syndrome."

Not surprisingly, Alice felt the strain in *her* own way during this ordeal. The situation with her brother-in-law got her increasingly angry and frightened as the business took a downswing. She pressured Al to sell and go back to brokering, "if she meant anything to him."

But there was more. As it was unfolding, Al's experience with the hotel came to resemble a life-changing episode from Alice's own early life: She was eleven years old when her father lost his fortune in a miscalculated real estate deal. "I watched *everything* we had hauled away in trucks," Alice said. Her father never recouped. He was about the age Al was now when it happened.

Al feels he has betrayed both Alice's belief in him as an ideal and stable provider and his own image of himself as a success. The hotel business has shown itself to be riskier than the stock market, and Alice is panicky. Her idealized perception of Al is fast blurring around the edges. No matter how much she tries to refocus, Al is uncannily reminiscent of her father. She is more than ever frightened of "winding up on the street."

A force from the past is gaining momentum in Alice, prodding her unconscious. A lot of her anxiety stems from a conflict between wishing Al would reproduce her father's situation (a meteoric rise and crash) and the *fear that he will.* Then she's afraid to lose her security and Al's love. Alice is stuck *there.*

Al fears he's about to break his brother's heart, betray his father's memory, and lose everything. He feels his career has been derailed. He wants to return to a business he's good at that runs at a pace he understands. In the bargain, he also fears Alice will threaten to leave him because he's failed her. Al is stuck *here.*

In each of Al's two key relationships, 50 percent of the problem is generated by Alice or Carl by turns, while Al maintains the other 50 percent. The timing was impossible: A superimposition of three divergent life "scripts" clashed into a stultifying impasse.

For Al and Alice, the triple interaction was too great to handle alone. They sought professional counseling to unscramble their scripts, put the past in perspective, and redirect their professional goals onto a realistic track.

WHAT CHILDHOOD REFRAINS MEAN In talking with a variety of sociologists, social psychologists, and psychotherapists, regardless of their discipline, they speak in similar terms about the ghosts from the past. The unconscious mind is fragile, and when it's young, it hasn't the means to create a logical answer to why it was hurt. You just feel the pain and confusion. You wonder what happened and may even blame yourself for acts and deeds beyond your control.

New York psychiatrist Dr. Yvette Obadia thinks that when this happens—when things don't make sense—"you are effectively in a trance state, temporarily disconnected from reality. The brain can't compute or sort out the information from the emotions. And so you come to a conclusion about something that you carry with you into adulthood."

This explains why Al "freezes" with Carl, Alice is obsessive about money, and why Dory Previn both sought and feared confinement.

If you are stuck, you may be reenacting a childhood relationship—"unfinished business." You may benefit from someone close to you asking an unexpected or penetrating question as Joby did with Dory Previn. This could spark the association that leads you to the source of a problem.

More so than a close friend or relative, a professional understands how to demythologize the past and guide you safely through the processes: There is really only one key to identifying a childhood trauma but there are many techniques for uncovering it. By not identifying traumas, says New York psychiatrist Dr. Daniel Kuhn, traumas can become "like icons" and upset the balance in life. If you are not living fully in the present because of past "demons," this may be your chance to come to some sort of resolution about them. The reason most people go into therapy is to identify these "demons," and become unstuck. Therapists can help you put perspective on an event and help you see why you are holding on to it now.

It is possible to "de-demonize" the original experience, Dr. Kuhn said, "by stripping it of power, *banalizing* it—that is, diminishing its meaning, reducing the trauma in size and its power over you." Pushing it through a keyhole, in a way. Such imagery may transform a person from where a trauma controls him to where he controls *it*.

REALITY CHECK Events cannot change, but your *interpretation* of them can. To finish unfinished business from the past, you have a choice of either (1) undergoing a "catharsis" by reliving and letting go of the painful feelings associated with an event, or (2) developing a different understanding of it. Once you make a past event less important, it can take its place in your personal history with other events, not run your life.

Take this reality check, asking yourself these questions, to see if past events may be running parts of your life:

- How often do I talk about or think about my past during the day? Ask a person who's close to you to tell you *what* or *who* predominates your conversation. This patter may be so automatic you may *not* hear yourself talking.
- Do I think my past history is incomparably the worst—and my future, incomparably the most deprived, in one way or another?
- Am I overly fascinated by my past but afraid of the future?
- Can I make sound choices or do I let others with influence in my life make decisions for me?
- Try to identify your "icon" or "demon." How much power does this episode exert over you?
- Is the general nature of my upbringing (poor, neglected, victimized, rich with absentee parents but raised by servants, etc.) still the reason I have not achieved what I am capable of?

SELF-DEFEATING ATTITUDES

When you are stuck, a fixed *mind-set* may have temporarily taken over to obscure the truth of who you are and what you believe the universe has to offer. These mind-sets are negative beliefs that can either be the *cause* of your getting stuck or the reason why you *stay* stuck. Operate through these self-defeating attitudes and you cannot make a decision.

Among the self-defeating and counterproductive attitudes are:

Thinking in extremes: You impose limitations on yourself by putting opportunities in unattainable or undesirable ranges. ("I refuse to take another job unless it's perfect," and its polar opposite, "Why bother making another call? There are no jobs out there, anyway.")

False pride: You are overly concerned with status and the standards by which others may judge you. Stuck here, you tend to feel demeaned by work that doesn't measure up. ("What if people find out I'm working at a low-level job just to pay the rent?")

Lack of motivation: You diminish your involvement with work and its place in your life. You secretly fear failure, but it shows itself as passivity or contrition. ("Why bother putting out more energy on *this* job? I'm just here to get a salary. That's enough.")

Fatalism: Cosmic forces, genetics, and your place of birth take all the credit for your lack of achievement or job satisfaction. ("I'll never make it. Look at my father/my mother/my heritage/my education/my appearance/my lack of connections. Losing is in the cards for me anyway.")

Burning your bridges: You terminate a work relationship in so hostile a fashion that you can never use him/her for a contact or reference in the future. ("Everyone here hates you and I'm the only one with the guts to tell you.")

The "It Doesn't Feel Right" Syndrome: You impart a disproportionate importance to *feelings* before you take any action. You know that if action is called for, it makes no difference how you feel, but you choose to ignore the truth. ("Do I have to make a call now? I don't *feel* like it." "Maybe when I feel better, I'll do a résumé.")

While these factors came up as reasons for getting stuck, the four *most common* self-defeating attitudes my interviewees shared were:

1. Harboring revenge fantasies
2. Perfectionism
3. Interpersonal difficulties
4. Sensation seeking, either through drugs or alcohol

HARBORING REVENGE FANTASIES Of all the negative feelings connected with extreme disappointment and loss over work, the most unsparing would have to be *revenge.* At some point or other, you may have indulged in revenge fantasies—usually directed at the person or the company who took from you your source of survival. It's easy to get stuck when you are consumed with thoughts of vindication. It leaves no energy for making reasonable plans for moving on to the next place.

Revenge has been called "wild justice," but it's more a tormented *obsession* that focuses on getting even with someone you feel has betrayed, humiliated, or wounded you in some way. Loss, in connection to money and work, can inspire the kind of passions more often associated with love. Thus aroused and under the spell of wild justice, you can be transported by vivid and elaborate fantasies of blood fury let loose.

In most cases, any spoken or unspoken plots to get even ultimately go nowhere. If they serve any purpose, such fantasies can release tension connected to the frustration of losing your job or having been put in a compromising position. Even the most reasonable, upstanding, and thoughtful people have confessed to a few flights of revenge fantasy.

Former senator Phil Mastin knew of such vengeful feelings firsthand when his political career was cut short through an unexpected turn of events. His story is almost a fable of "wrongs" made "right."

A realist and a man with strong moral convictions, Phil Mastin was elected to the Michigan senate in 1982. When he took office, he discovered he'd inherited a nearly $2 billion deficit from the outgoing administration. When he was appointed to the state's taxation committee, Phil had the onerous job of putting into effect a short-term tax increase.

In 1983, Michigan was hard hit by a suffering automobile industry, and the country was coming out of a recession. The tax increase was considered bitter medicine, further souring a widespread feeling of general discontent.

The increase had been voted for by the Democrats in power but the *conservatives* in Phil's district had their own ideas about government, taxes, and those who serve. Three of Phil's constituents began organizing. Their plan: to circulate a petition to recall Phil Mastin and get him out of office. The grounds for recall were that by his supporting a tax increase, Phil did *not* serve the people of his district. And they wanted him out.

Phil's recall election was held November 20, 1983, on the twentieth anniversary of John F. Kennedy's assassination. To add insult to injury, Phil *lost* the recall vote by a margin of two to one, while he had originally won the district by defeating a three-term incumbent.

A newspaper reporter asked Phil how he felt about losing. He said, "Terrible, but it's better than getting shot." But to Phil, the recall was a kind of *character* assassination. He'd only been in the Senate eleven months—voted out before he had a real chance to prove himself. He said:

> I felt wronged, like a terrible injustice had been done to me. There were three original petitioners, two men and a woman, whom I could hate with undying passion for the rest of my life. I didn't know this when I was younger but I know it now: the most destructive thing you can do is harbor feelings of hate and revenge. You only hurt yourself.
>
> When I saw that, I had to get to forgiveness by constantly telling myself to do it. I can't live with bitterness in my heart. It consumes your life and your time and can ruin other relationships.

Phil's first step toward forgiveness was to look at himself and realize that *he was better than what these people thought of him.* He came to understand that they were not "evil" people who were out to ruin his career, but people with a serious disagreement with him. "I kept telling myself," Phil said, "this is a *political,* not *personal* rejection. Don't personalize it."

It wasn't an easy road to healing for him, but after two months he was able to pray for his antagonists, and his mind and spirit was freed. "The load was gone," Phil said. "I wasn't carrying these people around with me anymore." Three weeks later, he got a job.

REALITY CHECK Revenge has built into it a way of doubling back on itself, punishing the avenger as much as hurting the avenged. An act of revenge—played out—more often than not leads to tragedy and accomplishes nothing.

The Spanish have a wise aphorism: "Living well is the best revenge." To "live well," ask yourself these questions:

- Have I based my future on "getting even" rather than getting ahead?
- Does everything I see, hear, or read remind me in some way of the person who reneged on a promise or betrayed me?
- Has revenge made me a cynic or pessimist? Have I lost confidence in all mankind, or can I forgive and forget?

PERFECTIONISM I was talking about excellence and perfectionism with the dynamic and highly articulate Pat Cook, a partner at the executive search firm Ward Howell, where she specializes in placing CEO's. Pat has an uncanny gift for "reading" people and in her experience perfectionism is less an asset than *having failed.* She explained what sounds like a paradox:

> You can be a perfectionist and get the job done and never make mistakes. That's fine. But I'd never present a candidate for a CEO job who hasn't failed at something. If I have a history of how a man failed, I know more about him. I don't want him to fail for the first time on my client's payroll.

A *Working Woman* magazine survey on turning points in careers examined similar standards: It pinpointed the effects of the personal traits known to help or hinder progress. Not surprisingly, hard work and personability still count, but *perfectionism,* while it looks good on paper, can "backfire." Perfectionists, the surveyors added—and Pat would agree—"do no better than others."

Celia Barton illustrates how perfectionism gets you ensnared in a fear of failure by obsessing over "history-making" mistakes.

Hard-working and original, Celia helped establish a huge share of the market for the California women's wear manufacturer where she was head designer. When a large conglomerate offered to bankroll her and give her her own label, Celia leaped at the chance.

Celia set up shop. Her first "spring line" was late getting to the stores, but it was a hit. Her fall line sold out in advance from samples, but Celia was still bound to her drawing board, frantically redesigning what should have been on the cutting tables.

Full responsibility for decisions and delays rested with her, but Celia "kept seeing flaws" in the collection. Never satisfied with the final sketch, she was unable to let the work go. And the seasons changed. Since she couldn't ship her orders, clients lost faith in her and began canceling.

It was said that no one worked harder than Celia, but she did herself in by spinning her wheels, obsessively reworking designs twenty to thirty times. Such perfectionism eventually sabotaged her business. Her investment in succeeding "with her name on the label" was so great that the fear of making a wrong decision drove her to make *no* decisions at all.

One year later, she closed her doors. She eventually got another job designing for a manufacturer. There, she could function without perfectionism getting in her way.

Perfectionism often begins with good intentions. But it has a way of creating a confusion between honestly doing your best and the morbid belief that others are keeping score of your achievements and failures. Celia is a victim of this kind of faulty thinking. Overconcern with how others judge you endows *them* with power over *your* productivity. Perfectionists take arbitrary reactions from others as law. This makes it hard to state with confidence what you think and feel.

Perfectionists typically share a common foundation for this obsessive behavior. If you're a perfectionist, this may be relevant to your experience: Early on, you're taught to equate self-worth with failures and successes. When you learn that nothing is good enough, eventually you believe that all your efforts are inadequate. Your ability to judge your own work fairly is sacrificed, too. Later on, you get *stuck* confronting challenges that test your capabilities or put your work or ideas on the line.

Perfectionism reflects low self-esteem, harsh bouts of self-rejection, and an overdrawn need for approval.

It's normal to want the approval of others and to be liked and applauded. Disapproval is a natural aspect of life. But if you get stuck fearing it and constantly shift positions in order to be liked or, as in Celia's case, redesign a dress until it is too late to do business, you forfeit too much for too little.

All learning is a matter of trial and error and adjustments. Perfectionism keeps you stuck replaying the same song . . . or sewing up the same old seams.

REALITY CHECK Perfectionism is overworked *excellence.* Doing your best is blameless, unless your best is an unreachable goal that becomes an obstacle.

Most of all, perfectionism delays gratification and cheats you of life. Test your feelings about perfectionism by asking yourself these questions:

- Can I make a distinction between perfectionism and excellence?
- Does my obsession with "getting things perfect" really mask a fear of what others might think about my work?
- Does my perfectionism cover a fear of finishing a task and having to make a decision about what will be next?
- Does my perfectionism give me a chance to turn down opportunities because *they* aren't perfect?

INTERPERSONAL PROBLEMS "I've seen people who've been dragged down by whatever happened to them in the past. It comes through to me, right across the desk, and I can't present those people *as they are* to my clients," said one executive headhunter.

"Sometimes I interview a guy with fabulous credentials, but when he talks to me, it's clear he lacks humor or vision, or he feels victimized or angry. Basically, he comes off *lost* . . . like a loser . . . when he shouldn't," another told me.

These placement experts and others agree: Of all the credentials you bring to a job, *personability* is the most important—it's what others see first. People work with people. Cooperation, flexibility, professionalism, and an ability to admit mistakes insures compatibility and promotion.

When you have been passed over for promotion or fired because of clashing personalities it is especially hurtful. The tendency is to blame someone else, and it may be true on occasion. But it's to your benefit to scrutinize these clashes and see how you may be participating in them. If you are stuck in your career because of interpersonal problems, you can still change.

Genevieve Bazelmans, a vice president at New York outplacement firm J.J. Gallagher, agrees that interpersonal problems can cause a career crisis. She told me confidentially of a recent experience with a woman she called Annette, a woman in her thirties who lost a plum job quick on the heels of her having been fired from a long-term position. Now she was stuck.

The reasons both employers gave for firing Annette were identical: belligerence, personality clashes, and an inability to take criticism.

Genevieve explained: Although her career was being punctured at the sharp turns, Annette's image of herself was as the smooth, high-ranked professional worth a six-figure salary. Life was telling her something quite the contrary, but she wouldn't listen to the words: *interpersonal problems with coworkers.* She was blind to her own behavior. "She doesn't accept that her personality is the real issue," Genevieve said. "Instead, she demands of me to 'get on with the process' of telling her how to get her ideal job." Paradoxically, Annette is a human resources counselor and is effective counseling others. Genevieve said:

> Annette is knowledgeable, gets good results, but *she doesn't get hired.* I've attempted to caringly give her feedback. But I find she manipulates information so she can restate the issues. This way, she doesn't have to accept a solution.
>
> Here's an example: She says she knows everyone in her field, but she'll come up with a blank if I ask her to name two good long-term contacts. At other times, she says she's called her con-

tacts to see what's new and expects to hear about a job any minute.

Annette wants magic—for a job to materialize where she can be herself as she is now—or for *others to change.* It's difficult for her to accept new ideas openly. She's full of her own thoughts and fears about not succeeding and losing the prestige she feels she's earned all these years. She's stuck in a fantasy world where her skills are accepted in lieu of cooperative behavior. And although she won't admit it, Annette's hurt herself by going back again and again to the same few contacts who don't have anything for her, nor will they.

You may not be as extreme a case as Annette, but if you sense that interpersonal relationships could be holding you back, look at the dynamics of what you're doing.

REALITY CHECK People with interpersonal problems are usually driven by unresolved anger and deep-seated feelings of inadequacy. Their "self talk" or internal dialogue focuses on angry confrontations or intimidating tactics. If most of your mental output is taken up with self-sabotaging thoughts such as believing you can never have what you want or that you don't deserve success, you cannot live fully in the present or plan a better future.

Take a reality test about your attitude:

- Do I feel entitled to behave abrasively toward others, dismissing their objections with comments like, "This is how I am—take it or leave it"?
- Do I believe that being congenial is tantamount to being weak?
- Do I make demands of others but put up a bitter fight if the same demands are made of me?
- Am I willing to look objectively at how I interact with others and do something about improving these relationships?
- Do I really listen to what others have to say, or am I too quick to jump in with my own opinions and judgments?

SENSATION SEEKING Alcoholism and drug addiction affect millions of Americans; others are addicted to food, to shopping, and to work. No one knows the extent of these addictions, but the numbers far exceed a reasonable guess. In terms of substance abuse, we know that approximately 600,000 people are being treated at the nearly 5,000 rehabilitation centers, hospitals, halfway houses, and clinics on any given day. If you need them, there are 100,000 daily meetings of Alcoholics Anonymous and several thousands more of similar "twelve-step" programs such as Overeaters or Gamblers Anonymous.

Whatever the sensation, addicts are stuck needing the "high" or mood change that makes them feel better.

Being stuck can also be addictive. The excuses and inertia that take over when you're stuck don't always insure a distancing between you and further disappointment, pain, or a fear of failure. These are some of the feelings addictions attempt to cover over.

Serious addicts, the experts say, seek a relationship with an object, not a person, to feel good. It's the work, the drugs, the credit card, the chocolate cake—this is the high. Since the drug only provides a temporary illusion of relief from the stresses of life, an addict needs constant replenishment at ever-narrowing intervals.

Rob Pointer, a Boston man in his late thirties, typifies the sensation seeker/inertia seeker who "hit his bottom" before turning his life around. A onetime workaholic who lost all sense of priorities, judgment, and self-esteem in a ripple effect of addictions, Rob told me his cautionary tale over tall glasses of iced tea.

Numbed by early experiences of a brow-beating, competitive father who set up challenge after challenge for Rob, he succeeded almost as an act of rebellion against the elder man, who gave him a dual message: dare to succeed and don't dare to fail.

Rob did both.

Three years ago, Rob was vice president of a large manufacturing company with 300 people reporting to him. Full of energy and ambition, Rob suffered from a tendency toward heavy drinking; Rob's life centered on the company and he had no interests in anything but work and getting high.

Rob sought power, but pressures got to him and he couldn't cope with them without alcohol and drugs. Substances soon took him over and Rob was soon in debt. "I was thirty-eight and on top of the world," he said, "but underneath it all was despair I couldn't face."

Confused by alcohol, drugs, and compounding debt, Rob made the wrong decisions at work too many times. He was fired.

Because he was well thought of in the business, Rob was unemployed a week before he took over a small division in another company. He was on the street again two months later. Humiliated, Rob knew he was in trouble. Instead of looking for an executive job, he chose to drive a cab "to think things out."

Rob soon realized he cared about nothing but achieving, yet he was emotionally distanced from the work itself. Stuck in a world of denial, he didn't allow himself to face the truth about what he had become and what he was feeling. Denial kept him protected, as did drugs.

And the drugs took on a life of their own. "No one starts out saying: My ambition is to end up a useless bum on the street. I drove that cab feeling I'd lost so much. To retrieve it, I had to clean up my life."

Skeptical, Rob went into therapy, then left it. In and out of Cocaine Anonymous and Alcoholics Anonymous three or four times, Rob was eventually able to face his demons. This was when the universe provided.

One morning Rob got an encouraging call. He said:

> A guy I hired, a marketing chief, worked for me eight years before moving to a rival company. He called me about a position that was right enough for me. I was pleased that he remembered me and thought enough of me to call. It was exactly what I needed right then.

Rob got the job and slowly rebuilt his life. Now he spends time counseling people who have been stuck in similar life-draining addictions. His energy and commitment is put into caring for others and saving lives. He emerged a whole person.

REALITY CHECK Drugs and alcohol foster uncaring and irresponsibility. When that happens, you cannot live life fully. You need support to clean up your life and this can be found in the specialized groups whose members all have been where you are.

Ask yourself how you connect to sensation seeking with these questions:

- Is there an unspoken link between drugs or alcohol (or even cigarettes and food) and accomplishment? That is, do I believe that without the "substance" I cannot produce anything? For example, am I a smoker or drinker who believes that, without a cigarette or a drink, I cannot think or act?
- Do I start thinking about taking drugs or drinking sometime around midday at work—and feel a great sense of expectancy for the "high"?
- Do I find myself telling elaborate lies or vehemently denying my actions, especially in regard to the frequency and quantity of substances I take each day?
- Have I come to believe that other people have pushed me into a drug or drinking problem?
- Do I have to give myself a reward of drugs or alcohol when I do anything?

AVOIDING RISKS

"The tongue is the enemy of the neck" might be the catchphrase for anyone who is stuck, unable to take risks or put their necks on the line.

When I asked people who were stuck, "What do you think about in terms of taking *risks*?" responses swung on a narrow arc:

"I don't shoot too high," a credit manager said. "It's out of order for me to think big."

"I worry I want something so much and that I won't get it because I don't deserve it," a paralegal told me.

"I'm afraid I'll be turned down," an accountant told me.

Women more than men tend to think in terms of limits and what "others may think" if they veer off the traditional paths.

"My husband likes me to consult with him first before I do anything," a Texas shop owner said.

"If I do something too different, I may lose my friends. They may not like me," an assistant producer at a Denver television station said.

A commercial artist tells me that she's barely making it freelancing for advertising agencies. Her problem: asking for money. Tonia is stuck being unable to charge rates that are competitive and make sense to her and to others who are buying her work. However, Tonia starts her negotiations at or *below* her bottom line.

"I need the business," she said. "I take what I can get." Tonia fears she might lose an assignment by charging more than her ridiculously low fees; therefore, she warns herself to not take a risk and make a change in how she does business.

Why is she so fearful? The explanation for her low rates stems from an "unchangeable need to be liked." Therefore, she's too insecure to ask for what she's worth.

"Insecurity" is a synonym for fear. If you're not willing to play your aces, you're dealing yourself a losing hand. Commitment to your work demands that you set equitable standards where you do not cheat yourself by devaluing your work through *others'* eyes. Getting unstuck means you need to face your fears.

Beverly Kievman, a dynamic Atlanta businesswoman for whom risk taking comes effortlessly, is guided more by curiosity than caution. Insecurity appears to be unknown to her. Now in partnership with her ex-husband in a real estate business, Beverly's career began when she bought a bankrupted talent and model agency from the previous owner. She made the purchase knowing that "it was an absolute risk."

What keeps her from getting stuck? She told me:

> I am willing to say, *why not?* and not worry about the consequences or think about failing. I just bought the agency and started making phone calls. To me, the thinking process in being an entrepreneur is a cycle of creation, development, and seeing the needs.

Wendy Snyder, a charming New York art dealer with a voluminous upsweep of brunette curls, did not have Beverly's natural sense of adventure when she first started out. Wendy gingerly felt her way toward it. Early in her career she took a job with an architectural firm that did not fulfill their promise of promotion. Instead, she floundered there with no structure. When she was offered what sounded like the perfect job, she was willing to move to Texas for it, but it too was the wrong fit. She said of these years:

> What became most apparent to me was my lack of motivation. I didn't have the skills to create work for myself or the skills to administrate what I was given to do. I just sat there waiting to be told what to do. I took no chances at these jobs at all. The single most important change in my approach to work is learning to initiate and take what comes.

Risk can imply failure as well as success, and without failure we don't learn much. Always having a plan can make sense, but being inflexible and overcommitted to routine is limiting, repetitive, stifling, and even unhealthy. Risk takes you a step into the unknown. You may be bored with certainty, but if you fear a loss of security, it is appealing enough. You may yet discover that nothing is certain but change and surprise.

Risk takers may seem irresponsible to those of you who seek predictability over possibility. But there are many people like Harry Peters, a gregarious New York restaurateur with flair, who enjoys the adventure of riding chance down the middle of the road. He's a *cautious* risk taker who makes his decisions and deals with change armed with enough information about what he wants or has been offered. "There's a gamble involved in taking a risk," he said, "and I feel better if it's not entirely out of my control, like a horse race."

What Harry does is calculate some sort of feasible outcome with a "worst scenario/best scenario" game plan. This plan makes good sense. By asking questions based on the information, the players, and any other relevant factors, including the "unknown," Harry can estimate his possible loss or payoff. The questions lead off with, "What's the *worst* thing that could happen if I . . ." then conversely, "What's the *best* thing that could happen if . . ." Then he makes his decision.

New York career counselor Leslie Rose finds that many people are trapped into limiting their progress because they don't ask themselves the right questions at all. They calculate outcomes from a mistaken view of themselves and stay stuck. She said:

> Someone may insist, "I am not a risk taker," meaning they always play it safe. When I question them closely, they'll often reveal circumstances where they take risks. They'll tell me about risks taken on the tennis court, in being very open and generous with others, in being tenacious about getting something they want. It turns out they *do* understand what taking risks is about after all.

Through the simple exercise of examining your life and seeing where you do succeed at risk taking, the faulty perception that "I am not a risk taker" is transformed into the more accurate "I am able to take risks." By recalling these positive episodes, you also confirm the *feelings* of confidence associated with risk taking. You already have the experience. Now you need to apply it to *work.*

REALITY CHECK If you are caught in the myth that you cannot tolerate anything new, take a chance on yourself. The true reality test is in testing yourself. Real inner security means you can trust yourself to deal with the unexpected as it comes your way. Do you ever say, *"I'm committed to a breakthrough as long as I know how it will work out"*?

Ask yourself these questions to see how you deal with risks:

- Do I have a sense of adventure about life in general or am I overly concerned with maintaining the status quo?
- If I am offered a golden opportunity, is my first response one of believing that it will be inconvenient in some way?
- Do I yearn for progress and change in my life, but, paradoxically, wish change could occur without making any changes?
- Have I created a mystique about my personality—that is, have I turned myself into someone who is "different," "overly sensitive" to the world, or "fussily eccentric" so I never have to take chances?

CAUGHT UP IN CREDENTIALS

While nearly 80 percent of the people I spoke to who were stuck recall having experienced a lack of passion for any kind of work, nearly the same percentage of people worried about losing the status connected to a position or title. This identification and personalization of credentials can reinforce a poor self-image and encourage inactivity. As long as you remain "labeled," and give yourself a name that defines you, you limit options and restrict change.

In speaking to many professionals about this, I found they concurred about one motive in particular: When you've worked hard to get the title or the degree, or you've reached some point of social stratification, you don't want it threatened in any way. The problem, they emphasized, is when the credential becomes the absolute symbol of confidence. Then the title or position encourages you *not* to look beneath it for real competence and desire.

When you are stuck in a self-imposed caste system, you come to think of credentials as the single measure of your worth. Such identification and personalization of credentials can work against you. Instead of getting you what you want, they'll reinforce a poor self-image: If you are stuck always wanting "what was *in the name of* . . ." your credentials will limit your options. You will resist change on "principle."

Credentials are an easy way to label yourself. A label distills and describes for others what you do. It's a comfortable, if general, picture of your expertise, experience, and social circle. These descriptions are true, but they're incomplete.

They aren't what you *are*. As the world changes, labels *can no longer define your interests, your potential for growth, and your ultimate goal.*

Not surprisingly, work associated with a credential may not be satisfying. A lawyer I interviewed feels he's fighting other lawyers, not fighting for justice; a social worker, disillusioned by city bureaucracies and disturbed by human suffering, clings to her civil service job for security. Among the 400,000 people each day who are shifting gears, a large percentage feel job dissatisfaction acutely. For thousands more, there's a very real and painful ambivalence. It isn't easy to give up a credential even if the work isn't gratifying. Meanwhile, you can get stuck deciding what your work means to you.

New York career counselor Linda Jerris discovered another nuance about the power of credentials: false expectations of how they can transfer from one career to another. "People get stuck in the *wants,*" she said. People *want* to leave one job and do something else, but they have overblown and unrealistic ideas of how they will fit in.

Linda cited a case of a teacher with ten years' experience and a master's degree who believed she could easily drop into a corporate hierarchy with no difficulty. "This woman," she said, "had no idea that she would most likely have to start at a lower-level job and work her way up to get the salary and position she wanted. This fact alone kept her in teaching."

Others who are caught up in the mystique of credentials are the once luminous stars or "rising stars." These people thrive on the rewards of public approval, applause, access, and notoriety. Athletes, performers, corporate titans, "movers" of infinite variety, and public figures belong to this group. Stepping out of the spotlight and into the shadows is one kind of adjustment. But being close to gaining national fame and having it taken from you is another kind of grave disappointment. A shattered career can make credentials seem more than they are.

Don Brenner is a strapping, thirty-five-year-old man whose imminent success was stripped from him in one fluke accident. For one magic season, Don played with the Dodgers. His only dream was to "go up against the best."

Fate held a different hand for Don one afternoon. He was playing a game of *basketball* when he turned, tripped, and broke his ankle. The injury was so bad that he could never move fast enough to play professional baseball again. His career was over before it began. Don told me:

> First I was a superstar, then I had nothing. I knew the broken ankle was an accident, but I felt like my chance for success was blown. I get angry about it every time I watch a game and think: I would have been better than that guy up there now.

When he was forced to give up this chance in the major leagues,

Don experienced a sense of utter failure. He has been stuck regretting his loss for fifteen years. *Nothing,* in his eyes, can measure up to what he might have had.

Don's "superstardom" was the credential he sought for himself—he wanted to be another Tom Seaver and be given the same rewards for talent and celebrity. In truth, Don was unknown and he never got the chance to see how far he could have gone—he didn't even have the opportunity to fail completely and properly.

Don's sense of loss brought on an uncontrollable phase of mindless drug taking and, with it, he entered into two marriages with an equal lack of conviction. He was stuck in a state of self-pity and self-destructive action. Eventually, he pulled himself out of his slump. He opened an electrical contracting company that is now doing well, but it hasn't given him the rewards he fantasized about. "I don't feel like a success. Not when I look at a baseball game and think of what could have been."

Success for some people can be alternately shocking, a matter of fact, or, as with Don, it can take on mythological proportions. Success has fabulous rewards, but it can isolate you. Celebrity makes you an object of love or a target of misdirected envy. Dr. Kalin added that if you want to be loved, nurtured, protected, and cared for, "success doesn't offer it no matter how golden it looks. If you've never developed ego strength or the intervening needs weren't met, you can't deal with success, failure . . ."

. . . Or twists of fate. You get stuck, as Don did, in loss, regrets, and bitterness.

Losing your moment in the sun is painful, but fifteen years is a long time to mourn a lost career. Don might have gone beyond his grievance and used his credentials and talent for helping other people—coaching high school ball or Little League teams, for example. There he might have found the rewards and satisfaction he sought in public glory.

Opportunities are everywhere. There are all sorts of things to grab on to by adapting your experience. Cut loose from the false standards of defining yourself in the name of credentials.

In the end, nothing is as important as how you see yourself and the world you want to affect.

REALITY CHECK People who have grown through setbacks in their careers often cite an unexpected consequence: They discover, or rediscover, abilities, resources, and inclinations they were not aware of, or had neglected. *These* "new" credentials ultimately help in successfully bolstering confidence and rebuilding careers. Is your image of yourself threatened if you think of giving up your credentials to start something different?

How much do credentials mean to you? Take this reality check:

- Do I judge others by their profession, titles, managerial level, or "who they know" and believe others judge me by the same standards?
- Do I believe the credentials I have now will determine my future or am I able to improve them?
- Are my goals based on getting the title/the money/the notoriety to impress others and have power over them?
- Am I willing to give up my title/profession for a job I really want where I must be a "beginner" for a period of time?

STAYING ON

Routine. Inertia. A "good enough" job. Your work is second nature by now and you're comfortable with the work load, the location, your coworkers. You want something more from your career, but the thought of disrupting the status quo stops you from taking action. You're stuck in a kind of complacency.

Perhaps you've reached a threshold of toleration at work—you've about had it. Yet the thought of leaving upsets you: "It could be you're happy where you are, but you don't realize it," says career counselor Linda Jerris. She continued:

> When you're in a state of confusion, you start looking for something else. Why? I think people reach a plateau—even in great, exciting jobs, and feel restless. They're so close to the situation, they don't feel productive or creative, they've lost touch with what they have. Anything looks better. It's like a middle-aged man who

goes out and has an affair, but who after a while, realizes it's not the affair he wants at all, but his wife.

People who are frustrated at a plateau may also be *vague* about what they want. This gets them stuck at, "I want to do something meaningful," but they can never quite define what that means.

Others are *bound to* the plateau by one or two appealing qualities the job offers—salary, title, or the prestige the company has in the field. Or, like Anne Bright, an account executive for a large Tucson public relations firm, you have reached burnout from overwork. "It's impossible to muster the energy to search for a new job. I work sixty-hour weeks. It's too exhausting to think about moving." You're stuck hanging on.

And so you hold on.

Companies also reach their levels of inertia or limitation: Perhaps the company is myopic and has no vision for expanding in a shrinking market, or they occupy a tightly guarded, albeit small, corner in an isolated industry. If your company functions within these narrowly drawn lines, analyze how their limitations affect you and your future. If you hold on, would your skills become obsolete and your opportunities end with your weekly paycheck?

On occasion, an industry begins to change its personality to accommodate growth and innovation, while its employees are the ones to object to the change. These mainline traditionalists adhere to old-guard thinking that soon proves counterproductive. Nowhere is this more prevalent than in banking. Ron Carter, a vice president of Professional Resources at Banker's Trust in New York City, spoke to me about the irony of this phenomenon.

A banker may believe in his "cluster of skills" so fervently, Ron explained, that the bank's new policies may not be compatible enough with the banker's line of thinking. When this occurs, his choice is to leave or adapt to the shock of the new. And a number do neither.

And not just in banking.

Getting stuck in company policy would have been preferable to Vic Halpern, who was unable to leave a sinking ship. Vic dwelt in a mode of *denial,* setting up a false sense of security for himself and invulnerability for his company, even as it steadily crashed around him.

An assistant director of corporate benefits for a large industrial conglomerate going through a huge shake-up, Vic watched the dust rise as coworkers around him were fired. He denied the inevitability of his termination by burying it under a blanket of ego-bolstering bravado or self-deceiving excuses like "I'm too indispensible to be fired" or "I can't possibly know what's *actually* going on here." Eventually the field narrowed, leaving him little ground to stand on, and he was fired. He told me:

> I believed my sphere of influence would keep me immune, even though my own boss was forced into early retirement. I thought, I have too many financial controls in this company. I wasn't hit on the first go-round of firings, or the second. So I gained confidence. But I was hit on the third round. When it happened, it was a relief that at last it was over.

Vic bought into the myth of the imperishable company, believing that his security would be in holding on as long as possible. Ultimately, he was stuck trying to rebuild his career from the outside, after he was fired. Instead of using the last few months by trying to get relocated and then *quitting,* he got caught up defending an indefensible position. More damaging, he said, was not realizing that "I had more in me than this corporation would ever be able to use. I found I didn't have to be trapped by the parameters of the job, but I could make decisions without asking permission . . . I could be my own person."

Eventually, Vic gained control of his destiny. After a period of deep introspection, he accepted a lower-level job than the one he'd left. Rejected too many times for positions he wanted, Vic finally was able to swallow his pride and work his way back up again.

If you are stuck staying on, you may understand Vic's *emotional* attraction to his job: The company provided a sense of belonging. This was of great value to him. He got a kind of recognition at work on a daily basis that his family, as supportive as they were, often could not give him firsthand.

Vic had one kind of attachment to his job. But in another, more claustrophobic, version of this false sense of family, a company may subtly ask you to give yourself over to them. The demands are much greater, and leaving can be even tougher. When this happens, the company manipulates your need for security, going so far as to *infantilize* you—treat you like a child. The company accomplishes this by stressing your dependence on it.

Such companies are not above using psychological tactics to undermine your confidence. They remind you of how well you're paid, how fortunate you are to be employed by them—because basically, they may imply, you're *not that good to make it elsewhere*—and promise you benefits and *understanding.* Executive search specialist Pat Cook has seen how overprotectiveness can create an illusion of the all-giving parent. She said:

> Certain large corporations and most bureaucracies are characterized by paternalistic tactics. It can become a stranglehold on employees. An authority figure controls your destiny, your pay, and all the elements that reinforce your being there. To be a good boss in such a situation is to be a good manager of children.
>
> There's a cadre of people who believe in the company as the answer or the cure. And, I think, no matter how entrepreneurial you are, it's possible to fall under the spell.

The need to be taken care of is a natural one. And a company skilled at playing "the good parent" can bring out this need in even the best of us. Devotion and loyalty to an employer is admirable within limits, but it's not a substitute for taking responsibility for your own life. Sacrificing yourself is a high cost for membership or "belonging."

REALITY CHECK If you're stuck hanging on, your options narrow year by year. Evaluate why you are still at a job that you have outgrown. Decide what you are most willing to *give up* if it means getting a better job or be clear about how you need to adapt to changes within your company or the industry itself.

Take this reality test:

- Would I rather stay on no matter how bad it is rather than face the discomfort of starting again?

• Do I say to myself, "At least I know what I have. It could be worse," rather than looking at change as a positive force?

• Is your unhappiness on the job worth the sense of security that comes with a paycheck and benefit package?

CONFLICT BETWEEN CAREER AND PERSONAL LIFE

Feminist Betty Friedan once confessed in an interview that there were times she'd lose her purse on payday rather than face her husband—whom she outearned. Deprivation was preferable to possibly insulting his male pride.

Today, there is no longer one interpretation of life. The contemporary woman may never have a husband or family, but she need never lack a career to fall back on. Women are equipped differently for the world than they have ever been before.

Nevertheless, the twenty years since Betty Friedan's *Feminine Mystique* have not totally eased the tension between working spouses: Many women are still stuck in conflict over their dual roles of wife and career woman. While men, too, feel the stress of economic pressures on the one hand and the pressure of making it on the other, the percentage of men who function as "househusbands" is very small.

So it is women who usually are stuck, feeling discontent, guilt, or confusion about managing a healthy marriage and an achievement-oriented career. How is it done? How should she feel? Should she hold back so she can be the support system to her husband? How would she manage a relationship in which she outearns her husband? What if she's asked to give up her career and stay home?

Terri Browne repeats these questions to herself on a daily basis. She knows firsthand that losing a purse isn't the only self-inflicted crisis in a marriage. Terri was in partnership in a fashion consultancy, struggling to make it, while her husband's career was "zooming." She'd pulled back a few years to support his career, and she needed him on her side now. But there were difficulties. Terri told me:

> I was going through conflict with my partner at work and turmoil at home. John's career was going great, but under our roof he was suffering, and so was I.
>
> It's painful to keep a marriage intact when you're trying to keep a business afloat and your husband isn't especially interested in hearing about your problems. John wanted me to tend to him at home. He was wonderful before this when I worked for a company. I could help him then. Now that I'm in my own business, he's jealous and angry.

Terri was unsure of her future in business—and in marriage—until a decision was made for her. Her partner pulled out, and rather than put further energy into a losing concern, she closed her doors. She feels the failure of her business might have saved her marriage.

Thirty-three-year-old Lynn Moore, a striking black woman in the communications field, summed up what many working women feel now: confusion and ambivalence about a career. She goes through days when she regrets not having jumped right into a traditional dependent marriage. At other times, Lynn is struck by the glamour of a socially acceptable form of perfectionism, "having it all."

As with many women, her desire to achieve all her career and marriage options has gotten her stuck. The image of the perfectly realized woman of the 1980s not only haunts her, but blocks the process whereby she can actually make a decision. She said:

> There are moments when I just want to give up on work. Other times, I cling to my job and worry that everything I have will be pulled out from under me. Then I think I'll hang in, hit my plateau, and become a "Lifer." Then that scares me, and I think about having children and worry that if I leave to care for them even for a short time, I'll be setting my career back five years.
>
> My generation was brought up to have a career, but I need a personal life and I want a family. And I want a great job. I fear I won't be able to handle it all.

While some women struggle with such demands of a two-career marriage, other women destroy the possibilities for themselves, sometimes unwittingly. Career strategist and author Betty Lehan

Harrigan commented in *Working Woman* magazine that capable women still sabotage their careers out of outdated "female linear thinking." Basically, this thinking includes a struggle with the baggage of "adolescent reveries" about what makes up an ideal job or marriage, a closing off of options by deferring to a spouse, and, most pernicious of all, a diminishing of one's abilities and accomplishments.

Relationships have individual balances and trade-offs, and each one is both simple and complex in its own way. Yet, there is a common denominator: In truth, marriage is a business partnership as much as it is an alliance of love. For a partnership to work, it needs a strong, joint goal.

REALITY CHECK When one person in a two-career marriage suffers a career setback, it brings up feelings of vulnerability that need to be eased during such hard times. Ideally, there is open communication and a sharing of burdens. A crisis of any sort will test a marriage and reveal its strength.

Take this reality check to see how you fare and where you stand:

- Do I prioritize my responsibilities to home and work, or, when I juggle all the balls, do I forget which ones are made of glass?
- If I had to give more weight to one side of my life, would it be my home life or work life?
- Does an imbalance in pay scales affect the relationship with my spouse?
- Do I have greater aspirations for my spouse (or significant other) than for myself?

BE WILLING TO CHANGE

Society is more complex than ever. Our social relationships and communication processes are not only sophisticated, but advances in technology change on a near daily basis. To survive, you need to develop and refine problem-solving skills and levels of thinking. You must be willing to change, to adapt, and to get unstuck.

If you've stopped growing because you've been tripped up by any of the reasons I've discussed in this chapter, you have an opportunity *now* to take action and really change your life. In the next two chapters, you'll learn about the techniques or approaches you can use to *sort out* what you want and how to go for it.

A friend once told me that when he got stuck in his career, he always asked himself: What does my life stand for? For him, the important question was not, "What am I working at?" but "Who am I and where are my commitments?"

When you make a commitment to yourself, you can get through any fear and any downward trend and rebuild your life. With commitment, you have pride in yourself and in what you're doing. When you're not stuck, you can contribute to the world and feel like you are part of a group making a difference.

5

A CRASH COURSE IN CHANGE

If there is a universal tie that binds the human condition, it is getting a grip on dealing with change. Along with love, spirituality, and money, *change*—even more than power—is most likely to shake up human psychology. Change implies:

- Gain
- Loss
- Movement
- Growth, and, most provocative of all,
- *Alterations* in the people and things we know so well.

And when change is connected directly to work, you may be talking about money, power, and relationships, too. Work is not an emotionless endeavor. All these factors add up to a lot of potential movement to deal with at once. No matter how you fight it, change shapes your life directly or indirectly; the closer the encounter with an actual change, the more you *feel* it.

Change is as natural as the wheeling of the heavens. It is inevitable for all of us. And feeling *comfortable* with change makes good sense in the face of the astonishing future that's on its way. Change gives life color, sweetness—it's not all storms and challenges of survival. As anyone who has shifted gears successfully will tell you, change has its triumphs.

To understand the nuances of how you change in terms of a career, it helps to take a closer look at how you face change emotionally. The two are irrevocably connected.

CHANGE: AN OVERVIEW

Following World War I, the French built a seemingly impregnable series of defenses along their border with Germany that was meant to keep the Germans at bay. It was called the Maginot Line, and it *was* impregnable if you saw it as a Frenchman looking across the border to Germany, or vice versa. What was kept in was kept out. Then during World War II, the Germans invaded Belgium, crossed the Somme River, and, in effect, marched into France by doing an end run around the line's northern border, making it a useless defense.

Elaborate defense fortifications set up to fight and win wars are not so far afield metaphorically from our own defenses, and often *equally* elaborate and impregnable when it comes to change. There are times when change feels like a battle, but we are capable of doing triumphant end runs around the borders. First, we need to define the line.

DEFINING THE EMOTIONAL LINE AROUND CHANGE

The *idea* of change evokes an immediate response in each of us as it approaches us at different speeds. Change can be slow to come about, taking a few generations of evolutionary permutations, but finally it's *here* face to face with you.

You may create change yourself and meet your future instead

of letting it *happen* to you. Perhaps you go into business for yourself.

Change can be set in motion as a strategic response to offset a situation you find yourself in. You see the writing on the wall and before you are fired, you find another job.

Finally, change can erupt suddenly, coming about as a shock. The company goes under, is destroyed in a fire, is hit by a long-term strike.

The people I spoke to reported a whole range of emotions and defenses in relation to these variations in change. You may feel any of the following as change touches your life:

- You embrace it; you banish it.
- You believe change makes you more yourself; you're convinced that change will make you a stranger to yourself and lessen who you are.
- You're first in line to try an innovation; you don't understand why the line is forming.
- You enjoy weeding through the possibilities in change; you dread the possibilities. You become confused by new information and how it could apply to you.
- You think you know your limits and you're willing to give change a try; you believe you know your limits and turn down the opportunities, judging them unreachable.

And often you fall somewhere between the two poles. At the gut level, change makes you feel alive, exploratory, modern, *with it;* at the same time, it makes you feel threatened, dumb, irredeemably old-fashioned, out of sync.

Mention change, and it may bring on a flood of unpleasant feelings like fear, a "flight or fight" impulse, general anxiety, a "clutching" sensation; other times, it can spur a rash of positive anticipation and an increased energy level.

Evolution provided us with instincts about change, and if we were to survive, we had to *commit,* but we also had to adapt or create adaptations. Originally, we were programmed to be territorial and tribal and protective of both. But we could also figure the obvious—when out of all sources of food and water, quench the fire, decamp, and move on to better fields. As thinking creatures, we learned how to adjust to every kind of environment on earth and now we're discovering how to adapt to life in space.

We may be far more sophisticated than our forebears, but some theorists believe we may still be triggered by that less evolved, "primitive' instinct that warns us to "beware of the unknown," often signifying change, or the specter of an uncertain future. The intense commitment to "one's way" is, in a sense, a built-in defense system. It is meant to keep us allied to a tribe, its belief systems, its rules, and secure within it. If we were to change our minds and alliances each time another asked it of us, we would be lost.

Most of all, we'd lose our individuality.

The character "Zelig," in the eponymous film by Woody Allen, was an example of the "chameleon" personality, the extreme version of an overly willing "change master." Zelig so sought acceptance by others, he willed himself not only to change his mind, but his *race* if need be, to belong somewhere, to fit in with those with whom he was associating at the moment.

How much change is enough?

Among the more than 300 case studies in this book, I found that *projected* worry about the outcome of change tended to cause more anxiety than change itself. The greater the fear of loss connected to change, the more self-defeating were the ongoing internal conversations about "what will happen" in relation to, for example, a change of salary, needing to retool job skills, stepping into a different profession or title.

Excessive worry about change is just one barrier to real constructive change. Others are equally as counterproductive to making important life decisions. At times, we all make excuses for ourselves to keep us where we are.

The following scenarios are the most common obstacles to change that people identified in themselves. Sometimes, the simple matter of recognizing them in yourself will be enough to get *you* back on the track.

THE SEVEN OBSTACLES TO CHANGE AND OVERCOMING THEM

THE CRISIS OF "NO"

Of all words connected to the process of change, "no" carries more trepidation than any other. We tend to fear hearing or saying this word, believing something terrible will happen. Some of you will avoid confrontation of any sort—you won't ask for a raise you deserve; you won't make an important contact call; you won't go on an interview because the answer might be *no.* This fear of rejection is the greatest dilemma of all.

When we were toddlers just learning about the world, we exercised great *will* and persistence—as two-year-olds, we tested everything around us with the power of our own *no.* Two-year-olds don't take "no" for an answer lightly—they fight for what they want. We have been socialized into being more accommodating, so much so, in many cases, that we have turned our lives inside out to accept others' judgment of us over our own best interests. *No* is not the worst that can happen at all. The "child" in us knows this.

In truth, *no* has two real advantages:

First, a firm *no* completes an event and kicks off a new beginning. When someone says, "Sorry, we've chosen someone else," and even, "You're fired," it may not feel good, but it creates *closure* and opens a space for the next endeavor. *No* can be a release from the past and a relief—now you can go on unencumbered. It is a simple statistic: You will get a certain number of nos to every yes. And no is often preferable to maybe: Being strung along with false hope can be time wasting, manipulative, and counterproductive. "No" can be more painless than a falsely polite "maybe." You need to be astute, though, to listen for a "moving maybe"—genuine deliberation that leads to a *yes.*

Second, when someone says *no,* you can question why. This can be valuable information to you. You can learn under which conditions they would say yes, or what specifically you need to do to come back, or go forward elsewhere, with new strength.

"HAVE TO" DECISIONS

The path of least resistance is usually smooth underfoot and well lit, but it tends to wind back on itself. It's not the scenic route if you are seeking change and opportunities. "Have to" decisions may be easier to make, but they are often booby trapped: You *resent* making the choice you do since it is often based on what others tell you that you want for yourself or what they expect of you—and what you have mistakenly come to expect from yourself.

What do others expect? You may comply in any number of ways: You *have to* take a noncreative job or you will never get another offer. You *have to* stay in accounting because you know how much money you can make. You *have to* go into the hardware business or you will disappoint your family.

"Have to" decisions defy change unless you defy "have to" decisions. It is a matter of giving yourself a well-earned chance. Don't opt out: "Have to" will always be there.

MULTIPLE CHOICES

Are you someone who can't make a decision because you have too many options? Do you tend to "bank" your many career choices to delay change? If so, *declaring yourself* and making a single decision from among your "assets" may create a fear of making the wrong choice.

I spoke to Sandy, a buyer at a department store, who keeps a lengthy list of "goals"—from returning to school for an M.B.A., studying dress design, opening a GAP franchise, getting backing for her own shop, even going to dental school, and more. Ironically, Sandy's goals are not quite options as much as they are *notions.*

Although listing career possibilities makes total sense, after Sandy's interest in a career is piqued she adds it to her inventory. Eventually, these "interests" have a life span of a few minutes to a few days. All this motion is just Sandy "thinking out loud" in the presence of others, testing *their* responses to options she will never act on. Her "tag lines" to each option always explain why she must stay where she is. ("But, I can't get a GAP franchise because I don't have the money, and who will lend it to me?" and so on.)

This keeps Sandy believing, falsely, that she's making progress.

The trick, of course, is to investigate the possibilities, inventory the choices, and narrow the field down to where you can *act.* If you act, you will find what is right for you directly, indirectly, or serendipitously. And if more than one choice is legitimate, you may find a career that combines them. So it was with the multi-talented Dorothy Hafner, "Queen of Tabletop"—a top designer of dinnerware for Tiffany & Co. and Rosenthal China—who "played out her choices" before coming to ceramics.

While on a trip through Europe, Dorothy, still indecisive about a career in art, academia, or business, told people she was in one profession or the other "to see how it felt talking about it." Such innocent auditioning of a future occupation actually helped focus her talents back to art—and eventually business. Back in New York, she rented a tiny space in a ceramics studio where she could paint. There, she picked up some clay and made painted plates for fun; she didn't think much about them as a saleable product. When Dorothy gave a dinner party and used the plates, response was so strong, she took the encouragement, chanced it, and went fearlessly to Tiffany for an opinion of her work. They gave her a *commission.* And Dorothy found her niche.

POINTING THE BLAME

A setback or loss often calls up a different set of coping skills. First among them is facing your part of the problem and acting to rectify things. A business plan was rejected, you went over budget, a department was mismanaged: What went wrong?

If you believe that the difference between success and failure is in taking the credit for what works and avoiding the blame for what didn't, you are fortifying the wrong values. Acknowledging a mistake does not mean that *you* are incompetent or foolish or an unworthy person. It is this inability to separate the "sin" from the "sinner" that practiced blamers use to sabotage their own progress.

Blame gives an indirect message to others about (1) what you fear, and (2) what you expect them to do: make excuses to protect you. A heightened sensitivity to criticism is often allied to blaming—a nonflattering appraisal by others can stop you short. Rather than admit defeat or revise plans, you argue the blaming point.

One way over the blaming obstacle is to think in terms of *revision.* There is freedom in revision. If you tend to be too content with your first efforts, even "falling in love" with your work, you can't see its shortcomings or resent others who point them out. Revision is not a sign of failure but professionalism and craft—every car or spacecraft ever produced, every ballpoint pen that was made "dripless," every designer's "sample," has gone through revision. Blame doesn't produce a finished product.

BUILDING A CASE FROM "POOR ME"

Blurred hindsight and vague insight are fine-tuned for those who brood about what might have been and never can be. Sadly, real and present opportunities rarely inspire such people; rather, opportunity tends to remind self-pitying types of past disappointments and why they can't make a change. Life grinds to a standstill as they browse through time and obsess over unalterable events or the tides of the genetic pool that made them one way or another. They believe only in the dooming powers of their "limitations"—no matter how minor—and set themselves up as victims.

We all know the "poor me" people. Their lament focuses on what is "lacking" or lost. They didn't get "the breaks," they didn't go to the "right school," they're "never in the right place at the right time."

Others' successes reaffirm *their* "inadequacies" and it makes them jealous, and often angry. In response, they either want the others "who have" to favor them with pity, or to hand over what they want unconditionally.

To be treated fairly and to be rewarded for one's efforts are reasonable requests. "Poor me" plays on sympathy, not respect.

Reciting litanies of real or imagined limitations and rehashing old stories are ways to avoid action now.

According to *Forbes,* 9 percent of America's richest men never completed high school. We can *all* summon an authentic "poor me" in our own lives. But to change and take advantage of change, the answer is to find your way around or through this obstacle.

STRADDLING THE EITHER/OR DILEMMA

Think in extremes and you may be treading the longest distance between change and career satisfaction. These either/or decisions mean you are not living in the disappointing past, but in a possibly threatening future. You may make changes, but not with much comfort—there's a tinge of anxiety attached to each move.

Either/or is a dilemma when the choice you make is either black or white; no subtle renderings give it a sense of security or depth. Those who choose "either" often fear that it will quickly turn into "or," its opposite, without their consent. Either/or figures you win or lose, fail or succeed; your work is either great or disastrous; you want to be seen as a fascinating, heroic figure or you fear you're a helpless victim, a cipher.

Either/or decisions are counterproductive. They put severe limitations on achieving goals and establish equally tough judgments about success. If you make a change shooting for the "top" or nothing, you are cheating yourself. But believing you are destined for low-level jobs is a self-fulfilling prophecy. There's a wide swath of life between either/or. It's here you'll find your real choices.

THE "PRISONER SYNDROME"

Fear of change haunts prisoners who are about to be released into a world where they are free to make their own decisions, not follow institutional commands. However, freedom can be a cell of another sort. Emotional stress—insomnia, illness, loss of appetite—strikes some as the release date nears; others, once they have left, cannot cope with a changing world outside and find a way back to jail.

Although liberation is a much better place to be, many of you worry about the "release date," and the onset of change as bitterly as some prisoners do.

You are *free,* yet you may be bound by rituals that keep you imprisoned—for you, the "jailers" are quantities of incomplete projects or never-ending busy work. When there is so much work to do at a dead-end job, it's hard to spring out into a change. As with the "prisoner syndrome," the closer you come to completion of a project or task, the more anxious you are. Afraid of what's next, you drag out the work at hand and avoid change. When you know what you have, you stay where you are.

Satisfaction, fulfillment, relaxation, and a reward follow real completion. For someone feeling overburdened by present tasks and anxiety about the future, completion is followed by a feeling of being let down—there is a sense of loss. If your method of operation is to feel contradictory about completion, recognize, define, and acknowledge each completed step as it occurs and give yourself credit for accomplishment.

MAKING CHANGE WORK: BEING ADAPTABLE

This is the key to change.

Social relationships and communication processes are not only mega-sophisticated, but advances in technology change them on a near daily basis. To thrive, we need to develop and refine our problem-solving skills and levels of thinking. We need to learn how to adapt our skills and competencies to fit in and succeed. And once you've identified any of the seven obstacles to change, you can begin to concentrate on your strong points and make the progress you deserve.

Adaptive action opens up to possibilities, no matter if you're a Lifer, a Synthesizer, a Builder, or a Reinventor. A belief in limitations closes a door.

There's a difference between skills and competencies. Skills are learned—working with a word processor, giving an injection, mastering tax forms. Competencies are talents you are born with that allow you to learn these skills and improve on them—a "gift" for business, for mathematics, for dance, for deftly organizing six people or six thousand, for acting.

Adaptive action lets you examine your skills and competencies, and if it is necessary to fit into a different corner of the marketplace, translate them into another career. Dan Marsh, for example, clung to the vice presidency in a small mail-order business that was mismanaged around him into near bankruptcy. After eight years with them, he was forced to assess the field, his location, his obligations, and what he most wanted to do. He told me:

> I don't have to stick around here. I'm great at managing people and the constant movement of products. If I have to, I can learn how to operate a machine—I have the knack. If I can't get a job in management, I'm willing to do a 180-degree turn.

Adaptation is an ongoing process. It's part of your life; it happens every day. You respond to the changes in your environment and to spoken and unspoken rules and customs that occur within it. How well and successfully you adapt is generally influenced by two basic factors.

1. *Your personality:* This refers to qualities that make you an individual—qualities such as skills, belief systems, your attitudes, and even your physical condition.
2. *Your personal history:* This history includes environmental influences—where you grew up and where you live now—and the nature of the situations you've confronted over a lifetime. Some of these situations include family structure, cultural rituals and norms, social conflicts such as religious and racial strife, wars, and natural disasters.

And so, who adapts?

Comic Jackie Mason, a man begat from fifteen generations of rabbis, knew he couldn't survive in a world structured by laws and ancient customs. He joined the secular world and became a comedian. Why is he different from his brothers and sisters who follow strict Jewish orthodoxy? His siblings may have Jackie's comic timing, mumbling delivery, and hilarious wit—and we may be able to teach them these skills if they don't. But we may never be able to move them *out* of their structured existence and expect them to adapt to the world Jackie has chosen.

What is the answer? Personality, personal history, and the "x" factor in each. Many of life's most agile adapters come from secure or traditional backgrounds, as with Jackie Mason; others battle through torn childhoods, family tragedies, frequent relocation confirming a perpetual sense of being an "outsider," poverty, and excessive privilege combined with unstable parental relationships. Some people can move out of a stable life and be flexible—early strife and stress teach them early on *who they are.* If you are so "cursed," then you may be later blessed.

Actress and playwright, Synthesizer Diane Kagan feels that much of her adaptability was formed by a sudden unconventional change in her once status-conscious and conventional parents. Her childhood experiences, she believes, have helped her adjust to the fickle and financially precarious world of theatre.

She told me of the history-making move from a socially prominent enclave in New Jersey horse country to a "virgin" Florida beach:

> One day, my father came home from work and said, "This isn't the way we were meant to live." He sold everything and *his* father disinherited him for leaving the family business. Suddenly, I was in Florida on a deserted beach. No houses, no people, just some Seminole Indians in teepees.
>
> My father founded a town there, named it Juneau Beach, and made himself mayor. My mother named the streets. First it was fox hunting up north, then it was barefoot with nothing.
>
> At first it scared me to death, but it gave me a lot of courage to live on the edge. I found out early that there is no security, no matter what you plan for.

Diane got accustomed to the insecurities, and the resulting resilience she developed as a child. It is a part of adaptive action.

USING ADAPTIVE ACTION

Figuring out how to apply adaptive action so you can change, nearly painlessly, follows three simple steps:

1. *You need information.* This includes, first, information about *you*—that is, a thorough evaluation of what your skills/competencies are, where you want to go, what you need, and what your future plans are; and second, *the marketplace*—specifically, information about the areas of your interest, trends, and understanding how your field is changing, technologically or philosophically. It's knowing what may be available to you and how to get it. Once you have a clear sense of the information, you can list the possibilities or create them.

Narrowed down to realistic choices, you need to *commit* to change. Commitment forms a strong foundation for what follows.

2. *You need to change your attitude.* As any psychotherapist will tell you, information alone rarely changes how you act. You may be able to pinpoint the traumatic episode that left you unable to do *this* or spotlight the early affirmation that lets you accomplish *that,* but unless there is a shift in attitude about an issue, you will stay the same. Attitude is the first determinant to tell you if you want to change.

3. *You need to change your behavior.* An attitude change sets up the chance for you to behave differently and see the connections between your skills, interests, and the marketplace. If you are someone who is highly skilled, bright, and ambitious, but you do poorly on interviews, you need coaching on *presentation*—how you sell yourself to others. When you change your behavior, you *accept* the fact that you need assistance in interpersonal skills. To change, you must take the crucial step of finding an expert to guide you through the process, build your self-esteem, and gain a skill critical to success.

Behavioral changes can be internal or external, but you will need to practice the changes until all action is *effortless*—fully and naturally part of you. It's like learning to shift gears in a car; you learn to coordinate the clutch, the accelerator, and the brakes until you can drive without thinking of each step.

ANYTHING'S POSSIBLE

Shifting gears is about starting over—trading in the comforts of familiarity for some serious self-effort and the chance to build a better life through work. Getting over obstacles is part of the challenge.

There is no understanding the world in six easy lessons. We all go through an apprenticeship in life and in time. Though we wish it were so, we can't create a capacity to change and flourish in a world of such rapid change *overnight.* We each have unique personalities and certain responsibilities to others. Change is never easy, even for the greatest risk takers. But what matters is that change takes *declaration* and *commitment*—and giving up any single-minded point of view that keeps you where you are. You need to make an inner effort to overcome entrenched attitudes and positions. Then you can work through the obstacles that cause doubt and delay.

When you make a change, it's natural to go through a phase where you feel off balance, uncomfortable. Missing your "old life"—even the familiarity of a dreary routine—is a common part of the process of change.

But how important it is.

Present environment is always creating a force that influences your livelihood—circumstances change economically; companies go under or merge; there is suddenly a job to strive for; new products change a market. Personality and personal preferences determine how you decipher these forces—you take the "temperature" of the world around you and, from there, you figure out how to adapt and survive. A shopkeeper in the Hindu Kush and a boutique owner in Trump Tower, for example, have an occupation in common, but they must adapt to different cultural values, trends, rituals of bargaining, and methods of dealing with the public in order to prevail.

Movie mogul Sam Goldwyn once said ironically about a film beset by numerous problems, "It's an impossible situation, but it has possibilities." Seeing the possible in the impossible is the ultimate in adaptive action. Giving reality to the "impossible" and making something happen for yourself assures greater mastery of your life.

6

SORTING OUT I

Following Your Own Star

The story goes that the start of the Chrysler Corporation followed the sound of a slamming door. Walter Chrysler, who had worked for General Motors, got into a dispute, was fired, banged the office door behind him, and went on to make history. Chrysler built his dream when he could no longer work on someone else's.

In a way, he represents one picture of the American individual—a gritty innovator who reaches his limit in another man's company and leaves to found a successful organization of his own making. It's happened millions of times over.

That disaster precedes progress tends to be the case for those of you who use adversity to free yourself to be yourself. And the truth is, sometimes you do not know you *are* an entrepreneur, or a minister, or a therapist, or a painter until you've slammed a door—really or metaphorically. At that moment, or shortly thereafter, you find the key to fulfilling work.

Self-discovery is a lifelong quest and there are never any easy answers. Some of you, though, like Chrysler, are lucky—whether you come to it early or later in life, because of adversity, an epiphany, or an item of news, *you are, or will be, true to yourself.*

In this way, sorting out will be easier for you.

You're every man or woman who is captivated by possibilities or driven by curiosity, inner need, or some source of restlessness to find out what lies beyond your immediate reach. It's what an astronaut said was the reason for joining a mission into space, ". . . to bring back the wonder of it all."

To capture your version of the wonder for yourself, you've no doubt considered, "what if . . . someday . . . could *I?* . . ." A percentage of you will never make it past the excitement of an idea or pricing the airline ticket. Family responsibilities keep you home, careers look too precious to give up, or an idea, on closer examination, really belongs to another time and you've outgrown it.

Others of you *do* make it, with the same set of "obligations" but possessing an ability to fine-tune your goals. You are the ones *who know who you are* and eventually act on that knowledge.

I spoke with a self-made millionaire, a woman who earned $15,000 a year at a desk job until she "had enough of not being enough." She got into specialty sales when she was forty-six years old, found her niche, and now, ten years later, Betty is worth $2 million and climbing. She has a modest perspective of her success. Betty told me, "I'm just an ordinary woman who wound up doing extraordinary things."

I believe that Betty, the eight people you will read about in this chapter, and those of you who *act* and change your life *are* extraordinary. You can live in the everyday world with ease, but you can just as easily push back the edges of the conventional world and reach inside yourself for something that allows you to set out on a journey of discovery—and self-mastery. This ability often baffles others less able to take the risks you take.

FOLLOWING YOUR OWN STAR

If you share the impulses, interests, and/or the deep spiritual faith that characterize the eight upcoming profiles, you have a number of qualities in common with them. These are:

1. You no longer ask, "What does life mean," but "What does *my* life mean?" When the answer is finally apparent, you possess the readiness to meet your destiny, wherever you may find it.

2. You are honest with yourself. Goals have less to do with activity (the busy work of getting a job done) and more to do with self-acknowledgment (the pleasure of doing your work).

3. While you may suffer from periods of self-doubt, ultimately you have faith in yourself and your judgment. You don't get caught up in obstacles to change, such as the "poor me" syndrome or "either/or" dilemmas.

4. You are more often than not self-motivated and spiritually grounded.

5. You are a cautious risk taker who can give up the routines that also give you comfort. You are not wed forever to a nest or to status quo thinking.

6. You are sui generis—unique, not out of focus. You may appear offbeat to others, but you are purposeful and committed.

7. You don't fear money. No matter how much or how little you have acquired, you always act from a sense of abundance. Neither a "poverty mentality" nor an infatuation with greed marks you.

8. You are open to opportunity and are willing to test yourself again and again.

You also know that *following* your star is a matter of timing and circumstance. This star may appear to you in any number of ways. They include:

- The Twist of Fate,
- The Call of Talent,
- The "Someday . . ." Dream, and
- The Spiritual Voyage: Serving Others

THE TWIST OF FATE

The three people I spoke with here each started out *sure* of themselves. They believed they knew themselves, knew that work was right for them: to work as a social psychologist, to be an orchestra conductor, to be a nature writer. Strong willed and artistic, they got to their goals by the book, got the credentials, the experience, a valid sense of the future. They were goal setters, occupied with concrete realities about doing the best they could at a chosen career.

Proving the adage that if you begin with certainties you end up with doubts/begin with doubts and you end up with certainties, three "certain" lives were diverted or upended, each by a twist of fate. Such diversion may characterize your experience.

FROM BLOOMINGDALE'S TO BALI . . . AND BACK Abandoning a high-octane career as a retailing star at Bloomingdale's, Barbara Ashley leapt out of the tough New York race for achievement and landed in a mythic "paradise." Hers is an interesting case of a traditional Synthesizer turned Reinventor *re*turned Synthesizer. Inspired by a desire for "harmony and personal growth," Barbara moved to the island of *Bali*—knowing no one, having no job, no home base, and no idea of the cultural nuances of taking up residence in an Indonesian island.

It was a drastic move, yet a surprisingly effortless one.

Rooted in convention, Barbara is guided by an unconventional fearlessness that guides her decision making. If many phases in her life and career are in high contrast to each other, it's no accident. Barbara has a real willingness to make change work for her even in situations where she has little foreknowledge. Where does this willingness spring from? She told me:

> It is the blessed ability to trust that things will work out. I was born with a sense of adventure and a strong gut instinct . . . I follow my nose and if it feels right, I do it.

Bloomingdale's and Bali exist within parentheses in her career. She began in social services as the only nonmedically credentialed administrator and psychotherapist at a clinic affiliated with Harvard. After seven years there, she was advised to earn an advanced degree, which, ironically, was to provide her with the credentials to qualify her for the job she *already* held.

The demand made her angry but it also brought with it a clarity about work that made sense to her. She wanted a career where advancement was based on strength and merit, not academic degrees. She quit the clinic and took a trip with Club Med to sort things out.

The trip resulted in the first of Barbara's successive—and serendipitous—career changes. Gregarious and full of energy, she was asked by the Club Med staff to come work for them. It was wildly different from her intellectually based job at the clinic, but she accepted. It served as a pleasant bridge to her next career move: a sales job at Bloomingdale's—another accident of fate that came through a friend's recommendation.

With no retail experience and no reservations about starting over in a new career, Barbara took the job. Again, it was the Synthesizer's ability to use opportunity to advantage, and instinct, the Reinventor's strong card, that told her it was the right thing to do.

Her career at Bloomingdale's was successful, but the light was extinguished after a few years. Operational struggles at the store and a "devaluation of her abilities" led Barbara to quit. She had no backup position in the wings. An unexpected small inheritance provided the opportunity for another "thinking" trip, and this time she found Bali. Instead of going to just "refuel," she discovered "simplicity, cooperation, the most beautiful place on earth." She rented a house, learned how to "do everything"—including living with no electricity or running water. She stayed five years.

In the States a year later, Barbara took a high-level job as director of retail analysis at a large Michigan company—another right fit for her. Although she was out of the competitive American marketplace for five years, luckily going to Bali hadn't cost her five years of career advancement. She has resumed her career *as if* she had stayed in retailing all that time.

She told me what makes this company uniquely right for her:

> The reason I took this job was that the company values the qualities I most value in myself. They see my having been to Bali as a plus. It means to them that I'm a self-starter, that I stayed

there and saw things through with a strength of conviction and commitment.

Barbara's side trip to Bali taught her that she didn't have to feel guilty if every moment isn't consumed by productivity—one of modern man's stresses. It's a blissful gift—to "just be" in a tropical paradise and find one of life's answers, inadvertently.

THE CYCLE OF SYNTHESIZER/REINVENTOR/SYNTHESIZER If you are like Barbara, you get the signal for change and act. Whether it's a change of job or a change of lifestyle where work is incidental, you can sell yourself into the next opportunity, and succeed at it or "go with the flow."

Also like Barbara, some very adaptive Synthesizers also go through periods of achieving at jobs for which they are overqualified. These are really "fishing" periods—you're still looking for the *work* that feels right via the *job itself.* This genius for adaptability and skill transfer can lead to "coasting" cycles. Since you're so able to learn the particulars of a job, you become caught up at fitting in and excelling, rather than racing the true limitations of the job.

On the practical side, you can stay in one place until it's time to move on. On the down side, you overachieve and expect too much from a job/company that can't fulfill what you need.

Such disappointments and changes brought out the Reinventor in Barbara—as it will for you if you are so inclined. These experiences will enrich and clarify what you want to do next.

FOLLOWING ANOTHER TUNE While someone like Barbara found her way back to an executive position without specifically *targeting* that goal, Ilana Rubenfeld, a musician cum psychotherapist, knew only specifics. Her trail followed the Lifer's intense devotion down one path—and to her surprise, she came to a welcome fork in the road.

When she was a student at Juilliard School of Music and the only woman in a class of fifteen men, Ilana Rubenfeld was sure of a shining future: conductor of a symphony orchestra. A serious musician, Ilana had no glimmering that her experience in conducting would, years away, lead to a fascinating synthesis of mind/body therapy called the Rubenfeld Synergy approach.

When she was a student practicing the conducting art four and five hours a day, the sheer physical labor—vigorous, concentrated action—was hard on her. "There was never any instruction about how to use our bodies. The work," she said, "took a serious toll." It was always vigorous, concentrated action. As a result, she developed back spasms; doctors treated her and she got temporary relief so she could perform. Then she developed a problem with her arm and it looked as if her career in conducting would be threatened unless she got help.

Athletes understand that sports injuries are inevitable—increased exertion soon reveals the body's weak spots. If one is lucky, therapy and massage is enough to regain strength. Musicians can fatigue muscles in the same way.

Among the therapies she used, Ilana was most relieved by the Alexander Technique, a method designed to teach you to use your body more efficiently, as well as promoting a healing process through subtle physical *adjustments.* It helped her, but more, the technique started a rush of ideas about *why* it worked. She learned that she didn't have to change what she did, but the *way* she was doing it.

Following Juilliard, Ilana faced difficult times. There was little enthusiasm or support for women conductors. She suffered a few disappointments, including when the invitation to be Leopold Stokowski's assistant was rescinded. The maestro instead replaced her with two men. She was twenty-two and hurt. It was a lesson to her that the music world wasn't necessarily lofty and principled, but simply the music *business.* But with the Stokowski rejection came a great sense of loss. A painter or writer needs only his materials and enough space. A conductor needs her gift and a population of musicians; without them, a conductor is powerless, unexpressed.

Ilana recalled the rejection and how it shaped her next move:

> I felt like a failure, but it was failure that was handed to me. Everyone in the world knew I was going to be Stokowski's assistant,

> and then I wasn't. I thought I'd never get over the blow. I cried and said: What can I do? How can I *come back* from this?

A resilient Lifer who did not get stuck clinging to good credentials in a prestigious career direction, Ilana went on to found her own chorus, the New York Lyric Ensemble, and hired twenty singers. Operating at first from grants, the chorus was soon a commercial success. Ten years later, she became the choral director at New York's 92nd Street "Y," a highly regarded cultural center in the Jewish YMHA system. Under her direction, the choral society grew from twenty to eighty members. Still, she yearned to conduct major orchestras and programs, but she concluded that, except for one or two rare exceptions, women were excluded from taking the baton. An able administrator, Ilana took over as director of the "Y"; when a number of internecine battles erupted, she was dismissed.

Ilana's first career choice had been stymied, but her ability to succeed in other "directing" professions—building a chorus, running a cultural center—set her apart. A commitment to stretching the boundaries of her talent once again materialized with her Lifer inclinations: she redevoted herself to "mind/body" work. The real foundation for her work as a psychotherapist and bodyworker arose from a gush of emotional memories during a session with the Alexander Technique. She recalled:

> I began crying and my teacher suggested a therapist. But when I got to one, "talking" therapy was equally inadequate. I now had in my life a therapist who would talk but not touch and an Alexander teacher who would touch but *not* talk!

The incompleteness of each discipline led her to question how she might incorporate both aspects in a new approach. "I set out to heal myself," she said. She began teaching the Alexander Technique and had the good fortune of meeting and working with Fritz Perls, the founder of Gestalt therapy. It was a critical turning point. When she asked him, "Why couldn't a therapist work with *both* verbal and nonverbal expressions at the same time?" he encouraged her to experiment. Sometimes, she and Perls would work in tandem, combining the Alexander Technique with Gestalt therapy—Ilana conducting the physical adjustments on a client, while Perls guided the verbal aspects of a session. She observed reactions, conscious and unconscious movements connected to psychological material, and how aware the client was of his/her own responses.

Perls died suddenly and it was a great loss to her. Shortly after, she met another pioneer in movement therapy, Moshe Feldenkrais. In the late 1970s, she developed a synthesis of her own theories along with her mentor's contributions.

THE LIFER: FINDING SECOND CHOICES Lifers are not as versatile as Synthesizers or Reinventors at career transitions—change is simply harder for them to get through. But they're fighters, like H. Bud Walters (who, I noted earlier, virtually won his job back with a relay of chicken soup to an ailing boss) and they're right on the pulse of what they *need.* So it was with Ilana. Combine the three factors—fight, need, and single-minded devotion—and it will get a true Lifer through any obstacle.

Ilana's Synergy technique resolved the great anger she'd harbored for years about the ongoing frustration of not being able to conduct. For her, the "active awareness" of her feelings and their physical manifestations—aches, spasms, disease—finally freed her to take greater risks and help others.

If, like Ilana, you're a Lifer with a long-range plan in which you place your confidence, destiny may well rearrange it. There will be the shock of loss—giving up the only work you'd ever conceived of doing—but there's also the surprise of what takes its place. Even more important for the Lifer, it may be for *this* second choice where your true gifts lie. The joy is not only in its discovery, but in how your work will affect others.

Betsy Barlow Rogers, whose case follows, was similarly transformed. Hers is a "therapy" of another sort.

SAVING CENTRAL PARK "Everyone needs to invest their lives with meaning, and *causes* gives meaning to life. My cause is to rebuild Central Park," said the gracious Betsy Barlow Rogers, speaking of what became an astonishing achievement. Betsy was moved to take action when prevailing apathy for the park in the mid-1970s resulted in its falling into tragic disrepair.

The lofty goal of saving a sprawling urban park, pretty much without the help of the city government, might have daunted other women, but not Betsy, a true Reinventor personality. With determination fired by her goal, the slim blonde who "never thought she had it in her," moved ably through bureaucracies, committees, and fund-raising crises to bring the park back to its original beauty—a "masterpiece of landscape design."

A totally inexperienced administrator when she began the job, Betsy, an award-winning nonfiction writer, learned what she needed to do step by step. Her fascination with the park began with her introduction to the work of Frederick Law Olmstead, designer of Central Park and, subsequently, the subject of her second book.

In 1975, she ran a summer youth program through the parks department. She began to develop an awareness of how to be an *administrator,* a skill she never believed was within her grasp. "I had to turn myself into a very different type of professional to do a tough job," she said candidly. "If you're an artist, temperamentally, you always feel business has little to do with you."

New York City politics that year were problematic; the job of Park Commissioner was up for grabs—*no one wanted the job.* There were firings, no budget, no projects in the works. This left the park on the edge of neglect. "The park was too precious to walk away from," she said, "so I took the challenge. Someone had to try and save it."

Betsy agreed to raise all the money for park maintenance and staff salaries herself. Officials gave her a tiny office where she learned the basics of fund raising. She also raised the consciousness of New Yorkers by launching special programs that increased donations and committed volunteers.

What came with the checks were hundreds of testimonials of people's affection for the park. In her first year, she raised $2 million; in the last two years, she's raised $22 million and has 104 people on the payroll. The work has sustained her for a number of reasons:

Not too many people get to invent their own careers as they go along. I feel lucky to have done it, but you need people to believe in you . . . and then you have to have guts and persistence.

In the beginning, in the dog days, I was naive. No one knew what I was doing in the Parks Department and [everyone] wanted me out. Bureaucracy sort of instinctively rejects things that are innovative. But if I wanted to save the park, I had to stay and do everything I could.

It's not enough to have a cause. You have to get up in the morning and do a specific set of tasks to make it work. Idealism isn't enough.

THE FIGHTING SPIRIT: ONE MODE OF THE REINVENTOR Twists of fate grow out of a belief that the world provides, not *de*prives. Reinventors, with a sense of adventure, curiosity, or a "cause" to inspire them, take such twists more easily than others. If you are like Betsy, you understand that "fate," or the unexpected, will always insinuate itself into your life in some way. Fernando Flores is another example of the Reinventor's nine lives: A onetime member of Salvador Allende's cabinet, then a political prisoner in Chile for three years, he escaped his country, came to America, and wound up on several career tracks. A computer software entrepreneur, linguist, and philosopher, Fernando, among others, founded a human potential program called Logomyth.

You may believe that things will always be as they are; that your politics will always insulate you from persecution; that the more far reaching your control over your life and the lives of those in your immediate circle, the safer you are. The twist of fate may, in the long run, surprise you.

THE CALL OF TALENT

When I see the paintings of, say, Gauguin, or listen to the work of a composer that moves me, or wear the clothes of a designer with a knack for line and fabric, I have no doubts as to *why* they did what they did: natural *talent.* I think: what other path could they have taken?—they had no choice. And although Gauguin, for example, worked responsibly in a bank until he was thirty-five, his destiny was art—and he made the meeting happen.

We tend to consider the talents we don't have as mysterious, awesome, enviable. Where do they come from? Talent is a blessing, but exercising it, directing it, and making the most of it is a choice.

Some of us have talents we put off to the side because we have to go through the very real concerns of earning a living; our "talent," we found at one point, did not support us. Others of us reach some degree of success with a talent, and have to *reinvent* a way to use it because times change and so do we. I know an art director, for example, who worked at a magazine for fourteen years. It folded last year and Peggy was out of work. Rather than look for a similar job, she opened a small printing company with two associates. Yet others of us always had a *knack*—for writing, for crafts, for carpentry—and found a viable, paying niche to express it. But there's another side to talent, too.

The two men I interviewed about career choices in this section are men I consider gifted in their own way—one is a former world-class athlete, and the other is a great editor and writer. Both men characterize for me the *grit,* the discipline, and commitment without which "talent" is simply a lofty unexpressed ideal.

You may be at a point where you want to shift gears and develop a talent you have and apply it to your next profession, or perhaps you simply want to use a gift more productively in the career you have now. Bruce Jenner and T. George Harris, I believe, may inspire such goals in you.

THE CHAMPION: WHAT FOLLOWS A GOLD MEDAL? With his clean-cut good looks, charm, and dazzling athletic prowess, Bruce Jenner had America cheering as he took the gold medal at the 1972 Olympics—the decathlon was his. Not just the best at one event, but at *ten,* Bruce was that year and for many years to follow, as he says, "one on one with the world." He was a champion and everyone loved him.

When you look at Bruce now—he's a sportscaster for NBC—you still remember his Olympic triumph and wonder if "things came easy to him." He radiates the confidence of accomplishment and "peace with himself," but it belies an ongoing struggle he has learned to deal with effectively: As talented an athlete as he may be, and as *verbally* agile and engaging though he is, Bruce suffers from severe dyslexia—a learning problem that once caused him great pain.

Of the many people I spoke to, I think Bruce is one prime example of someone who didn't get stuck in childhood refrains or tangled in a snarl of self-defeating attitudes. It might have happened. Instead, he used the pursuit of *excellence* to guide his life. It started early on. Although he had a difficult time with his academic subjects in school because of his reading problem, Bruce focused much of his energies on what he *could* do well—athletics. For him, eventually training to enter the Olympics was a natural step. He applied himself to it full time and full throttle. He told me:

> When I was trying to break a world record at the Olympics, it was something important because it was *me,* the dyslexic kid, trying to do something that no one had done before. To get to this step, I gave myself the challenge and took it. There's no other way.
>
> There's the other side to winning, and that was in my mind, too. Maybe you know how to take all the right steps to win a race, but there is also a fear of accomplishment—a fear of having people look up to you, a fear of what to do next once you *are* the best. . . . What then? So do you put yourself on the line? *I gave it my best shot.*

Once the games were over and he decided to no longer compete as an athlete, Bruce had to confront the reality of setting up a career—starting over and "growing up," as he said. The difficult part was gaining confidence in himself to make the right decisions about a career. His talent was athletics—where could he fit in? At first he relied on a friend and his wife, Christie—who he was married to during that time—because he thought they were "smarter than me at creatively coming up with ideas about what I should do." His background still haunted him; Bruce Jenner, "the dyslexic kid" could not think. How could he succeed, or survive, without athletics?

Bruce proved he had another talent—he was a natural interviewer and commentator, although an untrained one, and good at talking in front of a television camera. Still believing that skills counted—that he had to be good, to ask questions, to learn how to work with everyone, and that he couldn't coast through life as "Bruce Jenner, Olympic Gold Medalist"—he was determined to learn the craft of television sportscaster. There was also the practical side: He figured he had four years to learn the business and establish his reputation before the next Olympic superstar appeared.

He's been on the air since then as well as doing competitive auto racing. A risk taker with great energy and drive, Bruce is a great Synthesizer. He's someone who's not afraid to gamble on himself, who's not afraid to fail because he knows he's gone in as prepared as he can be, and, mostly, that he can only learn and grow from his mistakes. He told me:

> The hardest thing for me was gaining confidence in the decisions I made. I had to realize that my mind is as good as anyone else's. It turned out that I'm a good idea person, and over the years, I've developed that skill one small step at a time. But I know, as with sports, you don't win all the time.
>
> I accomplished something at the Olympics that I'll never be able to equal again, and I've accepted that. I'm fortunate enough to have had that day. What I have in my life now is personal satisfaction, for example, the pleasure I get being with my four kids. To me, challenges don't have to be about breaking world records all the time, but to have an idea and develop it into something productive.

GOING FULL MEASURE When he was a boy in rural Kentucky, someone told his mother that he would grow up to be a man with a mission, and, in his way, T. George Harris has embodied that prophecy. The brilliant, dynamic editor of *Psychology Today,* George has guided his career through the magazine business fueled by "trying to improve people's perceptions of each other." He's succeeded in many ways.

The first national investigative reporter to cover race relations full time during the landmark years of protest marches and sit-ins of the 1950s and 1960s, George soon built his reputation as *Time* magazine's favorite son. When he was thirty years old and the youngest bureau chief at the Chicago office of the magazine and on his way up, Henry Luce, founder of the *Time/Life* empire, brought him to the New York office, and then to the San Francisco bureau. George was, he says in retrospect, soon caught in the trappings of success and "so misled" he "forgot what the basics were."

Then two events triggered George's decision to leave the magazine after thirteen years and go elsewhere: His second daughter was born with Down syndrome, bringing about a more profound connection to his family, and Luce appointed a new managing editor at the magazine whose strategies and values clashed with George's. He said:

> I had a wonderful job and I was intrigued by Luce. But the tension at the *Time* organization eventually got to me. My hands were freezing on the typewriter—I was trying to do writing tricks, not reporting. The new managing editor played a slick game of internal politics and wasn't doing the kind of work I wanted to do. I wasn't being who I was or doing my best. Once I recognized that, I knew I had to leave.

It was difficult for George to leave for a competitor, not only in terms of his sense of loyalty to Luce, but there was the practical aspect, too. *Time/Life* then had the prestige *and* the resources most writers/reporters appreciated. He "hung in" for a year, all the time negotiating with *Look,* then, one day, he went across the street and accepted a job with them.

For a basic Lifer personality like George, it soon became a matter of solving the universal problem of pursuing a career as well as caring for a family—and achieving a balance. Many people cannot take the chance when there's an opportunity presented to them—they're stuck worrying about security for their family and stay at a job that isn't working for them any longer. Such choices to leave the "secure" job are never easy to make. Here then was George: His family had grown to four children—one severely retarded—

and his wife remained his support system, uninterested in a career outside their home.

It was the "family load" that led him first, through his "godfather," the economist Peter Drucker, to then leave *Look* and become editor of *Careers Today.* It appealed to George: It was a chance to create something new, even though the odds of failure were high for new magazines. It went under after four issues. Then the original editor of *Psychology Today* stepped down and George was appointed editor. He finally found his niche and a balance between meaning of work and connection to family. He said:

> My dream was to do honest, important stories in terms of human activity. I can't tell people what the world should be like, but I think that if you can help people understand each other in some profound way, my bet is that the divine spark in people will work it out.
>
> I always lived a lean life. I never wanted to be captive of my lifestyle. I've learned that the little things you worry about aren't that important. War and combat help you simplify life; if you figure you're not coming back, you grow. And having a retarded child wipes away petty middle-class assumptions about life.
>
> I don't think there's any security in caution. I believe in going the full measure—no shortcuts, in terms of marriage and in terms of work. And the joy of reaching into the unknown.

THE GREAT "SOMEDAY . . ." DREAM

In a tale of two ironies, there is Barbara Ashley who didn't plan to live in Bali until she got there, then there are the Bakers, a couple who floated on a dream for twenty years.

You can understand how it happened, if you've planned for *someday,* a word packed with great hope. The power of *someday* is that it takes us into a future when we are *free* to pursue a lifelong aspiration. "Before I'm too old, I want to . . . ," "When I retire from teaching, I promise I will . . . ," "I'm living like Scrooge now so I can travel for two years and. . . ."

Someday sets up a time frame—sometimes indeterminate, sometimes precise. What ignites the someday dream is the underlying *magic* of fulfilling it. For the Bakers, it was adventure.

She was a teacher with a flair for acting, but basically a Lifer, and he was a civil engineer, already a strong Synthesizer. Traditional beginnings. They married young. From these roots surged a passion for exploration.

Like Sir Richard Burton, the nineteenth-century explorer and translator of the *Arabian Nights*, who said, "discovery is mostly my mania," Mary Ann and Norman Baker, too, were captivated by the mystery and diversity of the world's cultural landscapes—and yearned to see what they could.

Whether it is the intensity of "mania," competitiveness, or simple interest "because it was there" (Sir Edmund Hillary's understated remark about *why* he chose to climb Mt. Everest), authentic adventurers are a bit different from you and me. Explorers are curious, but what *moves* them once the pin is in the map? The underlying motivation is a powerful *belief* in their goals. It's fueled by a willingness to invest the time in reaching a destination and an understanding that they will have to make some sacrifices before getting a toehold on the craggy peaks. They are not tourists.

Those who trek the earth or invent a better potato peeler—the rule breakers rather than the rule makers—see the world through a different prism. They are explorers with a vision.

And this brings us back to the Bakers.

It was Norman who had the itch for exploration first. Once he coaxed his way aboard a ketch voyaging out of Seattle to Tahiti, Norman's first such trip, his destiny was sealed. He thought next of circumnavigating the world, but he was called back to work in his ailing father's construction business. Ultimately, he went into partnership with his brother, intermittently joining expeditions.

When Mary Ann married Norman, his dream of circumnavigation became hers. The Bakers vowed that after their tenth anniversary, they would sell everything, buy a boat, and go. Their three children grew up with the excitement of the endeavor, and soon it became the family dream. It was put aside "just for a year," when Norman met Thor Heyerdahl, the history-making Norwegian anthropologist known for his Kon-Tiki expedition. Heyerdahl was organizing the "Ra" expedition, meant to prove that transmigration to the Americas was possible thousands of years ago by *reed* boat. The Ra, a reed boat built for the trip, was based on a reconstruction of one depicted 5,000 years ago in ancient Egypt. Norman signed on as navigator.

Following this trip, Norman lectured, wrote, and worked with his brother in the construction business. Then when the Baker children were in their teens, circumnavigation again became a feasible goal.

Everything seemed to fall into place. They were *ready*. What they needed was the vehicle. They searched for a boat and found the historic *Anna Christina*—the oldest wooden sailing ship in the world, still in service since 1868. The dream was taking shape and the possibilities grew. With an eye on the future, they thought the trip could be the subject of a movie or book. It sounded like a natural: A family of five circumnavigates the globe on the oldest sailing ship in the world.

A major snafu stopped them. The ship not only needed work, it required rebuilding, not repairs. The task took *four years* of work, relocation to the Caribbean where she was docked, and further delays.

Some people might have reappraised the situation and given up or redesigned the dream. The Bakers had a commitment and a loyalty to the decisions they made. Four years later, they were still holding on. The *Anna Christina* had seriously disrupted or rearranged their lives. What kept them going? Mary Ann told me:

> Norman and I don't give up easily, so we stuck with the dream. We thought things would always move faster and we'd say, optimistically, "Just a few more months . . ." The kids were still willing to join us when we thought the boat was finally ready for circumnavigation in 1986, but then we had major *engine* problems.
>
> That meant another eight months of waiting until we could get the right parts to fit it. *Leaving* port was always right around the corner. We would think it was time, then things would fall apart.
>
> Eventually, we went through our money and had to stop. We'd even sold our house to finance the trip.

The sacrifices they made were costly, yet their spirit didn't wane until the final knowing blow of engine trouble. In 1986, they sailed the *Anna Christina* from where she was docked to New York. It was to be their only voyage aboard her. With the trip, they faced the finality of their dream. But they had some moments of pleasure from the *Anna Christina*: They participated in the breathtaking parade of tall ships up the East River, commemorating the centennial celebration of the Statue of Liberty.

After more than four years of consuming labor, the Bakers now had to deal with the question of what to do with the rest of their lives.

Mary Ann had been fired from her teaching job, Norman had virtually left the construction business he'd been in with his brother, and their house of twenty years was gone. Their three children went on with their lives. After four years of stoking heart, blood, sweat, the family's joint efforts, and all their money into the ship, it was virtually *all* they had left.

The ship of dreams was their only asset.

The Bakers eventually got work for the *Anna Christina* as a sail-training ship in Nova Scotia, then moved to rural Massachusetts. There, they got distance from the ship and perspective on the two-year circumnavigation that became a five-year construction project.

If there is a happy ending to this comedy of errors, it is that the Bakers may have been disappointed that the dream deflated so terminally, but they don't regret the investment—or the experience. Mary Ann said:

> I think it's important to have the courage to change if you want to. I know we were privileged to live as we had. It's not to be taken for granted, and after it was over, I had the luxury of time to reflect on what happened.

Norman, true to his Synthesizer's nature, is now working part time with his brother, writing a book, and spending summers on the *Anna Christina*. Mary Ann, still a focused, single-minded Lifer, does a lot of community work in the town they live in. They've mellowed a bit, moved to a house on top of a mountain, and find that life is still an adventure. When Mary Ann says, "I don't think I've ever felt bored or lonely," you know why.

TAKING OFF ON A DREAM If you feel as the Bakers do, you are among those people who can delay gratification without losing the passion and commitment for what will be—someday. It's very clear that a good part of getting there—or taking it to the point where you know it can never go—is great inner strength, greater tenacity, and, greater yet, belief in the goal.

The Lifer holds on fast, problem solves, and provides a foundation for others; the Synthesizer can figure the angles and act on them. Either one working toward realizing a dream has a forward focus—an ability to deal with and adapt to abstract future goals. It is not uncommon to find among you those who live one life—the career that provides the basics—in preparation for the life that will most express who you are.

The *inner quest* has less to do with geography and more to do with a purposeful voyage meant to get in touch with spiritual and emotional centers. The four people whose stories are coming up have struck out on this journey and have, in their own ways, discovered their faith. Above all, they are uncalculatingly *giving* to others.

THE SPIRITUAL VOYAGE: SERVING OTHERS

Existential philosopher Jean-Paul Sartre said, "Hell is other people." Such cynicism sweeps into mind upon viewing the wreckage of a work relationship or a fractured emotional involvement. Power struggles get us one way, stress another. We're hard on ourselves—we feel guilty, anxious, conflicted. In moments of weakness, we blame others for an unsatisfying life; we don't feel charitable toward them or toward ourselves.

When hell isn't others, but your own demons, it takes a deeper kind of faith beyond ego to feel renewed. Such renewal of faith—a *transcendent* faith—brings you to a spiritual relationship with a new sense of purpose.

A CONVERSION EXPERIENCE: "SAUL BECOMES PAUL" "The timing of events is perfect even if it *seems* like what's happening is total chance," said the remarkable Reverend Jack Boland, minister of the Unitarian Church of Today in Warren, Michigan, and, in type, a Builder. Jack Boland was speaking about the shocks and confusion, the unanticipated moments of surrender that come with a test of faith. His own life was reconstructed out of a period of dissolute aimlessness, "my own skid row," he said, candidly.

He was a salesman then, out of work, at the end of his unemployment insurance, and drinking heavily. "Not only was I unemployed, I was unemployable," he told me. One afternoon, drunk, he couldn't remember where he'd been or where he was going. "It was like my ego had gone and I was suddenly a two-year-old kid deserted on the street:

> I turned a corner and saw a friend, who I thought was worse off than me, leaving an A.A. meeting. I always said that if I ever got as bad off as Joe was, I'd quit drinking. What I couldn't see right then was that I *had* gotten as bad as Joe and seeing him on that corner at that moment was destiny.

A few days later, Jack called him; they met and talked. The concept of recovery had gotten Jack's attention, but he wasn't quite ready.

Desperation can sometimes be a teaching experience, but if desperation is a trigger that's pointed at you, it may backfire. The person who *does* end up on skid row—a person with low self-esteem to whom all decisions are threatening—is one such example. Under the influence, "poor me" takes a stronger position than adaptability. Reciting the obstacles to change can become a way of life. Others in desperate situations have what it takes to pull back into life, recover, and rebuild. Alcoholics Anonymous declares that no one will get cured "until they've hit their bottom." When Jack Boland hit bottom, intellectually he knew recovery was his only chance, but he was immobilized by fear, unsure of himself, and an atheist. He told me,

> There was nothing else to do but pray and so I did. I said: If there is a God, don't help me. *Change me.* It never occurred to

> me that I needed a different belief system. I didn't even know what that meant. I became willing to do anything to have my life change.
>
> In my case, it was giving up willfulness, being a smart aleck. I knew how to run the world but I couldn't even run my life. At the moment of speaking to a God I didn't believe in, I had a moment of inner clarity to forgive myself and forgive others. It came in the middle of what I now call a prayer, and while the answers were coming to me, the prayer was an *event*.

On this hot August day, Jack Boland became a minister, but he did not know it yet. His ordination was a few years away, but this plea for change triggered a momentous redemption. In an unexpected flash of certainty, with a new calm and loss of fear, he knew he'd be all right, and what that would take. His behavior was unacceptable and he was finally willing to pay attention to that.

In beginning the process of his recovery, Jack had also committed himself to helping others. Eventually, he moved to Michigan and built a small church into a great spiritual network. His Church of Today has the largest system of support groups of any church in America, as well as including his own "Mastermind Program," a strategy for change based on personally built support systems.

Jack Boland's conversion and transformation has a universal context—he inspires others to bring out the best in themselves. The gracious Virginia Kiser, in answer to her own spiritual awakening, took a different journey in the service to others.

THE INNER QUEST An actress who's played a wide range of roles, from the president's wife to a character in the futuristic TV show "Max Headroom," to Bo Derek's mother in *10,* the elegant Virginia Kiser—with great chiseled cheekbones—put her career on hold to work at a women's shelter run by Mother Teresa. What led her to make such an exceptional pledge was a lifelong desire to help others, the "seed" of which, she says, "was always there."

Not long ago, Virginia, a versatile Builder, was committed to a high-profile acting career to which she turned for "meaning" in a number of ways. She grew up in a ruptured family structure where, in order to survive, she believed in fantasy and endowed it with great credibility. Rather than getting lost in "childhood refrains" as did Dory Previn, an acting career provided an extension of her confidence in the unreal and its effect on her. Judging herself by her ability "to be someone other than me" became a way of life. In short, Virginia measured her *self-worth* by having been chosen for a part over hundreds of other actresses. Her *identity* was connected to whatever role she would be playing next.

It all seemed right enough on the surface, but inside something else was happening. A clearer inner light seemed to be casting the glamorous life in the shadows. As it grew brighter, she discovered what it meant. "That life wasn't me," she said. "I didn't want to play roles anymore. I wanted to be who I am."

I asked her what brought her to this point:

> There was too much of the exterior world in my life. I'd just done a TV series and everything I *thought* I wanted was out there, but it wasn't. It all seemed empty. Then I married a man and went on what was supposed to be an incredibly romantic honeymoon, but this marriage wasn't what I wanted, either.
>
> I knew I couldn't stay.

From this milieu of achievement and conformity, where everything was "correct and pretty," Virginia reached a point where rightness and beauty had more to do with self-surrendering love and her deep inner *faith.* She contacted Mother Teresa for guidance; Virginia's answer was to move from southern California to a women's shelter in New York's Harlem, her assignment.

Virginia lived there for eight weeks along with seven nuns—the most "selfless extraordinary people I've ever met," she said of them. The daily work there was hard and hard work was expected, but there were also meaningful connections with people, most of them homeless, who looked to the shelter for hope. Virginia cooked for twenty-four of them, every day, by herself. There were days when she had to improvise these meals, making due with meager ingredients. With moldy bread she cut way the mold and made bread pudding.

When you feed the starving from authentic spiritual generosity, your act transcends simple ego gratification. For Virginia, the experience at the center left her with an intensity of caring more plausible, loving, and healing than she had previously known. From her months there, Virginia understood how she wanted to live part of her life.

First was a need to live with "every ounce of truth that I could breathe." She has not given up acting, but she is ready to use the money she has and live prudently, choosing to do only the things she wants to do. She told me further:

> If it means making choices that don't fit the mold, then that's because I'm not in the mold.
>
> Working at the center felt as if it was where I was supposed to be. *It humbled me.* I don't think there's a day I live when I don't look at life differently. It's something I want to do again. I expect to go back.
>
> The pleasure of living is giving, more than receiving.

UNLOCKING DOORS AND OPENING NEW VISTAS Michael Lee, yoga teacher and founder of the Stockbridge Health Center in Massachusetts, followed many signposts until he found his path with a heart. A sinewy man with a stentorian voice and easy manner, Michael grew up in Queensland, Australia, with a sense of wonder that went beyond the borders of small-town Toowoomba, his birthplace. It was a place where a ten-mile train trip east was considered a daring adventure. But Michael was always inquisitive and he followed his quest to be educated and to educate others. After his graduation from college—the first such achievement in his family—Michael began teaching.

If it's true that the army changes men, whether in or out of combat, Michael discovered one finer aspect of conscription. Drafted during the Vietnam war, he was sent to New Guinea where this Reinventor first "broke loose." Living in another country and experiencing another culture confirmed for Michael that it wasn't "bad" to do things differently. Impressed by the opportunities there—it was a country that supported risks and change—he and his wife stayed on when his army tour ended. He took a job teaching at a college in Port Moresby until he returned to Australia in the mid-1970s.

A government cutback ended a six-year position as a consultant in a highly controversial program and Michael went back to teaching. Although he was a natural at it, he didn't know what he wanted to teach—or if he should. In search of an answer, Michael—as with many introspective self-starting Builders—took a trip to sort things out. He traveled to America, visiting ashrams and health centers, investigating New Age philosophies.

His peregrinations brought his goals into focus: to teach yoga and open a health center. Attracted to the study of yoga, partly because of its focus on the flexibility of both mind and body, Michael ultimately left Australia and returned to America to be trained in this discipline and in holistic health education.

He arrived first at Kripalu, a highly regarded yoga health center in Massachusetts. There he came face to face with the reality of his intentions. It was the test.

Michael always strongly identified with being a teacher, or in some sort of role where he was leading, initiating. At Kripalu, he was asked to install locks on the doors—*manual labor.* The request, at first, was a comedown. He described what happened to him in the process.

> I thought, who are they to think I should be doing manual work? I was working on the locks, but my mind was saying, *I should be teaching, not this.* I was creating unhappiness, feeling bitter and resentful.

Michael wanted to complete the exercise in a meaningful way, and to do it, he had to "give up his ego"—relinquish his investment in the role of teacher. This meant "objectifying the situation"—shifting his awareness from *why he wasn't teaching* and refocusing his energy to the task of putting in locks. It was a good lesson.

> Yoga teaches you the process of being an observer of your own life. This is what I did. I used the locks as a vehicle for engaging my mind, rather than indulging what my mind originally wanted to race away with.

> I observed myself applying my energy and talent to the task, and at the end of two days I was a craftsman at putting locks on doors. I had a sense of doing something wonderful and valuable.
>
> What I do externally is only part of the story. Where I'm coming from *internally* is all important. It doesn't matter if I am washing dishes, putting in locks, or teaching.

How you get to the philosophy that "it's all the same—teaching or putting locks on doors" requires real enlightenment and a sure sense of self. For Michael, the connection meant that he needn't feel as if he must achieve something or else "feel like a failure."

With all his spirituality, Michael hasn't suspended mundane efforts of setting goals or of taking care of himself and his family. After getting his master's degree in health education, he began the Yoga and Health Center in Stockbridge, Massachusetts. Opening his own business made sense. He wanted the opportunity to create something on his own rather than continue working for someone else. He made the shift confidently "by giving myself permission and *knowing* it will work out."

A TRUE HELPMATE If half the game is *believing* you can win, the other half, for a man like Christopher Jones, is *facilitating* the win for someone else. Such altruism not only may strike you as uncommon but also inauthentic in this decade of supernormal strivers. But it's real: being a helpmate is normal for Christopher. In the competitive world of interior design and real estate, he is, above all, at peace with who he is, with the limits of his ambition, and how big a piece of the pie he wants. A man whose spiritual life is rich, his psychological strength comes from being a team player.

And you *want* him on your side.

Although he is the paradigm of the "service-oriented" person, this Synthesizer has the passion, commitment, and lack of doubt about his purpose that are the hallmarks of the high-energy achiever. He gets things done, and with utmost dispatch and congeniality.

Christopher started out studying architecture, but he opted for work over school and left the program. When he moved to New

York from his native Massachusetts, he knew he didn't want to be an "uptown decorator," skilled in design though he was. Instead, he worked as an editor at a number of national interior design and women's service magazines.

The man whose hope is to be "the walking personification of love," while genuinely modest, is also tough when pursuing a career goal that really appeals to him. In a show of world-class persistence, Christopher applied for a job with the now-defunct *American Home* magazine and decided to make his intentions resourcefully apparent. He waited to run into the editor in the office lobby three times over three days, each time asking if she filled the position and reminding her confidently, "I'm available." It worked. When he was hired, he felt it was a victory.

His spirituality makes him able to adapt easily to changes that transcend the business world; it has slanted every choice he makes. But for him the universe always provides. When he left his last editorial position, he was invited to be the design affiliate at a real estate office. It turned out to be a compatible collaboration. The realtor sells or rents an apartment and Christopher, on assignment, advises on decorating ideas. He took the opportunity, but what mattered more to him was his relationship with the realtor and her family.

He explained:

> It's an incredible world and my thinking has to do with believing there is a greater power in charge of the flow. All the changes in my life have to do with realigning myself with my original goal to be a loving person. I believe I'm here to serve others. I was molded by the Christian Science philosophy—to see the highest in man. In a way it hinders me because I am always looking for the spiritual side of things.

Believing "there's only so much you can do" makes him content to enjoy life; he's not driven to leave his mark. *Caring* is the key to his career goals. For him, a *career* has a broad thrust with points "a" through "z" that include everything to complete the picture. He concentrates on a narrower range of points and focuses more intently on issues of personality and personability. And if you are concerned about having to prove yourself beyond what really matters to you, taking Christopher's fervent belief in himself and his values as a model of soundness is understandable.

"Never stuck but just evolving," Christopher said of himself:

> I've never had a regret. The regret is to look back, to be stuck, and to want something you can't have. Things work out for the best for those who make the best of things *the way they work out.* Shakespeare said, "Nothing is or isn't and thinking doesn't make it so." I've always been a master of that thinking.

SORTING THINGS OUT FOR YOURSELF

Only a few of the exceptional people in this chapter work full throttle at nine-to-five jobs, but they are equipped with the inner resource that travels in any world—self-acceptance.

When it happens, self-acceptance will ignite in you an emotional master switch. It will turn you on to a new tempo of life—you no longer need worry about keeping a prudent and safe distance from your inclinations, talents, and career drives. Self-discovery may not be *easily* won, but it is worth the crusade.

On the way to self-acceptance, most of us get stuck, especially if we aren't willing to wait and trust in "the dream." That's 25 million of us. And for those of us who are shifting gears and willing to take action now, self-discovery *is* possible through more "nuts and bolts" traditional approaches—among them, testing, counselors, and other techniques such as outplacement services and support groups. These approaches follow.

7

SORTING OUT II

Seven Ways to Define a Career Path

Zen philosopher Alan Watts remarked that, "Trying to define yourself is like trying to bite your own teeth." It's a provocative picture—a metaphysical Ripley's Believe It or Not. If you are at a career crossroads, defining yourself *does* feel as impossible a task as pressing tooth into tooth, and as limiting in scope. However, I believe that defining yourself has less to do with metaphysics and boundaries and more to do with simple nuts and bolts methodology.

DEFINING THE CAREER PATH THAT'S RIGHT FOR YOU

A variety of sorting out processes that *work* can clarify and resolve what you seek in a career. And while they answer the question of what career is best for you, they also isolate the attitudes and actions that are required to achieve your goals.

You may find the answers you seek by pursuing any of these six specific paths. Sometimes *one* of those processes will click for you immediately and you'll be clear about what to do. In other cases, you'll need to go through a few of them. Be encouraged!

1. Outplacement Services
2. Career Investigation: Research, Planning, and Counseling
3. Self-assessment Techniques
4. The "Twenty-page Résumé"
5. Support Groups
6. The "Safety Net" Audition

OUTPLACEMENT: GRACE AFTER PRESSURE If you have been fired, you may have been escorted through the wrenching process of leaving a long-term job and being prepared for your reentrance into the job market—all with the aid and comfort of an outplacement firm. While most of these specialists *do not* find you your next job, their range of benefits can serve you well.

More than three-fourths of all Fortune 500 companies and thousands of smaller organizations employ such firms to take the sting out of sudden job loss. Essentially a one-on-one counseling service—although some firms will handle mass group services following a major layoff—outplacement serves both the needs of its client company and the terminated employee.

Companies who use outplacement services do so for a number of reasons—some of which are meant to uphold a "good guy" image in the face of "bad guy" terminations. Ex-employees, or "candidates," once they are in outplacement, are *immediately* put to the task of coping with goals and finding their next job. Rather than allowing any negative momentum to build up, energy and emotions are redirected toward a constructive plan.

In all, outplacement is good public relations and it counts for a lot—the service belies the theory that employees are expendable and business, big or small, is devouring and uncaring. Some companies keep an executive who doesn't make the grade simultaneously on staff and *in* outplacement until he/she finds another job. Outplacement has been even known to divert a newly axed employee from suing a former employer.

William J. Morin and James C. Cabrera, Chairman and President, respectively, of Drake Beame Morin, the largest outplacement firm in America, and authors of *Parting Company,* pointed out a few significant attitudes about terminations that I agree with heartily. A *worse fate* than getting fired is allowing a company to "placate you," to wedge you into a niche and "not give you meaningful, productive work." Equally counterproductive and self-defeating, they wrote, is for you to "abdicate responsibility and turn over the control of your life to a corporation."

While losing a job feels as if you have lost control of your life, say Morin and Cabrera, "you can turn what feels like a devastating tragedy into a personal and professional triumph. . . . In fact, your former employer will actually pay you to find a new—and better—job."

This is the key to outplacement and how you benefit from it. The charming Millie Asher, for example, learned to deal with the shock of losing a job she loved; having a backup therapeutic system such as this helped her through a rough period. She also found the process fascinating.

Millie had been an associate publicity director at a multinational corporation for nine years when the company merged with a larger conglomerate and phased out her job. Within two weeks, her new boss moved into the office vacated by his predecessor, started reorganizing the department, and fired Millie. With a polite reference to regrets, he accomplished the task in a few simple sentences. Millie reported:

> My boss asked me to be at his office at *precisely* one in the afternoon, which immediately made me suspicious. Why call a meeting during lunch hour? I found out: five minutes later, I was out of work.
>
> He told me they were eliminating my job and that I "won't be working here any longer." I felt ill. Before I had a chance to say anything, to cry, or run to the phone and call my husband, he added that the company was putting me in the hands of an "outplacement counselor."

> Then my boss brought me back to my office and, there, sitting in my guest chair, was the counselor. She immediately began talking to me about my career; our talk lasted nearly three hours. From that point, I was officially in outplacement—and still stunned.

The average person in outplacement has been at a job for eleven years—near Millie's experience. The average outplacement firm spends about twenty-five to fifty hours on introductory material—sorting out skills, goal targeting, writing a résumé, practicing for interviews. This was the process Millie found important in reevaluating her goals. Here's an interesting sidelight to Millie's case: A classic Builder, Millie's skills also include being a talented writer—over the last ten years she's been free-lancing after work and she's sold many articles to national women's magazines. She held this aspect of herself separate from her nine-to-five life. So while she developed this creative side, Millie, paradoxically, had a different perspective on her creative efforts at work. During the counseling session, she discovered that many of the activities she discounted were valuable and worth noting on a résumé.

Besides the usual psychological and vocational testing to determine if Millie wanted to stay in public relations, the outplacement service had her examine exactly what she did at work. Instead of just describing the jobs, Millie discovered, it was possible to give her abilities a different twist—*accomplishment.* One of the extra-curricular activities Millie organized at her last job was the yearly company show. She mentioned it to her counselor and added that "it was an absurd thing to spend a lot of time on at work. You wouldn't mention it in a résumé."

The outplacement counselor had another thought about the show. She called the personnel office and got their opinion of it. As the counselor suspected, the company defined it as "an important company benefit." Some employees, they said, actually stayed with the company to appear in the yearly show—it gave them that much of a sense of importance. Millie said:

> I can't bring the skill of doing a company show to another job, but there is something wonderful about my being able to make it an employee benefit. Rather than saying flatly on my résumé,

> "highly developed organizational and directorial skills," I can describe the task *and* what it accomplished. I was shocked to find out that the company actually used the show as a selling point to employees . . . by the way, we have this wonderful yearly activity. . . ."
>
> I'd been doing the show for seven years, and never once had I been told directly that it been given such significance.

Other than clarifying her true accomplishments, the outplacement counselor helped her understand that there may never be a job exactly like the one she left—"I'd molded it to myself," Millie said. It's natural for most people who liked a job they lost to try and replicate it, but it probably won't happen.

To Millie, another valuable part of the experience was that it gave her specific tasks to do immediately, "rather than sitting and mourning the loss." Most firms provide desk space and a phone to work from at their office; now, some outplacement services give top executives available office space or an actual office. This is an important psychological boost for people like Millie who work best in structured situations—they feel grounded and have a place to report to during the job search.

The immediate focus on Millie's understanding her skills more fully and applying them to selling herself for the next job bolstered her self-esteem. It took her three months to find another job as a director of public relations.

CAREER INVESTIGATION: RESEARCH, PLANNING, AND COUNSELING

The second area to look into involves your finding a way *in* to a career. As often as not, an opportunity is as likely to arise through smart and thorough planning as from trial and error or simple accidents of fate. You have probably gotten a job, even a plum position, because a sudden change in staffing put you in the right place at the right time. On other occasions, you started work on a temporary basis and were kept on and promoted, or you liked the work so much, you left and started your own business. A niche might have opened for some special expertise you possess in relation to a new development in your field—and it called for someone like you to manage or produce it.

These adventitious events notwithstanding, most of us will have to go through a more stalwart job search.

National Business Employment Weekly reported that the "most frequent tactics" 75 percent of job hunters used was to answer the want ads in newspaper employment sections. To adapt to a changing marketplace, another 45 percent, they reported, went on to learn new job skills or furthered their education; another 30 percent were willing to search for jobs in cities other than where they live. A "willingness to retrain and geographically relocate," said the *Weekly*, "were the most effective strategies for obtaining employment."

There are many avenues to investigate the career of your choice and to find a way in, other than through advertisements or needing to relocate. These are: networking and contacting former employers and mentors; checking with professional and trade associations; enlisting the services of executive recruiting firms; parlaying volunteer or free-lance consultancies into a permanent job; enrolling with college and/or graduate school alumni associations. Not to be overlooked is the "cold call"—borrowing from a sales strategy and calling a potential employer directly to let him/her know you are available and how your skills are suited for that company.

If you need direction clarifying your skills and defining yourself more fully, the third step—seeking out professional counselors and self-help sources—will be vital in sorting out and focusing on your career goals. Counselors have valuable information, maintain career information and sources, are trained to administer tests and recrudesce your interests. Both counselors and self-help groups can help you sort out the difference between dream- and reality-based aspirations and help you through transition periods.

Simply a side benefit in the outplacement process, traditional career counseling is available to anyone, employed or unemployed, who seeks professional guidance. Probably the oldest and most respected system, career counseling employs a combination of verbal and written techniques, designed for those who seek clarification of their interests and goals or redirection into a different career.

Who benefits most from a career counselor?

George Heard is a fascinating case in point: After fifteen years working in managerial positions at a large New England hotel, George seriously contemplated a partnership with an old friend in the construction business. His friend was ready; George was stalling. He cited two reasons he believed held him back. His wife was taking evening courses on Tuesday and Thursday nights and George had promised to watch the children those nights. Money also worried him, but not as much as reneging on his promise to his wife, who wanted to get her college degree.

George's partner-to-be worried that George didn't have the resilience it would take to run a business, and told him so. His doubt in himself grew and George went for counseling, to sort out "if he was an entrepreneur or just spinning his wheels."

George told his story; described his career and how much more he liked *constructing* buildings rather than working in them. Then, sincerely and seriously, he told the career counselor that he couldn't quit his job *and* work the long hours a new business would demand of him, especially since he couldn't have Tuesday and Thursday nights free.

The counselor listened and then concluded: If George was unable to figure out how to handle the babysitting issue two nights a week, he couldn't tackle much more urgent problems that would come up in a business. Therefore, she thought *he was right.* He should stay at his job.

It was an ironical twist to the story, one he needed to hear. George got the point. Now it was a *challenge.* And he went into business.

WHAT HAPPENS IN A COUNSELING SESSION While a new perspective on a life goal is one way a career counselor may help you, his/her other main functions are to help you document and analyze your experience and interests, target a goal, and develop a plan for reaching it. As with psychology, there are a number of disciplines and schools of thought that are brought to the counseling session. One such approach comes from the highly regarded Crystal/Barkley Center in mid-Manhattan whose techniques and views have greatly influenced others in the counseling process over the last fifteen years.

John Crystal's career changers' methodology is based on the pivotal question, one you may be asking yourself now: *What do I want to do with my life?* Following a course of discovery that is constructed to reveal the answer through tests, exercises, and interviews, Crystal's process then sets about helping you answer the next question: *Where do I get the kind of work I want?* Richard Nelson Bolles has written with Crystal *Where Do I Go from Here with My Life?* and on his own, the annually revised and eminently popular *What Color Is Your Parachute?* based on Crystal's ideas.

BUILDING "SELF-CONCEPTS" Top New York career counselor Leslie Rose, in private practice, utilizes a similar approach—one that is designed to clarify interests, motives, and problem-solving techniques for those in flux. The people most likely to use her services fall into four categories:

1. People like George who operate through *doubt.* This doubt sets up limitations—either in regard to recognizing their capabilities or in denying that their goals can be achieved at all;
2. Those who have no idea of what they want to do;
3. Those who have a passion, but haven't integrated it into their work lives; and
4. Common to nearly everyone who seeks career counseling, those who have a job but no job satisfaction. This dissatisfaction may spring from its never having existed in the first place. Or once having known satisfaction and having lost it, they wonder how to get it back.

What happens in the counseling process? Self-assessment exercises are part of it, but a counselor will also give those with "a weakened self-concept" the tools for confidence building. Through objective feedback, a counselor can help them see the extent of their competencies for the first time. The person who is caught in the "imposter syndrome"—believing his/her success is an unduplicatable fluke, more to do with being liked than being capable—learns to accept the truth about his/her own abilities and how to deal more effectively with the business world.

Leslie employs a technique that is provocative and effective. She will ask you to write a "press release" dated in the future. The subject of the release describes an event that, if it happened, would make you, the writer, feel like a success.

What comes out of an exercise like this? Leslie said:

> The release answers an important question: *What could you have that you don't have now?* In some cases, people write what's in their hearts and what they value—recognition, opportunity to do their most creative work, being visible or famous. It puts a focus on the key points that particular person needs to feel successful.
>
> In other cases, people will hypothesize what they should be working toward. Many people build their lives and work on satisfying others' expectations. They may still operate from a state of denial—hiding the truth from themselves, even when they have the freedom to write what *they* want.

This is the tricky part to any counseling exercise and payoff: The only thing that will change a counterproductive belief about yourself is to act differently. The real test is to put yourself in a situation where you get positive *results* and candid feedback from other people. This validates your abilities and your efforts; it's a good measure of whether you can do something or not.

Going through the transition stages in career counseling may not be easy. Ideas, attitudes, and feelings out of which change evolves are turned upside down. Being uncomfortable or unhappy during the transition is not a test that something is wrong or that you need psychological counseling. Leslie added:

> The little successes that happen as you move through the process should make you happy. What matters most is getting through it—what you eventually do with your life.
>
> There is no one right way to do it. Most of all, you need structure, support, and experience to "reality check" the plan to move forward and change.

The value of counseling sessions also includes access to basic information about oneself—specific skills, interests, strengths, and the kinds of work that utilize them.

SELF-ASSESSMENT TECHNIQUES

How well do you know yourself? Self-assessment (or self-*awareness*) requires that you intently probe your skills, accomplishments, and interests—and how to make the most of them, or figure out how transferable they are to other targeted professions. By *assessing* key qualities, you can begin to hone in on a career choice that reflects the best of what you can do. When necessary, you can develop any new skills required for the opportunity you seek.

If you are as unique, self-motivated, and *clear* about your direction as the people you read about in the previous chapter, then you make choices with a different kind of confidence, even insouciance. Self-assessment lies along a slightly longer path for the rest of us, who require time and thought to dope things out. For those of you who are stuck *not knowing* what you want to do, what you like, or even how much of a risk taker you are, there are self-assessment tests that help provide the answers.

A word about testing: I found that even when in a state of great confusion, some people resist self-assessment tests. It can be problematic, if not threatening, for a thirty-five-year-old accountant or a forty-five-year-old chemical engineer with a long career history to suddenly face a battery of questions designed to reveal what they believed they always knew about themselves—but didn't. My suggestion is to put reservations aside. The point is to clarify your goals and not worry about false pride. Self-assessment tests are legitimate guides and if they don't provide an absolute answer, they can start a ball rolling in the right direction.

By the way, self-assessment questions needn't only be administered in check-off-the-answers-Q&A formats. Professional career counselors, whom I'll talk about shortly, either work with traditional modes of testing and guidance or employ a variety of "new age" approaches. Whatever the style, they all focus on understanding the totality of your abilities and long-term aspirations.

Career dissatisfaction and confusion about what to do next usually bring people to "aptitude" or self-assessment tests. Potential career changers are not the only ones who may benefit from such tests. They are good sources of guidance for unfocused younger people who have no real direction, especially those who feel they've made choices solely in reaction to parental influence. Older people who have never worked can learn specifics about applying their skills and interests to a profession. Another sector seeking testing is people in the arts. Caught in a battle of committing to their talent and what may be a continuing struggle for recognition, many opt to give up "art" for mainstream jobs. They, as with others shifting gears, need an astute review of transferable skills into a newly chosen field. But which field, and how do they choose?

Many people who come for testing have already explored options, read books, and a number have decided on a career choice that feels right. But is it? To ease the doubt, such cautious risk takers seek assessment services that focus on *what it takes* to work in the career they've chosen and *how it would actually suit them*.

Others explore the range of testing procedures. Among them are "forced choice" questions where you are obliged to answer yes or no; these uncover where your strengths lie and where you get stuck. Counselors have found that even with such a simple testing process, there are people with an inability to answer yes/no questions. Part of the problem may be a lack of self-confidence about making a decision or not being able to project how you would act in a situation beyond your experience. Other questions require more thought, lengthier plotting out of answers, even simple diagrams or drawings to illustrate your projected life path.

Although tests that measure aptitude, skills, and interests vary in style and scope, these are the kind of questions you might expect to be asked about yourself and a career direction:

What are your *goals*? Are these goals consistent with the kind of life you can see yourself leading?

If you examine them closely, is it your *job* or your *career* that you are dissatisfied with? Could you find more satisfaction with a job in the same general area or a career in a related field?

Are *working conditions* or *salary* the real motivating factor in wanting to shift gears?

Are you confined to a narrow *skill base* on your job, but see how you could use them more advantageously in another job or career?

Have you *acquired* any skills since beginning your job but have little or no opportunity to use them?

If you have an inventory of your skills, which ones are most *marketable?*

Is your job in the field(s) where your *interests* lie?

Do you find that you are unable to express certain *values* that are important to you on your job? In contrast, are you obliged to defend or acquiesce to values on the job that cause conflict?

If you are thinking of *starting over* in another career, how willing are you to make any inevitable sacrifices, such as a lower-level position and a salary cut? If other people in your life rely on you, how would they feel about such a decision?

If you want to change occupations or jobs, is *reeducation* or *retraining* required? What does this mean in terms of time?

Do you have an *alternative or contingency plan* if your targeted goal doesn't work out?

If you have figured out what you want to do, can you *try out* a new career without quitting your job?

Are you a *risk taker?*

How important are *seniority, retirement funds,* and *long-term benefits?* If you opt to give them up, can you rebuild future security elsewhere?

Are you being realistic about the *financial prospects* in a different career?

Are you willing to honestly confront *emotion-based* obstacles that are in the way of making a decision? (Some of these obstacles are procrastination, indecisiveness, obsessing over fear of failure or success.)

Will you invest the time to research or gather whatever information might be required to fully understand your targeted career? This may mean contacting professional associations related to the career, guidance counselors, library sources, or mentors.

TRACKING YOUR "LIFE LINE" A good counselor employs information, logic, and intuition, piecing together the connections between where someone is and where they are going. One such counselor is Allie Roth, a Ph.D. and career management consultant who has trained in many disciplines of counseling technique. Talented and insightful, Allie sees herself as "catalytic" in exposing people to their next stage of growth. Through a combination of testing, self-assessment exercises, and the interaction between her and the client, they come out, she says, "with a solidified self-concept and appreciate their own uniqueness."

One effective process Allie uses is the "life line" self-assessment technique. Unlike "Mainstream," a popular system that divides your life into nine separate chapters, Allie charts a twelve-part "line" representing twelve periods, each sector marked with key events. The sectors don't have to be equal in size—some will represent two or three years, others will be longer. Allie explains what the process clarifies:

> The "life line" is a graphic representation of their lives. I have them tune in to the energy of the time—when they were up, to see the slumps, the breaks, the decisions, and to make a list of past successes from the very earliest sector. The next step is to put stick figures along the line as pictorial representation of this movement.
>
> I look at the *connections* between events and look for all the various possible subtleties, components, and possibilities.

Over a series of sessions, Allie will employ a number of equally probing tests and interview sessions that help people begin to define themselves, if broadly at first. This lets them know: "I'm an idea person . . . a communicator . . . a healer . . . good at sales." Further questionnaires, as well as the Myers-Briggs test—one of the best career development instruments used by counselors—helps to narrow career options down. Tests such as the Myers-Briggs plumb the depth and range of your skills and interests while the Holland Vocational Guidance test helps determine which of six general areas of expertise or "themes" (e.g., "Social" and "Conventional") best suit you. For example, if your tendencies are to help, inform, or enlighten others, but you're now basically in a position where you deal with details and follow-through (the basics of the "Conventional" theme) a wise move would be in the direction of work that falls in the "social" arena.

Importantly, these tests not only draw answers, but you become clear on how you *use* information—each of us has a unique way of taking and perceiving data and reaching judgments, and these tests point them up. During testing, things may *click;* you have a sense of what you want to do. Typically, though, patterns will emerge by the third or fourth session in what Allie calls "success clusters." At this juncture, she is "reaching for the basic person," the things that have made people successful. Sometimes she will focus on skills, like writing, or values, like loving animals, or sometimes personality traits that make people special.

Another step in the self-assessment process, "perceptive judgments," instructs Allie on how you feel about structured and unstructured situations. The questions are designed to reveal the extent of your flexibility, spontaneity, and ability to explore new possibilities. It shows if you concentrate on data and facts; if you see in concrete and finite terms. If so, it may be more difficult to unscramble all the information you've learned in the process and apply it to yourself—and figure out where you fit. Conversely, a more "intuitive" person concentrates on the connection between bits of information, sees creative solutions differently, comes up with the possibilities between things, but may make assumptions without first looking at all the facts.

From this battery of tests, a *totality* emerges—a sense of oneself and how to gain the most career satisfaction. You make a positive connection to "what I'm going to be." Sometimes, you know what name to give this totality. Other times, you may need to consult "The Dictionary of Occupational Titles," which contains descriptions of over 45,000 occupations. When you find what's right, you can finally start moving toward that goal.

THE TWENTY-PAGE RÉSUMÉ

The numbers are astonishing: *100 million* résumés cross in the mail every year, either in response to the 130,000 jobs that are advertised in newspapers alone or those targeted to companies that might have a position available. Burdette Bostwick, in his book *Résumé Writing,* reports that the 200 leading companies each receive about 25,000 résumés a year and the top percentage of these manage up to 50,000 hopeful solicitations.

"Because the numbers can work against you," says John Langley, a master of résumé strategies, from his Detroit office, "you have to make a résumé *sell* you." The person who reads it must have a strong reason to *contact* you and request an interview: This is a résumé's primary purpose. When you realize that only two out of every hundred résumés actually leads to an interview, you may not be comforted by the odds, but you want a good shot to *be* among the favored two. If your résumés don't get attention, you can change the odds by learning how to properly analyze your experience and your skills and put them on paper. John said:

> Ninety-nine percent of all people have a problem writing a résumé. My contribution is in forcing them to write one that's a killer . . . fifteen to twenty pages, to start. I preach that résumés are important—they help people account for what they're good at and what they can trade on.
>
> I want their lives to pass in review so they can put it all in some sort of form. From this, they extrapolate, draw conclusions, then boil it down to only ego-building successes on two pages.

Within John's "killer" system are probing questions meant to extract personal qualities and abilities that help you sell yourself better; the "little things that reflect character." If John sat with you, he'd search for situations in your experience that show conviction—demonstrable personality traits that set you apart from simply knowing how to perform on-the-job functions. If you were, for example, a mid-level manager with low visibility in a company, how did you act if you had a good idea for increasing productivity or profits? Did you fight for the idea? Who did you take your idea to? What happened to it? If your action got a response, whether or not it was enacted, this counts. It is a detail for a résumé.

Handling a termination is a delicate matter; how should a résumé reflect it? Reggie, a senior manager with a retail chain, for example, sought to turn his experience of it around to ease an oppressive sense of self-blame and recover his self-confidence. In a precise and carefully structured exercise, John asked him to go back to when the problems started with management and to write them out in outline form. Based on the outline, John looked for whether or not Reggie spoke up, and how. "I understand the pitfalls in losing an argument with management," John said, "but my point is to bring up a number of instances where he stood up to the issue, even if they fired him. Was it a real reflection of money-saving strategy or his competence on the line?"

John, himself a classic Synthesizer—once a manager in a rug factory, a newspaper man, a retired top television executive, and of late, an expert counselor on selling yourself through résumés—believes that you have to plan your career, but you also have to gamble at what you're good at. The twenty-page résumé and its analysis is one way to stack the cards in your favor.

Some of the problems John puts before his clients are ones you can look at yourself:

Expand. Are you a specialist whose life is cast in niches or can your skills be employed along a generalist path? While specialization indicates a commendable concentration of knowledge in one area, it is a detriment if it limits your earning capabilities and promotability. If specialization is leaving you behind, you need to expand. *Megatrends* author John Naisbitt suggested the power of diversification in career skills when he said, "We are moving from the specialist who will soon be obsolete to the generalist who can adapt." A broader skill base equals broader markets.

Are you isolated in a declining industry or worrying only about a very small segment of the marketing world? What are your translatable and transferable skills? Look for the common thread to "layer" in another direction. If, for example, you're in accounting or finance, how can your skills translate into sales and marketing in another industry? If you objective is strategic planning in the toy industry and you come from consumer loans in banking, what can you tell a company on your résumé about your knowledge of profitability and the market? Translatable skills increase your opportunities. If you are overspecialized, expand your field of knowledge.

Figure out your goal. Your résumé should reflect this. Successful people know where they want to go and what they want to do. John told me of a man torn between his three interests and his inability to focus in on one. Paul had a master's degree in engineering, a law degree from a top university, *and* a master's in business administration—and he still didn't know what he wanted to do. Paul tended to job hop without showing any real gains. Because he applied for positions basically below his skill level and interest, he never stayed around long enough to get into a higher salary bracket. Loyalty to a company was unheard of for him. "I never advise, recommend, or direct," John said when Paul told him of his career crisis. "I let him figure out how to put all the disparate elements of his interests into one career. I just hung in there until he figured it out."

While Paul was smart at accumulating knowledge, he did not know how to synthesize information and "selectively eliminate" the details that were holding him back. It was a dilemma of interpretation, and a solvable one. He outlined his strengths and accomplishments in each of his three "careers" to better sell himself. Paul soon found a company where he could best apply his law and engineering background.

Establish a realistic time frame and strategy. The higher your goal and longer the range, the easier it is to fill in the blanks. What qualities do you need to work on to get what you want? What in your past experience demonstrates the skills required for your goal? Does your résumé reflect these skills?

Get motivated. The stronger your motivation, the more likely it is that your game plan will work out. What does your job history tell you about this? Are you self-motivated or do you need motivation and support from others?

Do you take risks or play it safe? If "the right thing came along," would you grab it or stay in a job or an industry that doesn't interest you any longer? Were there occasions when a lack of motivation and/or playing it safe turned out to be no guarantee of security? Perhaps a company shut down or relocated across the country and triggered a drastic change in your life where you had no backup and no choice. The safe position may prevent exposure to risk and guarantee routine, but it also tends to foster impatience and a sense of frustration. The conservative person tends not to see the future of an industry or the opportunities. He thinks in a litany of status quo rationalizations.

If you're motivated, self-confidence grows. You can say, "I haven't succeeded in the past by doing innovative things, but I see how I can now. I have an idea and I will give it a maximum of three years to make it work. If it doesn't, I will move on."

Do the research. Find out who to target. Know something about the company and the industry you are targeting. Check any number of business periodicals and standard business reference books to get a comprehensive background on the company. Find a company "deep throat" if you can to fill you in. Call people. Request annual reports. In the covering letter accompanying your résumé, openly show the company you want to work for that you know something about their operations.

When you have answered all the questions that highlight your strengths on each job, rewrite your résumé, condensed into two pages. Be clear about the position you are seeking.

And get the interview.

SUPPORT GROUPS

Valuable arenas for "sanity testing," goal setting and ongoing camaraderie, support groups are effective self-help outlets roughly fashioned after group therapy. Basically meetings between like-minded people in the same or different occupations, support groups are comfortably flexible, often with no declared "leader." The better groups are run with an operating schedule that focuses equally on the issues affecting their members and encouraging their participation. One such successful long-standing support group involves four New York actresses: Francesca Howell, Laurie Sanders Smith, Charlotte Patton, and Mimi Stewart.

The women met by chance, all of them having been at one time in the same acting class. Each woman discovered she had an identical goal: Each believed she was "put on this earth to perform," and each wanted nothing more than to be a working actress. They started the group trusting that support from other actresses in a highly competitive field was not only feasible, but likely to be beneficial. That was three years ago. They have since cared for each other very well in many ways.

Francesca Howell lived with her husband in Chile and became a television personality there, all the while teaching English "from the American perspective that you can be an overnight success and as easily an overnight failure." Back in the States, Francesca has not yet reached the same success; she teaches English as a second language and has acted in community theatre.

Laurie Smith "harbored acting desires" during her ten years as an advertising copywriter. When she was fired from her job, then married soon after, Laurie "took a break" to pursue an acting career. She now does free-lance copywriting, word processing, and performs singing telegrams.

Charlotte Patton, with acting and producing credits, also works in word processing for law firms to support herself.

Mimi Stewart has appeared in fourteen films, is a versatile actress, and she, like Laurie, does singing telegrams to support herself.

The group's primary purpose is to set goals and work through fears to bolster confidence, but their meetings may also involve personal life issues. An agenda structures the group's activities and accomplishments. They make lists each week to check their progress in furthering their goals—for example, in sending pictures to casting directors, dealing with auditions, or "fighting the fear" of calling agents.

The support group reached a high point with a "power breakfast" given at New York's Carlyle Hotel. The object of the breakfast was to act from a *compelling sense of future*—to pretend the breakfast was the occasion for a reunion among four highly successful actresses: them. They were to behave as if they had achieved what they wanted. And since what they wanted would have been made public by their projected success, they exchanged information about their "lives" the night before.

It was great repertory theatre that day: They met "in character" and not one of them broke the momentum for a single minute. They *were* their future—confident, working, fulfilled. Although the "play" was fun, internally, they connected with how real it could be and how right it felt. "Each of us could accept the facts of the others' lives," Laurie commented. "In this business, it takes so much to keep your dreams alive that sometimes it all feels like daydreaming."

Each woman's "future" had a trenchant reality the others could empathize with: Mimi had posters around town advertising her new film; she'd also appeared on Johnny Carson to plug it. Laurie was in rehearsal for a Broadway show, to be followed by a starring role in a film being shot in Italy. Charlotte hosted a hit TV series for which she was just nominated for an Emmy award. Francesca, whose husband is also an actor, produced a TV show with a starring role for him in it. All of them spoke of their "children" and their homes.

"Act like it's real," they all agreed, "and it will happen." What makes them believe their plans will come true because of having acted it out? They agreed with Charlotte's verdict:

> If you put it out there in the universe, you're not only clear about what you want, you stir up an energy to make it real. The acting reprograms your mind—you have to convince your unconscious that what you are doing is true. To be able to have it happen at all, you need to accept the concept first.
>
> Show business is rough and every time a casting director says, "you're too short or too dark or too old," you tend to believe you're not good enough. This breakfast gave us a real sense that we *are* good enough. It gave our ideas a reality. You quickly forget it was a role.

It was the kind of polestar in their careers wherein life resumed as "before" or "after" the breakfast. Its importance strongly established a renewed commitment to their work and a greater sense of confidence. The consensus in the group was that before the breakfast there were more obstacles—either they were saying, "I can't do this," or people were telling them, "You can't do that." After the breakfast, there was much more of their knowing "yes, this is possible." Before, Charlotte said, "I thought of myself as a newcomer, playing at pursuing an acting career rather than taking it seriously." Laurie affirmed: "I'd never have dared to go to Los

Angeles and meet casting directors, but I went and had the best time." Having dealt with each other as celebrities gave them all a "better sense of accomplishment."

Francesca summed up one core reason such support groups work for people in transition:

> For me, it's having people I know and respect telling me the truth. When I'm feeling depressed about work, I can go to the group and say, "I'm feeling bad about this." Sometimes, just talking about it with them gives me a different perspective.

THE "SAFETY NET" AUDITION

Entering into business is a major step, an experience that brings the basics of security, enterprise, and risk taking into an inseparable "eternal triangle." The fascination with going into one's own business provokes anxiety about success and failure, the desire to achieve and make one's mark—and for many, it means the big payoff. Independence. Creativity. Your own ship. But . . .

Then there is the wonder of job security, the paycheck, the pension, the perks; it has a nice shimmer, rumored to be gold dust. When you think about leaving all this and going out on your own, no small emotional conflicts arise. Your enterprising spirit, desiring independence, challenges the career "safety net" in a battle waged as strongly as any artist ever threatened bourgeois conformity. How do you change? Is there a compromise?

"Change requires a leap of faith and faith is so much more plausible on a foundation of successful prior experiences," said Rosabeth Moss Kanter in her fascinating book, *The Change Masters*. It is prior success in small, sure steps that can propel you out of the safety net and into the world of entrepreneurs. You can get your wish, as did Margaret Newbourg. A career management consultant and vice president of business development marketing at Fuchs Buthrell in New York, Margaret figured out how to ease into business slowly and steadily, avoiding the shock of the plunge. And succeeding.

Originally, she trained as a psychiatric social worker, got a master's degree, and worked for ten years at various positions at

Mt. Sinai Medical Center. Although Margaret generally liked the work, something was missing. When she realized nearly all the friends she and her husband had were in finance-related businesses—brokers, financial planners, bank officers—it told her something important. The affinity wasn't just social; she wanted to go into business, too. How could she do it?

This set off a search for the bridge to another profession, one that would allow her to use her ten years of counseling experience. With this idea in mind, she made a momentous connection quite serendipitously. She chanced upon an article describing the problems that spouses of relocated executives at Merrill Lynch were experiencing—many were either depressed over the move and/or needed help finding employment in another city.

Suddenly, the pieces fell into place and formed the big picture. Margaret struck a concept for a business. She told me how she felt:

> I wrote the words *relocating spouses* on a piece of paper and thought: I could do that. *I* could help them. I had experience counseling depressed people; I knew I could handle that issue. I had also gone to a number of career seminars, so I knew how to write a résumé and prepare for an interview. And, there were other aspects of job search I'd gone through myself, too.
>
> I heard myself recite the ups and downs. While I knew I could help these people, what I didn't know was how to sell the service—that is, I didn't know who would *buy* it.
>
> To me the down side was, if I lose, I'll get over it. That's not the tragedy for me—the tragedy is doing nothing.

When she discussed her idea with a friend at work "there were then two of us wanting to make a go of it." Still keeping their jobs at the medical center, they "opened for business."

It may seem a long way from transforming an emotional connection to an idea into an actual working business without clients, but so it was that "CareerScope" was created. Operating on sheer bravado, they ordered stationery, wrote a press release about their service, and sent it off to companies they knew were in the process of relocating personnel.

Taking another angle, they sought company visibility—publicity. The release also reached a number of select women's magazines, like *Vogue* and *Working Woman;* both of them cited CareerScope in "little boxes about this new service and the relocation blues." It started the ball rolling toward them at full speed. A *New York Times* reporter read about it and offered to profile them in an article. Margaret asked her to wait until they had a good caseload of success stories—which by the end of the year numbered ten people.

By this time, Margaret and her partner were putting in approximately two days a week in hours on the business. After the *Times* did the article, Citibank hired the service, but they soon asked Margaret to work for them full time, rather than use her as a consultant. After a year, she left the hospital and took her first full-time corporation job. Eventually, she left Citibank and switched professions to outplacement.

In reviewing Margaret's example, starting a part-time business that's cushioned by long-term job security looks easy. First, the light goes off—you have an idea you know you can do. Suddenly, you're operating on instinct, trial and error. One press release is so right, it kicks off a business that has found its time. What does it take to juggle a long-standing career and a budding enterprise? Margaret told me:

> My attitude was, I have nothing to lose. My employer didn't know I was working part time at my own business. I never let anything get in the way of my work at the hospital. I did my work for CareerScope on my own time.
>
> Because there was no conflict of interest between the two, it was fun for me. I got to see myself in a new way—that I was a *businesswoman.* Instead of sitting in my office at the hospital being depressed because I'm not in business, or thinking, how am I ever going to manage this and doing nothing, *I did something.*
>
> In the beginning it was like playacting—I took that leap, even though I had no clients. I didn't know how to write a press release. I knew how to write well enough to get my point across.

Margaret has a number of characteristics that make her a good entrepreneur.

• Margaret knew she could handle the service, using the skills she had.

• She's "a risk taker who will go out on a limb where someone else might not."

• She is fully committed to an idea. Her plans are carefully thought out and she has a willingness to experiment.

• She doesn't have to have everything in absolute order before starting up. Samuel Johnson said, "Nothing will ever be attempted if all possible objections must first be overcome." If things look right enough, she said, "I'll take the steps and improvise from there."

• She doesn't take rejection too personally. Some people are more vulnerable, oversensitive to others, self-critical and highly judgmental about themselves. Margaret doesn't stay with "I" disappointments.

• She can visualize herself in the position she chooses. It's an ability to use imagery to internally experience success and what it might look like.

• She thinks in terms of being able to do things, rather than being unable to achieve what she wants.

(I'll talk more about being and becoming an entrepreneur in Chapter Nine.)

With Margaret's capabilities and attitude, there is always an opportunity and always the adventure.

The saying goes that "brilliance can follow its own voice." If you start out a genius, you don't have to worry about the marketplace, but most of us *do* need to respond to changing times. Even the sharpest among us reaches a point where we seek advice, redirection, comfort, and guidance. It's worth the asking. It's a way, I think, of increasing our own light.

8

STARTING OVER AND SELLING YOURSELF

How do you get a job when no actual past experience says you can do it?

I'll give you an appealing example. In her autobiography, *D.V.*, the late Diana Vreeland, the former editor of *Vogue* and curator of the Metropolitan Museum of Art's Costume Collection, described her entree into the publishing world. She was being whirled around a hotel dance floor one auspicious night in 1937 when the editor of *Harper's Bazaar* spotted her. The next morning, Mrs. Vreeland was found and offered a job on the magazine. The offer was based solely on her style as seen across a crowded room—her apparent chic answered all the fashion editor's questions in advance. Well-traveled and married twelve years at this time, Mrs. Vreeland *had never been in an office in her life.*

It's a fifty-year-old success story that contains some of the magic we wish would be visited upon us. The effortless offer. Unconditional acceptance. The right contacts so you *can* be found. An employer pursuing you, not the reverse. An employer not only enchanted by your style, but one who intuitively sees how such enchantment can be marketed, if not made into a legendary style-setting career.

Depending on your point of view, such a stellar embarkation into a career was destiny or "smarts"—that is, when the opportunity was presented, Mrs. Vreeland seized it. *Selling herself professionally,* albeit unintentionally, she fulfilled a need for her employer and got what she didn't yet know she wanted. But she *would.*

Most of us have to let the universe in on our goals before we get them, but Mrs. Vreeland is a bit different from you and me. She is among the 5 percent of people in this world who are graced with such . . . beneficence. This 5 percent are the people who are remembered, get called, are asked, are invited. Then there are the rest of us. Within the boundaries of this diverse 95 percent, there are those of us who aren't called but who are likely to get our calls answered, and those who will have to do something *outstanding* to get a response.

This is what selling yourself is all about: *getting a response and getting the job you want.* Selling yourself needs thought, strategy, preparation, and credibility, especially if you are shifting gears. It's another kind of waltz, with different steps.

WHAT DO YOU WANT AND HOW CAN YOU GET IT?

Professional expertise is simply having the credentials to prove it. You've done the work; you've got the evidence. Your résumé tells the story. Selling yourself with conviction is the way to prove you *can* do something professionally when you lack the credentials. Suppose you're in advertising and you want to work in a winery; you've managed a winery for ten years, now you want to work for an environmental lobbyist; you taught high school French for twenty years and you want to work in public relations. You come from public relations and you want to move into fund raising.

You have your expertise, but there also exists your "handicap"—a lack of correlating career history, your age, or some other nonconforming factor that may strike your prospective employer as suspect.

Who will hire you?

Employers are cut of two cloths, says Richard Bolles in *What Color Is Your Parachute?*—those who would be "put off" by your handicap and those who would *not* object. Simple enough. Of these two options, you face a numbers game. Theoretically, ninety out of a hundred employers won't be interested in interviewing or hiring you unless you're categorically right. As a career changer, therefore, it is up to you to persist until you make contact with the ten who *will* accept your terms.

Sophisticated though they might be, the truth is that most employers compartmentalize you and the positions they seek to fill. It's a historical pattern that's thousands of years old, full of fissures and weakening from them, but *still* it stands, the unbreakable obstacle blocking too many paths. A single occupation—or two at the most—once identified who we are and made it easier to figure each other out. And while those hiring today talk about how they seek "renaissance" men/women, most hope you fit in and don't want to figure you out. In bottom-line thinking, it can be too expensive to train an inexperienced outsider rather than hire someone with appropriate experience who, in fact, may *not* produce at all.

Further odds decree that you will not get your chance at the job you want through a conventional route—newspaper advertisements, executive recruiters, even word of mouth—unless someone with influence is in your corner to champion your cause.

To sell yourself as a career changer, you will have to reach beyond ordinary means.

You will have to be *more* inventive, more attentive to details, more determined, and bolder than before. When you are shifting gears and want credibility, you *may* have to press forward with a professional "gimmick" that gets you noticed—problem solving, humor, or as with H. Bud Walters, cited in Chapter Two, getting rehired through steady applications of persistence and chicken soup.

Before you set out on a campaign to sell yourself, you need to be clear about the following: your goal, your skills, and your commitment level. Every employer operates from a half-dozen standard questions at an interview session. Being clear about the answers is a key part of selling yourself. Although the phrasing may not be the same, the content is:

- Why are you here?
- Who are you?
- What have you done so far?
- What can you do for them?
- Why should they hire you?
- Can they afford you?

To answer these questions, you must also be clear on the following:

The exact scope of your skills: What are they? *Prioritize* them so you are working from your strongest set of skills. You want to speak about them first. *Analyze* them so they have a depth of application, especially in your chosen job. Cite *explicit* results of your skills—how your successes benefited the companies you worked for and how you believe you can do the same for this potential employer.

Being passionate about finding the job you want: Can you persist and not become discouraged by the numbers? In every sale, the rule is to expect more rejections than acceptances. This is a fact of commerce, of learning, of experience. Tenacity counts. The Xerox corporation once did a study on salesmanship and discovered that the difference between excellence and bare mediocrity in their company was five phone calls. Salespeople who gave up did so too soon, even though the product they were selling was expensive office equipment—not an easy sell in the best of circumstances. Hanging in is part of the game.

Going forward with confidence: Daniel Porot, an expert in job hunting strategies, noted that the "job beggar mentality" defies success. Once you believe that an employer is doing you a favor by interviewing or hiring you, self-esteem and your career are in jeopardy. You are better served by thinking of yourself as a "resource person," someone who has something important to offer the company rather than presenting yourself as a grateful laborer.

Doing the research: If you are changing professions or "layering" into another industry, you move with greater strength when you have a destination in mind. Phyllis Bosworth, the Reinventor who went from television producer to top real estate saleswoman in Chapter Two, followed a lead, checked out the industry, estimated her chances, and got a job recommendation from a friend. Like her, you want as many advantages in your court as possible. Researching likely prospects serves you better than flooding the market with résumés and hoping for a response. Instead, *find the companies you can target directly.* Know them as best you can. What impressed you about these companies and why do you want to meet with them? How can you fit in? Most important, how will you sell yourself to them?

Learning what's necessary to best sell yourself: Selling is selling, even when the product is you. And to make any sale, you must close the deal. The "close" in this case means getting the job. What if you know you've got the goods, but your bête noir is the interview process? Do you think you've lost jobs in the past because a face-to-face interview reduces you to jelly with no memory, personality, or guts? If so, you need help with "presentation" skills—learning to sell yourself to others with confidence and grace under pressure.

Such training is no reflection of stature. In fact, it puts you in a pantheon of business, entertainment, academic, and political figures, among them Presidents Bush and Carter, who all needed coaching to best get their message across. Presentation skills techniques vary by trainer and some videotape your sessions to chart your progress. All of them work on your ability to communicate easily and help prepare you if you expect to be under fire at an interview.

Jon Rosen, president of Impact Communications, a New York–based media consulting firm, is one such specialist who trains executives for media interviews or speaking engagements as well as working with people who need preparation for the successful job interview. His training focuses on situations the potential interview may hold, including the "ambush" interview, where you may be asked tough questions. You or your company provide Jon with some of the questions that you *want* to answer with utmost cool and authority. Such training is the best kind of rehearsal to build confidence. Jon said:

> An interview isn't a conversation. You want your point of view to be understood, you want to look comfortable and be persuasive. The training gives people the skills necessary to cope with these situations, from getting the first words out to relearning body language. By videotaping the sessions and playing them back, you see how you look when you speak informally and what happens when the heat is on. You see your progress.

Media and presentation skills training is one way to go to "rehearse" the interview. If you have problems with simple interpersonal cues like eye contact, projecting your voice, demonstrating charm or humor, or speaking up to state your opinion, you may also benefit from other processes that stress such skills—assertiveness training, acting classes, and voice lessons, to name a few.

PUTTING ONESELF TOGETHER AS A PACKAGE

Here are eight ways I discovered to put oneself together as a "package" and make the sale—either to break into another field or move up in an allied area:

Make It Real I: Doing the Work That's *Not* Required of You
Make It Real II: The Fait Accompli
Make It Real III: Transferring Skills and the "Seesaw" Salary
Make It Real IV: Adjusting Ideals to Marketplace Truths
Putting a Spin on Rejection
Create an Opening Where There is None
Seize the Opportunity to Prove Yourself
Playing the Wild Card

MAKE IT REAL I: DOING THE WORK THAT'S NOT REQUIRED OF YOU

Most executives are overworked or overburdened and time is probably their biggest enemy. This is a fact of business life. Suppose you have an idea for a company and the company could well benefit from it, but you don't have the credentials to present it to the executive who could make it happen. This idea, you know, can further your career. How do you sell it and yourself when you face the key obstacle: getting the time from others to *make your idea real?*

This example demonstrates one method of successful approach.

My husband, Gordon Hyatt, is a documentary filmmaker seeking a crossover into dramatic films. He had been negotiating almost a year with a film company about doing the biography of a nineteenth-century artist. Gordon was not making any progress beyond his original proposal; the project was hanging in the air.

Finally, he had to take a step to get an answer one way or the other. Since he wanted funding for his film, he needed to know exactly what his chances were with the company. Instead of issuing an ultimatum—*Are you or are you not going with the project?*—he tried a more creative approach. He decided to extend himself and make the project real for the film company. Perhaps this would persuade them.

He wrote a strong "press release" on the opening of his would-be film. He described it so powerfully that it took on a new dimension. The film was no longer just year-old talk and words on paper, but an immediate hit. The right people read the release and Gordon got the word: He was on the way to a deal. Even though Gordon had never done a dramatic film before, he got his chance.

It's a cautionary tale that applies to any field: Be willing to go ahead with your project. When you are moving into a new area, you have to prove your commitment. The people you are waiting to hear from won't think through your problem without your help. They don't have time. But you do. A "press release" or a research proposal, on target, solicited or unsolicited, will help others make a decision about you. This reality is: People who get to do what they want to do often start out as the people who do it for others. *Take the initiative.*

This is another of Gordon's approaches that, coming in as an outsider, has an effect. He had been talking to an executive at a national nonprofit organization that manages exhibits of historical significance throughout the country. Gordon wanted to develop a film series based on their exhibits. The organization had never negotiated a deal with someone in the film business and hesitated to agree to any proposal. Filming seemed replete with too many unanswered questions.

A top executive there made his reservations clear: The group didn't know about public broadcast projects, so they sent Gordon's proposal to their legal department. They, in turn, replied that it would take a *year* of meetings to educate themselves in all that was involved in integrating cameras, crews, and a population of film people into their programs.

Gordon's response to them was: *You're right. You need education. But let me educate you.* He submitted a new offer: He would introduce them by phone to two lawyers who had experience with film projects produced in cooperation with nonprofit organizations. *In half an hour,* they could provide answers, examples, and precedents about procedures common to such special situations and answer all their questions. Following the call, the nonprofit group could decide if they wanted to be in the film business or not.

This is good salesmanship. The prospect cites an "objection" and you overcome it with an attestable solution. Again, the nonprofit group gave Gordon leverage by (1) not rejecting him out of hand, as in, "We can never do this because we haven't done it before" and (2) telling him they lacked an essential information base from which they could realistically make a decision.

Gordon made it possible for them *to be knowledgeable* in a very short amount of time; he arranged for them to get concrete information from sources they could trust. With their new knowledge, the group could sit down and cut a deal . . . or not.

No matter what the business, making it real for others always takes a dramatic turn—you are creating something out of nothing while convincingly projecting its future. But making it real also has its risks: There is also a downside. The company you approach may very well use your information and make a deal with someone else. It is not unheard of. But if you do the work and do it well, chances are good they will stay with you. By initiating an idea and bringing in experts to back you up, you become a visible force. It gives you the credibility you need to get a foot in the door.

MAKE IT REAL II: THE FAIT ACCOMPLI

My friend Arlene is facing a typical marketplace crisis: The company she works for has disbanded her market research division and she has been given five months to leave. This news set her into a panic. She feared the job search ahead. Not one to change easily, starting over is especially difficult for Arlene. Above all, she worries that she *won't* get a job and her final option will be the last one to fall back on: working alone in her own business. Arlene has a sharp business mind, but she is not entrepreneurial. Her gift is as a high-powered performer who thrives within a company setting—typical of a Lifer personality.

Arlene's chief worry was that there are few positions available at her level and the competition for them is stiff. She needed an angle, a tantalus to pique interest in her. After analyzing her skills and listing them, Arlene put her strength as a go-getter at the top. She could back this up: No one in her company matched her record for bringing in business.

Arlene finally looked at her two options. The first was to go the usual route. Using networking/contacts she would single out the companies to apply to, send a letter, a résumé, wait for the response, the interview, go through the process. Or the second option was to go in fait accompli—to prove to a company how great her skills were and bring business in with her. She told me:

> I called the people I worked with over the last fifteen years and explained my idea. Then I asked them if they would work with me, specifically, to write a brief letter stating that if I were involved with so-and-so's company, they would, under the appropriate circumstances, give me approximately $100,000 worth of market research business a year.

So far, Arlene has collected *one million dollars* of possible work, on paper. Buttressed by such a show of support, her attitude has changed from diffident to confident. Whereas before she wondered who would hire her, now the quandary has changed its tone: To whom does she want to bring her million dollars' worth of potential business?

The benefit of the fait accompli is that you are not just talking about your assets, but making it very real to a company that doesn't know you. What better proof of your track record than two or ten new clients and "x" amount of dollars in business written, as a strong possibility, in your name. The fait accompli saves a potential employer time in scouting new business and, importantly, you've removed any doubt that you are able to do what you say you can.

MAKE IT REAL III: TRANSFERRING SKILLS AND THE "SEESAW" SALARY

As the saying goes, prosperity is not without fears, and adversity is not without comfort and hope. However the paradox lives, when you've lost your financial assets and prosperity vanishes, your fears are that comfort and hope might elude you, too. You are not only starting again, you are starting over.

Coming back from adversity is the stuff of oft-told tales of guts, ingenuity, and just plain hardheadedness. Frank Ryder, founder of the truck leasing company that bears his name, went bankrupt five times after he sold the business. At a vigorous seventy-five years old and with a thirty-eight-year-old wife, Ryder is once again raising money for another venture in Florida, certainly full of hope.

Ryder has a direction—to succeed again as an entrepreneur.

What if, like Ryder, your career was single-minded, but, unlike him, financial calamity changed your plans? What if, out of financial insecurity, necessity meant starting over and changing your entire way of life? And what if starting over meant starting at a beginner's salary?

Such a financial dilemma struck Robert L. Green, one of the most respected style setters of men's fashions, a man whose advice and expertise were long sought after. Robert was very successful until a few unfortunate investments suddenly stripped him of everything, including his New York City townhouse. Instead of declaring bankruptcy, Robert paid back everyone.

By then, Robert, a Lifer who had thrived in one industry, was in his sixties and starting over. He knew he had to get back into the work force to reinvent himself, but how? The man whom others emulated decided he was no longer eligible for the station of fashion guru. Feeling that he was too old to be the arbiter of taste for twenty-five-year-olds, this onetime head of men's fashions for *Playboy* decided to change occupations or industries. Since New York City was too expensive for his budget, he moved to California.

Knowing a few contacts in films, he asked them how he might connect into the business. His great skill was in style, and he thought he might consult on films about wardrobe and sets. He got a piece of advice about the best approach to consider practically. At one time he was a known entity, accustomed to $50,000 in retainer fees. Now he was in a "foreign land," an unknown entity. Until he could establish his reputation, Robert was advised to trim his fees back to a fractional amount. He said:

> I decided on a reasonable fee—$2,000 a month—to be a consultant. And while $2,000 a month is not what I was used to, it was a way to get started. There was no question that I could do the work—look at fashion and advise if I think it's right or wrong for an effect. It was *what I always did,* but the approach was different, the language of the business was different, and I was different.

While his rates and goals were not anywhere harmonious, it was the kickoff Robert needed to get off the financial seesaw. He knew his service wasn't a budget breaker in Hollywood, where such a rate is considered petty cash. It was a sensible step.

Although financial loss often weighs appreciably on one's self-esteem, Robert's choice was not to act from false pride or *exception* and modification. False pride would have kept him lamenting the past and oppressed by financial burdens; instead, he went for the slow climb toward long-term rewards of rebuilding a career.

On the most basic level, cheap rates and mighty credentials were an alluring combination; it paid for the studios to hire a man like him. Between the credentials and the allure, though, Robert was practically aware that he would have to make dramatic or strategic moves to prove himself.

If you want to establish yourself in a new industry using crossover skills, Robert's appreciable example is proof it can be done at any age. And, if you have a passion for a business and it is tough to break in, you may have to lower your rates even more—give away your services. It may mean working at another job until you get the credits you need.

MAKE IT REAL IV: ADJUSTING IDEALS TO MARKETPLACE TRUTHS

Somewhere between lofty dreams and a drive for success lies real accomplishment. We've all sailed on that cloud, reaching for an ideal—in ourselves and in others. Having high standards measures us not only in terms of performance, but as functioning, civilized, ethical people. But having impossibly lofty ideals is high on the list of reasons why we don't succeed in our work. Wanting what appears to be "the best" and issuing the ultimatum to ourselves, "the best or nothing," is misplaced attraction to achievement. It's one way to get stuck.

Radiant blond actress and former talk show hostess, Mariette Hartley told me of her own struggle with upholding her ideals while steering her career along that course. She'd been acting since she was ten years old, doing a lot of stage and screen work; the growing "child" of technology, television, was not yet as great a force. She grew up in the fifties and sixties, a time when people "pooh-poohed television," and she pretty much agreed with the going wave of opinion. Stage and screen work was "best," was "art." All the rest was trade, marketing, "sellouts."

Even so, television was a force too powerful to ignore. There was work to be had. Mariette made "the TV rounds" and briefly starred in her own series. She worked with film director Sam Peckinpah in a western and her "old voices" haunted her over what to do next: "Don't do television, don't do soaps."

She wound up doing both. "I felt tarnished," she said. On *Peyton*

Place, a daytime soap opera based on the best-selling potboiler, Mariette faced another career crossroads when the series ended. She still thought she could have the dramatic artist's life. One of life's realities that was difficult for her to accept was compromise, and so far, she felt she'd been coasting on it.

She was looking for work when it was suggested she do commercials. The image of her selling a product before a camera was totally alien to her. Unacceptable. She told me:

> I'd see other actors doing commercials and I remember thinking, "Those poor suckers—their careers must have gone down the tubes to be doing this." I still thought of acting as art. But in the process of art vs. food on the table, surrendering art soon took me into many different directions. One was commercials.
>
> When I learned that commercials represented the kind of money it did and the kind of work I could get, I thought I had better start thinking differently. It started out feeling like the "end," but it turned out to be an adventure.

The adventure launched her on four or five auditions a day to sell "floor wax and tissues." She approached it with the aplomb of the professional actress, even keeping a range of outfits in her car to adapt her style to the "look" a casting director was seeking. If they wanted a "Candice Bergen" effect at two-thirty, she'd do that, then be ready to switch into an "Ali MacGraw" high-fashion cool by four.

When Mariette decided to go wholeheartedly into commercials, she faced the numbers game: It took twenty auditions before she was hired for one. Then "the roof started blowing off." By the time she played opposite James Garner in one of the most popular commercials of the 1970s for Polaroid, Mariette had logged close to a hundred commercials. Other than the obvious financial rewards and visibility of a career begun begrudgingly, Mariette also met her husband on a shoot.

Zen philosophy tells us that to make a perfect cup of tea is as worthy an act as ruling a kingdom. Most of us don't quite see the equanimity between the two—we make judgments. We give acts and occupations greater value than others and those who perform them greater or lesser importance. By accepting the reality of "lesser" work, not unlike Robert L. Green did in Hollywood, in her way, Mariette finally made her perfect cup of tea.

You may be like Mariette—high ideals on one hand, but, on the other, you're a *realist.* Work sometimes means survival first. Her choice was to act, and if it meant acting in thirty-second pitches for products, that was okay. How did Mariette make the leap to accepting and enjoying the world she previously disdained? She told me:

> When you surrender yourself to change, it's astonishing what can happen . . . astonishing and terrifying. There is nothing about change in my life that hasn't scared me. There's the fear of the unknown and the fear of judgment. How do I get through it? I think that needing to get to the other side of the fear is stronger than the fear itself.
>
> I have to attend to the panic. I cut off so much of experience when I'm afraid. As the jokes goes, if you worry about yesterday and tomorrow today, by the end of the week you've lived twenty-one days.

All business has compromise built into it; sometimes, it's called negotiation. All life has compromise; if it doesn't devalue others or yourself, it may hold a few surprises, such as opportunity, and even one's life work.

PUTTING A SPIN ON REJECTION

In all of the seminars I conduct, whether the subject is sales or failure, the same lament comes up as to why people do not *act:* fear of rejection. The result of this fear is clear enough: You are giving others the power to determine your worth and tamper with your self-esteem. Rejection, more or less, falls on the word *no* and its many verses.

If you are shifting gears and trying to sell yourself into another business, your chances of hearing *no* are pretty high (and as we've seen, constitutes one of the main obstacles to change). Some people take a single rejection as the answer for an entire industry and back down; others see it as predictable odds and press on. Yet others take a "no" back to the naysayer to get what they set out for. One way they do it is with guts and humor.

One master of the art of putting a spin on rejection is Denver artist Mario Rivoli. He started out waiting for the "big gallery show" that would make his career, a dream much like other fine artists work toward and wait for. But meanwhile, there was the rent. Originally a New Yorker, the city's diversity provided many opportunities for Mario's resourcefulness. He sold antiques, bartered drawings for necessities, designed and handmade leather clothing and bags that were sold in specialty boutiques and upscale craft galleries. Then he learned that he could earn nearly as much for designing a book jacket as he'd been charging for his pencil drawings. He decided to pursue it.

He put together a portfolio and, through a contact, made an appointment with an art director at a large publishing company. The woman perused his work and seemed to like it. Mario was sure by her response that he'd get an assignment to do a cover. To his great surprise, she handed his portfolio back to him and made her apologies. Mario told me:

> She thought I was talented, but so were there many *other* artists equally as good. Then she pretty much told me to *give up* . . . the odds were against me. Her exact words were, "Maybe if you're lucky, someone will give you a cover to do by the time you're ninety-nine."

Disturbed by her comment, Mario headed home, then retraced his steps midtown to Western Union. There, he composed a telegram that he sent off to the art director. It said, "Tomorrow is my ninety-ninth birthday. Where's my cover?"

Early the next morning, the art director called him and, charmed by his nerve, invited him for a "birthday drink" and gave him the first of twelve book jackets for that company. His work for them eventually led to his illustrating an award-winning children's book and establishing an authentic sideline as an illustrator.

When Mario sent that telegram, he was standing up to a judgment about him that may have been true—he had no chance—while asserting himself as someone to be reckoned with. Mario parried first with humor; he had nothing to lose by challenging a rejection that wanted to doom him to anonymity in the book business. He couldn't take "no" for an answer.

What Mario did was make a sale, applying a tried-and-true rule in effective salesmanship: He used the words his "prospect" used, he took the prospect's negative evaluation and turned it around into something positive. He took the risk and moved from place to place.

CREATE AN OPENING WHERE THERE IS NONE

The tailor-made job with your name on it is the best of all possible worlds. Since such a position rarely exists at the same time as your seeking it, the alternative is to "build your own"—create an opening where there is none. If you're shifting gears, creating a niche for yourself is the kind of option that can pay off in many respects. Marketing expert and intrapreneur Chuck Zackary is one such success story.

Good detection and practical experience marked Chuck's change of path out of advertising. Over a three-year period, he noticed tremendous growth in the sales promotion industry, while he also noticed advertising dollars declining. Sales promotions include coupons, special displays and offers, in-store merchandising, and even meetings and conventions.

In his own business at the time, Chuck also noticed that his clients were interested in sales promotion because of its immediate impact on sales results, faster than with advertising. When he ended his partnership and closed his business, Chuck decided to get back into the mainstream and get a job. He figured out exactly what he wanted: salary, location, cost of living, demand for his skills. Chuck did his research on livable cities and settled on three: Albuquerque, Orlando, and Providence. After honing in on his requirements for urban livability, Chuck decided to target Orlando.

In terms of business, things looked good. Disney and Universal were building studios—"it was almost recession proof because of that," he said. Then he did another intensive study to find advertising agencies that didn't have sales promotion capabilities. Hopefully, he would fill it. In sending out letters, Chuck inadvertently uncovered the clue to what kind of letter best summons an interview:

> In the first letter, I told them I was moving to Florida, moving my business and looking for a place to put it—I saw the benefits of us working together. I said I had many business contacts and could bring in sales promotion clients from all over the country. I didn't say I was looking for a job.
>
> In the other letter, I said about the same thing, but mentioned I *was* looking for a job. The responses were entirely different, even from the same company.

It was an interesting test for him, made most obvious by the response from one company president who received both of Chuck's letters. Three days after he sent the first letter ("let's talk") Chuck was called for an interview. Two days after the call, he got a form rejection letter from the same man in response to his *second* letter, saying there were *no jobs* available. When he went to Orlando for the meeting, he took the rejection letter with him. Chuck mentioned the letter; the man said it was how his secretary handled such inquiries—he hadn't even seen it.

In all, Chuck's strategy netted him *six* interviews from *ten* letters—a great response. Of the six interviews, Chuck got three offers to develop a sales promotion department—excellent results!

Now in Orlando, Chuck has happily created the job he wanted in the city he chose. Added to that, the company is paying him a salary base while he builds the business. "They're willing to invest in someone with my background," Chuck said.

You may have a similar plan in mind and are thinking out strategies to connect with the right people. Taking Chuck's example, you need to: *observe* the market, *see the need* and fill it, do the *research* and the legwork, *believe in yourself,* and take the risk.

SEIZE THE OPPORTUNITY TO PROVE YOURSELF

Call it opportunism, but opportunism in the best sense: If you see a way for you to make yourself helpful—and eventually indispensable—to a person who can boost your career, do it. He (or she) who hesitates, I firmly believe, loses something. I've been on both sides of the fence and what I remember best is those who *made an effort for me* without my having to ask.

When I had my research company, I once had to interview for a secretary on what turned into an especially hectic day. There was a line of people waiting to see me, phones were ringing, and there was at least one emergency. In such a melee, Lois Block sat down to be interviewed; she was the third candidate. I was juggling two calls; the papers were piled up on my desk. When I hung up from the last call Lois said, without missing a beat, "You need my help. Let me get you some tea and I'll tell you how I can best organize your life here." Whom did I hire?

Making a demonstrable and unsolicited effort may strike others as presumptive familiarity. Or you might get hired. These are the chances you take. Busy people are stingy about their time and they almost always need organizing and care. By showing people you really want to work for them, you probably will.

Your résumé tells people what you've done. *Action* tells them who you are.

PLAYING THE WILD CARD

Knowing that most companies operate on the theory that "if you haven't done it before, you can't do it," is no reason to stop you from trying. In fact, for some people, the caveat is motivation for them to try harder. The shrewd and savvy Jennifer Adaire twice sold herself into jobs, introducing herself as "the wild card," the long shot. If ever I met someone who didn't get stuck in "the crisis of no," it's Jennifer.

When she graduated from Princeton, she decided on a career in investment banking. A self-proclaimed "generalist," what she knew of the banking field interested her; it correlated with her strong points—a high energy level and good organizational skills. At the interview, Jennifer, going in with no business experience, set herself up as the ideal candidate for the job. Her delivery and approach were sophisticated, knowledgeable, and effective. She told me how that interview went:

> Beyond the standard questions—like: How can you prove leadership qualities?—I had to really sell myself, sound confident. I tend to be a steam-of-consciousness kind of talker, but I spoke in "bullets," point after point. I didn't deny my lack of experience, but I turned it around in my favor.
>
> I said, from my standpoint, investment banking is right for me. I'm good at details. I'm interested in the business. I can deal with the long hours. I told them I've always been successful at what I've done.
>
> Then I spoke frankly. I said, I'm a bit of a mystery to them, but I'm giving them the opportunity to expand their pool of candidates. I'm going to provide a point of differentiation. I'll have a different perspective in terms of background—they're not going to have all same type of person when they go to the client.
>
> Hiring me was to their benefit.

Strong stuff. Jennifer was hired as an analyst, working with public offerings, commercial equities, research assignments, real estate. After two years of not being in the "most creative end" of the business and very long hours—up to 90 percent of her weekends, too—Jennifer enrolled in Harvard Business School for her master's degree in business. Her decision to go back to school was a practical one: (1) she wasn't happy with the work she was doing, and (2) a degree in business would help create more opportunities for her future.

She focused on marketing, but when she applied for jobs with her degree, she was cast in a niche—no one believed she wouldn't quit marketing and go back into investment banking. Ten companies turned her down for marketing positions, focusing on her two-year employment history. Then she interviewed at Pepsico. The company felt right for her. She wanted the job with them. She had a purpose and she had to get that purpose across, despite their reservations.

Pepsico was looking for a strategic planner; Jennifer thought the job was "the answer to her prayers." Before her interview, she researched the industry and found out where Pepsico stood "on the cola wars." She knew all their commercials; who they signed to do them. She was completely prepared and focused. Her purpose was to get this job.

> I think it gets to be a self-selecting process—you find the company that you fit into. Sometimes the chemistry isn't there. You don't fit in and you know it and they know it. When it's right, be confident.
>
> When I interviewed at Pepsico, I let them know I wanted the job. I proved it by how I sold myself. I think that kind of drive is always what a company is looking for.

A FINAL NOTE ON SELLING YOURSELF

The heart of successful presentation is *self-belief*—the belief in your value and your sense of uniqueness—and tooting your own horn with conviction, not bravado. Once you have a clear vision of who you are and where you want to go, *persist* in making it possible. It is the passion of your own quest that will engage others along the way—others who will want to be on your team.

Setbacks and discouraging words will always be part of the bargain, but to keep up the best fight, do your homework. And if you have to, undercut the market to get what you want. It doesn't matter how you *feel,* but how you *act on* your convictions to build a fulfilling life by getting *results.*

The adventure is making things happen for yourself, exploring options and daring to act on who you are. You've come so far through the process; sell the best of who you are.

9

OPPORTUNITIES AND ENTREPRENEURSHIP

You never thought of yourself as a risk taker, but circumstances suddenly changed and you found yourself thinking: Maybe I should start a business.

You can set nicely rational goals, but you seem to have a knack for getting to them by some other, unplanned routes.

You're a bit of a rule breaker.

Stifled by organizational structure, you want to make your own money and your own career decisions, but wonder how.

You have a dogged intensity to succeed. You want to come back from a career low point to try again.

If any of these points resonate for you, be assured—you are among the many millions of people who are shifting gears out of mainstream industry and into your own business. It is *circumstance* above all that will steer you into an entrepreneurial venture. The industry you worked in has hit a slump and you're out; you're one of the middle managers who was forced out and cannot find a way back in. You've always been a bit of an oddball and no longer wish to make the effort to fit in. You've put your career on hold to have children, but wanting to keep your hand in or make your own hours, you consider starting a small business at home.

A thoroughly circumstantial entrepreneur, you didn't plan on this career direction at all. Business operations may even have baffled you, but now they engage you. Opening your own business seems feasible and the timing is right.

Yours may be the story of this decade as you join the ranks of the new entrepreneurs.

The Small Business Administration reported that there are over three million active corporations in America—many of them budding industries that did not exist two years ago. Large and established industries may be the hotbed of many scientific breakthroughs and offer tradition and security, but it seems they are getting a run for their money from original thinkers, like you, who have figured out how to tap the newer and equally profitable markets.

The idea of becoming an entrepreneur has captured everyone's imagination; those who take it up have no lack of support. Getting the know-how to make a business work is almost as much of an industry. Fifteen years ago, the number of colleges with a course in entrepreneurship numbered about ten; today more than 320 colleges offer such a course. Seminars, how-to books, tapes, and videos proffer expertise in every aspect of business from the "successful outlook" to the economic outlook. Finding more opportunity or tantalized by autonomy, four out of ten new businesses are started by women.

Opportunities are limited only by your imagination. You can create a business the way business has always been created—by filling a need.

There are, for example, *niche markets* for "nurturing networks," service organizations that tend to pregnant and financially or emotionally stranded "middle class" college age and working women; there exist special products, magazines, and services for "grampies"—Growing Retired Active Monied People in (an) Excellent State"—the over-sixty version of the yuppie. And for those less fortunate, there is "elder care"—a private health care system for the 9 million elderly people who need special services, and "senior *day* care centers," which provide social and health services for the same group of people. There are young entrepreneurs revolutionizing the mail-order business, the ice cream franchises, the hotel chains, the travel and tourism business.

Where do you fit in?

COULD YOU START YOUR OWN BUSINESS?

What makes a successful entrepreneur? Ask those who are in business (like Margaret Newbourg, profiled in Chapter Seven, who moved from social worker to outplacement expert) and they will tell you what they did and what they have within them to succeed. No matter what their business, they always talk about two things: risk and seizing the opportunities. To make it in business—to even tack your name on the door—you must take a chance on yourself.

Harvard University Business School has been studying the profile of the successful entrepreneur over the last twenty-five years. From their vast sources of material, they have distilled these eight chief qualities as representing the makeup of a *real* (versus a circumstantial) entrepreneur. Each is distinguished by:

Great drive and personal energy. Not only are they highly motivated, but real entrepreneurs are *willing to put forth the effort* to make things happen. They're good at juggling time and activity.

A *high level of self-confidence.* They believe in their goals and have a need to see them realized. They don't depend on luck as the deciding factor in their success.

Commitment to a long-term involvement. Real entrepreneurs are not in for the fast buck, but see business as an ongoing process. They can focus in on planning, building, organization.

A *view of money as a measure of success,* not money for its own sake. Theirs is the satisfaction of knowing they have money in the bank, equity, credit, and a personal sense of prosperity.

Persistence and problem-solving ability. The entrepreneur can "get from here to there" and not collapse under pressure. He has ingenuity, resourcefulness, and can seek advice.

An understanding of how to use resources and contacts. "Real" entrepreneurs have in their heads a "Wheeldex" of names—and what they do, what they know, where they are, who they may know. In wanting either information or a person who can make a project go, real entrepreneurs can get on the phone and put together what they need.

A tolerance for ambiguity. The entrepreneurial life is less predictable than the nine-to-five job and more fraught with unknowns. To make it, the real entrepreneur must be able to live with uncertainty while trying to establish a secure business.

An ability to use positive and negative feedback wisely. In building your own business and making improvements, you must be able to listen to others and what they think of your enterprise.

So while you may be an entrepreneur at first by fluke, you will need to develop these qualities in some measure to make a go of your business. You may fall in love with your product or your idea, and emotion may give you the momentum you need to take the first steps in opening a business. But, said *Entrepreneur* magazine, "It's not enough to be energetic and adventurous . . . you can't neglect to check out the market. Is the right product in the right place with the right price?"

Going into business means you need to think out these questions, too:

Why do you want to go into business?

Who are you? Do you seek a partner or is the business entirely your "baby"?

What is the big picture?

What industry are you breaking into? What stage is it at—embryo, growth, maturity, decline? What are the trends?

How much money do you want to make—realistically?

Have you defined your target customers? Who are they and how can you best reach them?

Have you scoped the competition? Who are the leaders? Where are they vulnerable?

How can you be different? How can you get the edge over them? Have you developed a sales plan?

IDENTIFYING THE ENTREPRENEUR

The following entrepreneurs came to own their own business from divergent beginnings. Some were educated and trained in business; others had dazzling instinct from a young age and worked relentlessly toward that goal. Both the "real" and the circumstantial entrepreneurs tend to fall into these categories:

1. The Planner
2. The Franchiser
3. The Partner
4. The Married Partners
5. The Initiator
6. The Sideline Entrepreneur

THE PLANNER: FROM BANKING TO SPORTS MANAGEMENT

A great idea, a generative business sense, money in the bank, and guts can add up to success. And it did for New Yorker Robert Fayne, a unique breed of Lifer with strong risk-taking abilities, who started his business three years ago. Trained and educated in business, Robert left a mainstream job when he saw a niche in the market and decided to test it out.

Radiating confidence, Tennessee-born businessman Robert Fayne is among a growing number of Black businessmen. Strongly persuasive while being soft-spoken, Robert was an investment banker with Kidder, Peabody in New York, riding the market boom and working his way up. His career was in high gear when he decided to make a move his colleagues did not expect: He wanted to leave banking and open a sports management agency.

Robert had a long-standing interest in sports that he hoped to combine with his expertise in business—the agency idea seemed like a perfect solution. He evaluated the possibility of consolidating a full range of financial, counseling, and legal services that would be available to athletes under one roof. It seemed feasible. But being astute and methodical, he first did some research on the industry. A graduate of Harvard Business School, Robert turned to a professor friend and a graduate student there to help him do independent market research, assessing the business.

From the research, he discovered, most significantly, that sports management was a "fragmented business" with some companies running quality practices and handling significant clients, others being small, specialized "mom and pop" operations that tended to concentrate on contract negotiations only. He thought his chances were good: By consolidating all the services in one agency, he could take advantage of the industry's lack of structure. He could offer to athletes services like tax and investment advice and career counseling as well as contract work. Thus was spawned Consolidated Management Group.

Robert left Wall Street before the fateful market crash in 1987—exiting in a measure of comfort, not as a casualty of circumstance. By that time, he'd been with Kidder, Peabody for three years—his only job following graduate school. "Comfortable with risk," Robert evaluated the trade-off of going from corporate life to the uncertainty of his own business:

> What I gave up at Kidder, Peabody was security. But I felt that opening my own business was not an unreasonable risk at all. I knew I had a chance and that it would be a lot of work to build a reputation.
>
> I saved a lot of money when I had a job so even if I didn't earn any money in the first year on my own, I would not have to change my lifestyle. It was something I had to do.

Robert started off Consolidated with a group of five people who were committed to working with him on an "as ready" basis—lawyers, a counselor, business advisors. Contacts helped put him in touch with prospects. Set up to go, the first few months were difficult for him. It had more to do with disengaging from the schedule, routines, and certain predictability of working for a large company than dealing with the vicissitudes of starting up. He was only used to an affiliation—and the steady salary. Now he had to establish his own pace and be responsible for the profits.

His idea soon took off. Understanding business, its fluctuations and cycles, Robert prepared for the typical first-year struggle by being adequately financed—an essential, if you are going to survive. In his second year, Robert doubled his number of clients and, now in his third year, he expects his company's growth to continue.

Robert's strong business credentials, quality skills, and personability mark the successful entrepreneur. He's not just selling a service, but selling himself and his credibility. "There is no greater satisfaction than succeeding in your own business," he told me. "It is more gratifying than anything else."

Robert was trained and educated in the ways of business. Others of us discover we have the interest, but we're not sure if we have the knack. Trial and error is risky and financially hazardous in many cases. Franchising can offer the kind of structure for those of you who prefer the known factor of camaraderie, product, and organization.

THE FRANCHISER: THE ENTREPRENEURIAL "NETWORK"

There's a Stonehenge "Blimpie," Kentucky Fried Chicken on the Ginza, and a Weight Watchers in Mexico City—seemingly incongruous locations for American fast-food outlets and a weight-loss center to thrive in. But a Druid landmark in Britain, a Tokyo thoroughfare, and a Third World metropolis demonstrate, if anything, that if you combine an enterprising spirit with proven marketing strategy, you can succeed in business anywhere. The "proven" strategy is, in this case, exemplified by *franchising.*

There are about *1,300 different* franchisers, offering every product and service from soup to weight-loss centers. Franchising can be a fascinating venture with benefits often outweighing the drawbacks in a start-up business. Someone else has invented the wheel for you; if you have the money, or the borrowing power, you can repeat their process.

Franchising tends to attract two kinds of people. The first type wants the appeal of *active* ownership—the entrepreneurs who plan to invest in and work their own shops. The second type is primarily investment conscious and operates a franchise through "absentee ownership," hiring management and staff to run the business; in effect, being an employer. If you are of either mind, franchising could be the right arena for you.

Choosing the type of franchise you buy into is a matter of personal taste, but what reputable franchises offer you personally will help you decide if you *will* buy. Franchising's main selling points are these:

1. It provides the comfort of belonging to an already established company with some proven staying power.
2. Because you belong to a "family" of businesses with the identical goals, it sets up the sense of a "safety net." The cautious risk taker who would not ordinarily risk independent action takes brightly to the franchise concept.
3. An independent business demands market research to test the feasibility of a product in a targeted location. As *Money* magazine pointed out, when you own a franchise, "you worry less about whether there is a market for the product or service." The successful company has already done the work for you.
4. This "worry" taken care of, your next concern may be day-to-day operations, and training. First-time entrepreneurs can benefit from learning the logistics of the business—ordering supplies, managing personnel, keeping up the "image," and so on—through the franchiser. As part of your purchasing fee, most franchisers will train you to run the business.

While franchisers take the worry out of what to sell and how, such a "cookie cutter" business may not suit the entrepreneur who is more the individualist—even the decor of the business tends to be standardized with less freedom for expansion and redecoration. And, as part of your expenses with a franchise, expect to give over to your franchiser a percentage of your revenues—up to 12 percent annually. But if you are less concerned with such details and prefer to concentrate on building trade and income, you have, according to the statistics of the franchising industry, a 95 *percent* chance of succeeding. A 5 percent failure rate is astonishingly low compared to a 65 *percent* failure rate among independent business ventures.

While franchises provide a network of business opportunities for those who buy into them, so is there another profitable side—the creative end. Those who *originate* ideas for franchises, also designing their management systems and marketing strategies, have spawned great empires. Ray Kroc, for one, is the legendary master of marketing the hamburger and turning it into an event at McDonald's. Newer franchising ideas grow and move with the times and include products and services, edible and inedible, of every sort. One such growing franchise operation is an update on the post office, a one-stop shop that is part of an overall $800 million a year industry. Called CMRA's—Convenience Mail Receiving Agencies—these franchises feature shipping, packing, and mail services, many with twenty-four-hour "prestige address" mailbox rentals. These outlets, among them Pak-Mail Inc., are growing at an annual rate of 25 percent, selling convenience around the clock much like the local 7-Eleven grocery store.

Another, the O! Deli Corporation, is a few years old and thriving. The concept of master franchiser Joe Sanfellipo and his partner, Rick Cardin, O! Deli is a unique high-quality, low-cost sandwich shop franchise targeted at locations in financial districts, office complexes, and industrial parks that operates five days a week. Joe began O! Deli—"a concept so simple it's incredible no one has done it before"—after twenty years of having owned and operated several independent and franchised operations.

At thirty-nine years old, Joe is the quintessential self-made man, a Synthesizer who made and lost and remade his fortune. A millionaire by the age of twenty-five, Joe was by that time on his own for half his life. Totally self-educated from the age of thirteen, Joe began his career by lying about his age to work in a Dallas transmission shop. Ultimately, he moved to California, and his career took off. He bought a transmission business, increasing the volume tenfold over a three-year period, and expanding into an eight-store chain. With his real estate holdings, he had $5 million in assets by the time he was twenty-five years old. Less than five years later, he "went belly up."

Resourceful and optimistic in the face of bankruptcy, it was Joe's reputation as an expert in the transmission business that made him decide to temporarily switch gears: Until he got on his feet, he led seminars for service station and garage owners on prospecting for transmission jobs. The success of the seminars "snowballed" into another life-changing shift. A man with a transmission franchising idea approached Joe to consult on the operation; since he didn't have the money to pay Joe a salary, he offered him a franchise. Within eight years, Joe helped bring Gibraltar Transmission Corporation up from infancy to more than a hundred franchise outlets.

I asked Joe to compare his first meteoric success and failure as an independent businessman to his ongoing success in franchising. He told me:

> I overexpanded my business to eight shops and went broke. I had hundreds of employees but *no* good management system. Being the person who's there physically running the business and showing someone else how to run it in your place are two different things.
>
> Finally, I created an effective management system by looking at what I did wrong, then went into the business of teaching it to others. It was because of management systems that I got interested in franchising. There's something to it. Now, I can take the skills I learned about franchising to any number of businesses from cars to golf balls.
>
> I found that most people who fail are embarrassed to do something other than what they failed in. I know a lot more about failure than most people and I knew I could teach people how to avoid it.

When Joe met Rick Cardin, a former director of the Cambridge Research Institute, they decided to create and build a franchise. After considering five broad categories—food, clothing, shelter, recreation, and transportation—they settled on "food" only because their accountant had some experience in it from which they could draw. Methodically, they listed and defined the ideal characteristics of their potential business, filling four pages. Out of this list, they came up with the concept for the O! Deli Corporation: to replace the "mom and pop" deli the way Baskin-Robbins replaced the corner soda shop. The partners built a management system for O! Deli while Joe simultaneously ran his transmission business and Rick Cardin handled daily operations. In 1988, Joe came on board full time with O! Deli, selling the transmission franchises to his partners.

Franchises, in the "big picture," look like paradise to some viewers—or at least a sure thing. But as with any venture, you must be properly informed about the process and your sights set on a realistic goal. Having the experience of building two successful franchises, Joe understands both the drawbacks in owning one and how dreams of glory can capture your imagination. Joe suggested to potential franchisees:

> *Visualize* what the business will be like—the good, the bad, and the *why*. The good side is that you control your destiny. The bad side is that when you are in business for yourself, you have to work hard. And while you can call the franchiser for advice, you are responsible for what happens.
>
> And in terms of "why," you must be like "Columbo," the TV detective. Go to "the scene of the crime"—the franchise operation you want to buy—work backward, and find your motive. Visualize the process. I even recommend you find a franchise that went wrong and figure out how *you* would have managed things differently.

Joe has an energy and what seems to be an undaunted positive mental outlook. Clearly a great risk taker and an independent thinker, Joe has the ability to turn his setbacks around into the bases for his next life change. With franchising, Joe Sanfellipo truly found his niche. Inspiration, though, can also be found anywhere, even among stacks of copper tubing.

While franchising offers structure first, many would-be entrepreneurs are motivated by an *idea* they want to see realized. It is this idea that enthralls them and refuels a real sense of purpose.

However, they may feel they can't do it on their own. They need to form a team, a partnership, and from this, businesses can happen.

THE PARTNER: TWO DREAMS ARE BETTER THAN ONE

Forbes magazine reported that in a study of 2,000 businesses founded since 1960, figures revealed that companies built on partnerships are *four times* as likely to succeed as those started as solo ventures. "Lone Rangers" may have the capital, the expertise, and the guts to go it alone, but it's interactive feedback and accountability to others that appear to be surer shots.

One reason for success among partners, the study said, is "discipline"—specifically, a commitment to hewing to your part of the bargain. Entrepreneurs going it alone were less likely to use time effectively, many procrastinated or labored over trivial details. The words "It's *ours,*" it appears, carry greater weight in the matter of growing successful than "It's mine."

But the event of partnership is not made in heaven. Business partnerships are serious relationships first—marriages of personalities, strengths, and shortcomings—as much as legalized teams of complementary abilities. Choosing an appropriate partner is as sensitive a decision as choosing the right business to invest in. While evidence shows that partnerships foster greater growth than solo enterprises, other studies indicate that about 60 percent of surveyed business breakups occurred because of personal conflicts or a change of interest.

How do you choose a partner? Instinct? References? The camaraderie of long-standing friendship? How successful are married couples in business? Can they cope with professional decisions without affecting their personal relationship? Two very distinct business partnerships were created by four very different people shifting gears. Each partnership was founded on a unique balance of familiarity, skills, and timing.

THE PARTNER: WOMEN IN BUSINESS: THE LOCAL FOOD SHOP BECOMES AN INDUSTRY

"Builders" Sheila Lukins and Julee Rosso opened The Silver Palate, a tiny neighborhood gourmet and catering shop that grew into an international line of packaged gourmet foods, three best-selling cookbooks, a video of all-occasion entertaining tips and recipes, and a *standard* by which others judge specialty foods. Neither woman expected such a rush of success. It was to be a sideline, a hobby at best.

They met serendipitously. Sheila, the smaller of the two and the talented cook, married and with children, ran a catering business from her apartment; Julee's boyfriend, a steady client of Sheila's, recommended her for a catering job Julee needed. At that time, Julee was the advertising director at Burlington Mills. When they met it was "love at first sight."

Impressed with Sheila's professionalism and style—"at six o'clock in the morning she had picked fresh hydrangeas that still had the dew on them for an important breakfast function"—Julee hired Sheila again for a four-day job at Burlington. By the third day, Julee mentioned her idea for a gourmet take-out food shop, something small and part time, and that she'd like Sheila to be her partner and cook. After a few momentary doubts, Sheila agreed.

The store, The Silver Palate, opened on New York's Upper West Side in 1976. With a third partner, the plan was: Julee would manage the shop part time, Sheila would cook three or four hours a day from her house and supplement her income from other sources, and the third partner would work at the store. They each invested $7,000—enough to open the doors and get started.

The store took off and their partner pulled out a year later. Julee and Sheila, still improvising and working on instinct, barely knowing each other and not quite sure of how to communicate, found themselves with a success on their hands. It was the right store at the right time—gourmet food and stylish entertaining was back.

The Silver Palate was getting a lot of attention and publicity; Julee was working double time—at her day job and in the store. Sheila thought she could get help with the cooking to free herself by writing down her recipes, but she "didn't know how. I just cooked." Both women were working from five-thirty in the morning until eleven at night; their personal lives were becoming sorely affected. In spite of all the rules they broke about making it in business, it was a dynamic that worked, almost in spite of itself. Sheila explained:

> We were exhausted all the time, but we learned every aspect of the business. It survived out of tenacity because we knew nothing! We couldn't even train a staff to do what we wanted done because we didn't know what we wanted until we did it.
>
> What we loved was the creative part—the menus, the catalogues, the newsletters, and, eventually, the books. It was addictive. Julee had the notion to think the whole thing up. She had a dream and she changed my life dramatically. I never would have done it alone.

Julee eventually quit her job to devote her time fully to the store and its products. She spoke of the partnership and why she thought it was successful:

> People always rooted for us and we loved the business. The burden was totally on us and we didn't want to let each other down. We went through an adjustment period in the beginning which might have backfired, but it became a remarkable marriage. Maybe it worked because we didn't have time for anything but getting the work done. We both always delivered.
>
> We brought in another third partner a few years into the business, but he wound up stirring up chaos, not being the answer. The magic was how the two of us worked. We never did anything the easy way. The fact that two women could stay together in business twelve years is remarkable. We were much more different years ago—I was corporate, task oriented, and not very effusive, Sheila was more the hippie and much more emotionally open. Now we both dress alike and we're more alike personally.
>
> Once we almost ended the partnership—Sheila was exhausted and she had enough and walked out—but she came back. The trick is that, together, we produce something special.

The Silver Palate products have since gone international from that first tiny take-out shop, and Sheila and Julee have sold their multimillion-dollar business, consulting with the new owner on a day-to-day basis. In analyzing their partnership further, they cited other factors as to why it worked for them and how it could have been improved:

1. They always acknowledged each other's contributions and value.
2. After a period of trial and error, they found that meeting on a daily basis to discuss operations was essential. Each was isolated from the other for most of the work day—Sheila in her kitchen, Julee at work or in the shop. While the distance gave them a perspective on what the other did, it kept them apart too much for day-to-day operational decisions. As a solution, Sheila met with Julee at her office to recap the previous day's business and to block out that day's needs.
3. In terms of expertise, partners should complement each other's strong points and not compete with each other. Julee won't cook professionally on her own; Sheila doesn't manage budget and concepts. Over the years, partners historically tend to learn each other's job and the mystique of the "other's" work is broken; sometimes the loss of mystique is coupled with a loss of respect, too. To uphold a balance in the partnership, Sheila and Julee have kept their specialties individualized.
4. If they had it to do over again, they would enlist the aid of a professional counselor—a disinterested third party—to meet with once a week to talk things out. Both women thought that with a therapist they could have resolved a number of little problems they couldn't deal with and let drag on too long.
5. If you are looking for a partner, they advise, don't start out as good friends. It was professional respect that sustained them. Friendship is a preconceived relationship that has nothing to do with getting a job done. More critical, friendship can be destroyed during tough times; is it also more difficult to confront the other when the air is emotionally charged. A lot of the decision-making process that is involved in business never enters into friendship.

6. Be clear on your goals, how much time you want to give the business, and what you want to get out of it financially, and how much you will sacrifice to get it.

Sheila and Julee were an interesting study in complementary skills—Sheila with her cooking ability and Julee with the marketing know-how. What they had to learn was how to get along as partners in a relationship that was, in many ways, as intense as a marriage. They succeeded with talent, trial and error, tenacity, energy, and a joint belief in what they were doing.

THE MARRIED PARTNERS—MAKING THE PARTNERSHIP WORK

Starting in a business that has a concept, a flexible plan of action, and a clear division of labor as with The Silver Palate seems the prudent way to go about building success. And allowing for some improvisation and early "on the job" training, they pretty much knew in what direction they were heading. Laura and Gerhard Gschwandtner, though, built a successful Wisconsin publishing company from a "one-shot" mail-order newsletter they never expected to take off. Quite inadvertently they had a business on their hands and were willing to take the risk to see where it could go. It went far.

Neither Gerhard nor Laura, two interesting Reinventors, had publishing experience. Gerhard, Belgian-born and living in America only four years at the time, was on the road giving sales training seminars; Laura, a painter with a studio in her home, was also taking care of their three small children under the age of five. Then Gerhard decided to package his system in an audiovisual course sold through direct mail—the first step toward reinventing his career. In one of his mailings, he placed an ad for article reprints and newsletter reorders at a nominal sum. The response was good and Gerhard thought it was a fluke. He tried again and the same thing happened. Laura congratulated him on having a business, to which he replied, "*Which* business?" Laura said, "*Publishing!*" Gerhard was not quite convinced. Laura said:

> I saw the newsletter as the start of something to pursue, even if we didn't know anything about publishing. I'm a big risk taker—I love upsetting the apple cart and constructing something at the same time.
>
> My husband said he'd make a deal with me to test it out. He asked me to write a half page ad soliciting subscriptions. He thought ten people would respond. We got 1,200 paid subscriptions at $12 each from a mailing to 30,000 people—a very good response on the average. Now we had a tabloid called "Personal Selling Power" and we had to produce it six times a year. Gerhard opened an office in our garage and hired a secretary. We quickly outgrew our home office and moved twice more.
>
> Now when I look at it I think, ignorance is bliss.

When Gerhard asked Laura to work with him on the tabloid, Laura had little idea of how to contribute. She had no office skills, but eventually, through necessity, she'd discover her abilities to edit free-lance articles and write about sales and selling under her byline. Over the years as the paper grew, she took on more tasks. But within their success the delicate balance of their personal relationship seesawed. Once the business was set up, Laura had to deal with a role change from wife to worker within a company her husband had structured.

When the issue is not "who's the boss" or "who is doing what," but how to accommodate each other and get the work done *without* the added burden of emotional baggage, then ties may really be strained. The marital relationship is always there—day and night. An office partnership is one thing and has certain practical demands; the intimate relationship is another issue, with other needs. How do two people walk the fine line between professionalism and intimacy, stay in business—and stay married?

In the beginning, Laura felt Gerhard was overly harsh in his criticism of her work and Gerhard thought she was overly emotional in her response. Laura thought Gerhard would have been more diplomatic in his approach if she were not his wife and he thought she should have been more professional in her delivery. Basically, Laura didn't see her husband as her boss and Gerhard didn't see Laura as a partner *or* a coworker. Neither one knew where the relationship was. Business had created out of it a whole new marriage. Laura explained:

> It took us a year and a half to establish a good working relationship. It was easy to see why. The direction our marriage had been going was in discussing vacations, sex, food, and the children. Now we were having board meetings at home and it was about business, *our fourth child.*
>
> We figured out how to deal with both. It's important to us to keep the family close, and with both of us working together, the kids can always find us. We set our own hours and cover for each other. Our future security is under control as much as it can be. And I like the fact that we see each other a lot. I know the problems he's dealing with and there are no power struggles in our marriage.

Laura, as a partner, "stocks the store," runs the publication, which now comes out eight times a year, and runs the editorial side of all their ventures. Gerhard creates new products and runs the business, as publisher and founder.

It takes a tremendous amount of energy and effort to run a business; when it's successful, you must keep pace with it. For the Gschwandtners, it means long-range plans, five or ten years into the future. They also feel they are building something for their children, giving them the option of joining them in the organization, spinning something off of it, or going on their own.

THE INITIATOR: FROM SECRETARY TO CONTRACTOR

Other such idea people can become entrepreneurs—they are the initiators. Intense, focused, single-minded, tireless, they are people like Susan Terry who are willing to go it alone. What motivates people like Susan to begin a creative enterprise or start a business is sometimes the sudden connection to a simple truth: Although not fully tested, you instinctively know that you are as capable of accomplishment as the person who hired you. When "*I can do that,*" is less a case of bravado and more a statement of gritty belief in oneself, it can signal a kickoff to a rising career. And if anyone has the opportunity for such epiphanies, it is the *secretary* with vision, street smarts, and ambition.

Susan Terry, a winner of Avon's "Women of Enterprise" award, was in such a secretarial position at a Des Moines plumbing firm, when she figured out how far she could go: She would be a builder of houses. She was only twenty-three years old then, but the idea *felt* right. Part of her interest in the trade was earnings: She'd met many builders through the plumbing firm and knew what their income was: a lot more than what she made. In fact, she discovered ditch diggers made more in a few days than she earned in a month as a secretary. Other observations spurred her on: All these men, she determined, were of *average* intelligence, but they were out-earning her, and she was as smart as they were. She was resolute about starting her own business.

Armed with a how-to book on how to build houses, Susan quit her job and enlisted her husband to be her partner. An estimator at the same plumbing firm, he was not only supportive, he agreed to help her get the financing for her first project.

Money was the big issue. At first, two friends of her husband's were asked in as partners, but as "non–risk takers who were afraid to invest," they quickly backed out. Susan's second disappointment came when the bank turned them down for a loan. She took the rejection gracefully and planned her next move. When she remembered meeting a banker at a party, she decided to call him and make an appointment. Thirty days later, Susan got her loan.

Still a little short of cash for a lot on which to build, she called a Texas friend and asked him to invest $5,000 in her venture. They agreed to terms and Susan built, and sold, the house and property. Susan still calls him to invest with her in real estate. She was on her way to "having it all"—a goal that appealed to her at the time. Her business looked like it would take off, she knew how to get backing; she was married to a man she loved and they were planning a family. I asked her how it felt going from secretary to entrepreneur:

> Since I'm a risk taker, I didn't give the change a lot of thought. Instead, I concentrated on how much the house would cost to

build and how much I could sell it for. I just took control, knowing I can do it. I used my skills in bookkeeping and managing details, which are important skills to being a good contractor. That was the easy part. The hard part was coming face-to-face with being treated like a second class citizen. I had some difficulty in being a woman in charge: some of the men I'd hired to work on the house had problems with my telling them what to do.

Then tragedy struck. Susan's husband was killed accidentally when a ditch caved in on him at a house she was building. He was thirty-three years old; Susan was thirty—widowed with a ten-day-old baby who was ill and hospitalized and a three-year-old child.

Susan credits her great spiritual faith in pulling her through the devastation of extreme loss. And needing more grounding, she joined a women's support group in Des Moines—called the "Survivors"—who met once a month over the course of three years. Each woman had survived a devastating event—incest, death of a loved one, rape by a relative—and convened to manage their feelings while learning to cope. The group recently disbanded, having accomplished their mission—including writing a book about their experiences.

Remarried in 1984 to her accountant, Susan's business has expanded enormously. She has several partnerships, real estate holdings, as well as lube center and car wash franchises. As with many women with successful careers and families, she seeks a balance within her life.

Susan's attitude incorporates spirituality, practicality, and the need for others—support groups, feedback, and reality checks. She has an aphorism she keeps on her desk: "Success is never final and failure is never fatal." It's something she believes in:

> Success is an ongoing thing. I know I'm in a volatile business. If I go broke, I'll do it elegantly and go into something else. If I fail, it's okay. I can live with it. I can always find other places to put my energy. I'm comfortable with who I am.

A "natural" entrepreneur, Susan focuses first on her goal, expending very little effort on doubts, downsides, and obstacles.

Although she sought backing from establishment sources and was turned down, she coolly put contingency plans—some of them improvised—into effect: Everyone is a likely investor until they say no. She synthesizes information in a smart and useful manner and, most of all, she is willing to take a chance on her dreams.

THE SIDELINE ENTREPRENEUR: CASTING A WIDER NET

When you hear that Gail Koch, partner in a successful recruiting firm and cofounder of a flourishing ethnic gift food shop, once thought of herself as an "insecure misfit," you may be surprised that this confident, robust businesswoman was ever unskilled and directionless. A wide-eyed blonde with an engaging personality, Gail's struggle and ultimate professional triumph—as with many women of her generation—evolved out of a financial need following the breakup of her first marriage. Along the road to simply earning a living, she discovered the range of her skills and how to accomplish the kind of goals worthy of a classic Builder.

Soon after college, a "sure paycheck" job as a caseworker for the city sustained her for six years. Gail knew she had potential, ill defined though it was. Motivated by a fear of failure and an urgent bottom-line sensibility, Gail agented craftspeople on weekends and nights. Gail was in the right arena, though the wrong product—sales suited her. When she was offered a job in telemarketing selling high-tech products to the brokerage community, she took it and excelled, meeting her year's quota in one month. After two years there, she defined her direction—to specialize in high-tech products and develop the kind of expertise that would separate her from the pack.

Over the next six years, she was recruited in managerial sales positions at a number of companies, moving up and now defining the measure of her success by the amount of money she made. Wanting to switch jobs, Gail went to a recruiter, who, instead of finding her a job, asked her to join the company as a partner. It was something Gail wanted for herself, and for the first time since her daughter's birth, she felt she could take a professional risk without worrying about money. Another circumstance had newly changed her life, making this career change possible for her, even giving her the "opportunity to fail." The circumstance was marrying her second husband—the brother of New York's former mayor Ed Koch—whom she met on a sales call. I asked her how she made the step from employee to entrepreneur:

> When I became a recruiter, I wanted to go in with some strength. So I specialized in what I knew from the sales end—high tech. I thought that throwing out my nine years of experience in the industry wasn't a good idea. Instead, I defined my skills, redefined and built on them. I was still a little insecure about my abilities, but I "packaged" myself as a business and sold my competitive edge.
>
> Being responsible for the care of a child 100 percent left me no choice but to succeed as best I could. I might have been fearful at my other jobs, but I went forward anyway. Then I married into a situation where I could test myself in a new business and not worry about survival. It was scary, but less so.

"New York To Go," her ethnic gift food business, came to her on a fluke. Former clients who'd been impressed with her from her telemarketing days tracked her down. They had a concept, not yet fully developed, about wanting to set up a small business at the airports around New York. Gail met with them and they came up with a product. They'd sell bagels as a specialty item, six to a box, the boxes designed and constructed to look like pop-art New York yellow cabs. Her partners put up the money and Gail handled the start-up details and store management.

As Gail soon discovered, opening a shop in an airline terminal was not a simple matter of signing a lease and moving in. A quick education on the complicated logistics of opening shops in airline terminals and a few lessons in decoding the chain of command among airline officials and airline terminal landowners led her to a conclusion: She needed leverage, a gimmick. Airlines were going through harder times, then, and Gail thought they would welcome extra revenue. She did a study of how many people used major airlines each day, projected how much passengers would spend on her product, and what percentage the airline would get. She packaged "New York To Go" as an edible souvenir and left six bagels in her logo box as a calling card . . . and Eastern Airlines said yes.

Still in partnership as a recruiter, she opened a kiosk at the terminal, hiring a manager to run it. Shortly after, her original partners sold their share and Gail reopened with a more experienced management at the Delta terminal. Gail expanded beyond bagels to include "edible New York," such as Mrs. Grimbel's Cheesecake, Yonah Shimmel's Knishes, and products from Sarabeth's Kitchen. A growing business, Gail hopes to take the concept on an international level.

A Builder with strong Synthesizer skills, Gail is a highly regarded expert in the high-tech recruiting industry and an entrepreneur—a dual career that equally demands of her a unique selling approach and marketing acumen. With all her triumphs, surprisingly, it wasn't until she established "New York To Go" that Gail believed in her abilities as a good businesswoman. In evaluating her own experience, she concluded about the process of shifting gears:

> If you sell yourself on the commonality factor of your experience—seeing the common threads in defining your skills—I think you'll be successful. If your energy is diffused, you'll fail. Being a generalist is a luxury—it doesn't have much power. I believe in using your history and knowing your strengths. If you sell in an industry and hate selling, stay in the industry and redefine your skills. *Adapt.* I wouldn't have succeeded unless I had.
>
> I'm a firm believer in knowing how much you want to make and working backward. You should know what your end goals are, then figure out how to get there. Take objections first, then see how to act.

Sometimes you don't know what you don't know—but you have an impulse to leap at a tiny opening—the possibility that tells you you have nothing to lose. You may not have any experience in business at all; what you do have is fearlessness. A naivete that propels you forward . . . into success.

EPILOGUE

This is the true joy in life, the being used for a purpose recognized by yourself as a mighty one; the being a force of nature instead of a feverish, selfish little clod of ailments and grievances complaining that the world will not devote itself to making you happy.

I am of the opinion that my life belongs to the whole community and as long as I live it is my privilege to do for it whatever I can.

I want to be thoroughly used up when I die, for the harder I work the more I live. I rejoice in life for its own sake. Life is no "brief candle" to me. It is a sort of splendid torch which I have got hold of for the moment, and I want to make it burn as brightly as possible before handing it on to future generations.

George Bernard Shaw
from Man and Superman,
dedicatory letter

Appearing as guests on a talk show, two popular newspaper and television film critics spoke about the business of being reviewers and how they got to where they are. One of them added a humbling footnote to the story of his ascent through reviewerdom. He said that while he's often envied for the work he does, and America, in general, may think he's doing just fine, it's not always so. A friend of his mother's frequently asks her "if her son has a *job* yet or if he's still just going to the movies."

As much as it's a quaint and funny remark, so is it a parable for our times: It expresses the conflict of beliefs about the worth and purpose of a person's trade. Whether or not you believe that film criticism is a plausible occupation for which you can be very highly paid or a frivolous enterprise will pretty much depend on your interpretation of work. And, clearly, film reviewing is not *work* as this woman knows it.

In a very real way, this telling remark raises questions that millions of people in conflict over their careers ask themselves every day. What is work for me—or am I "just going to the movies?" What is my life for? How important is it for me to like what I do? How much will others influence the career choice I made for myself?

This is what *Shifting Gears* wants to help you answer.

As you know, understanding what you want from work and what is expected of you can change with or without your input or effort. The business world is no longer a predictable, paternalistic force, characterized by the "powerful" and the "powerless" enacting ritual forms of behavior and manners. Business is about *fitting in* and, hopefully, *Shifting Gears* has provided a foundation of information, guidance, and inspiration to help you achieve this.

You're among the first generation of people who have radically affected the relationship between the corporation and the individual:

- "The company" is no longer the masterful giant that takes care of you for life and where, no matter how you feel about the work you do, change is unthinkable.
- The definition of company loyalty has changed from long-term acquiescence to short-term barter.
- Credentials do not necessarily imply a lifetime stay in one field of expertise.
- And the words "career change" no longer signify indecision or lack of commitment, but personal growth and expression and an understanding of opportunity in the marketplace.

FINDING THE ANSWERS FOR YOURSELF

Most of the people I interviewed for this book started out with certain beliefs about "work" and "career" but nearly all of them changed their opinions along the way. They learned that life isn't linear, predictable, and fully under one's control. *Exposure* to new ideas, technologies, and to the people involved with making the world interesting as well as keeping it running can be life changing. *Experience* in the marketplace validates your skills and competencies—you get a truer sense of your limitations and a valuable sense of how you can build, what skills you can "layer," and how you want to reinvent yourself.

As much as this book is about finding a fulfilling career direction, so is it a book about dealing with change. Joan Kron, the editor of the glossy *Avenue* magazine, told me something I heard similarly from a number of other creative people. At a few critical points in her career she wasn't sure what to do next but she could move toward something when she could say, "*I can do that!*" "That looks easy" is not said in vain by those who have confidence in their creativity but sometimes don't know where to put it. For them, change *is* easier.

My step-by-step examination of change is designed to prepare you for one thing: to shift gears successfully.

To guide you, think about these key five points again:

1. *Know Yourself:* Examine your work style in detail. Are you:

- a "Lifer" ("monogamous" and cautious of change, you tend to be fully committed to one industry or one job within an industry);
- a "Synthesizer" (more versatile and adventurous, you build up—or "layer"—skill/responsibility/power bases that can transfer from industry to industry);
- a "Builder" (you hew to one profession, but find a *second* one to work in simultaneously that is equally important to you);
- a "Reinventor" (using your skills and talents to really shift gears, you change professions one or more times).

When you clarify your style and determine where your strengths are, you free yourself to be the best of who you are.

2. *Change Is Your Friend:* Change is inevitable and to thrive in this world you need to accept it for its benefits—not damn it for its clout. New York career counselor Leslie Rose says that change

is not just about discarding things, it's also about making sound judgments to reach your goal.

Search *change* for the opportunities rather than counting the losses.

3. Understand the Trigger Points: Proof that things can never stay the same is never more apparent than with a trigger. It can blast into your life via *loss* or through a more thoughtful *internal* decision. If you've gotten fired or were the last Samson to hold up the walls while your company crashed around you, or the company merged and you were moved laterally into a dead-end job, you know that moment of truth has created a situation where you must make a change.

Perhaps you've committed yourself to a career, but five or ten or twenty-five years later you know in your heart that *it's over.* You're treading water, bored, going nowhere, and now it's time to reach out for something else. This revelation, too, is a trigger.

Triggers send you out into the world, and bring with them a range of emotions as you adjust to this limbo period. You worry that you'll never work again, you go through a crisis of confidence, you feel vulnerable.

You're not alone! You can get through this sensitive stage if you take it step-by-step and know that you must . . .

4. Take Risks: The trigger has given you another chance to live the life you want to live and do the kind of work you want to do. In the end, you have to decide how hard you want to shift gears and commit to something that is meaningful to you. What are you willing to do to reach your goals?

A restaurateur who lost his popular eatery after twelve years in business told me how he almost got stuck "with the bathrobe factor." Depressed over the loss of his place, Bob crashed, unable to look for another business or a job. For nearly three months he shuffled around the house, ignoring offers. One morning he caught sight of himself—a gray figure in a bathrobe, feeling sorry for himself—and he saw himself clearly. Normally a risk taker, Bob got caught up in his fears for his future and lived as if he had none.

We all fall, we all suffer. Taking risks is life affirming; the "bathrobe factor" keeps you trapped, literally or figuratively, within four walls.

5. *Find the Support You Need:* Nearly everyone I interviewed for this book asked for help. They sought advice from career counselors, psychotherapists, support groups, and mentors; they were willing to "audition" jobs to see what they were like; to take jobs in a different industry at a lower salary, just to get a foot in the door; they were willing to go back to school, if that was required.

To shift gears, you often have to go back to neutral before you once again can go full speed. If it's what you want, it's worth all the pain, all the efforts, and all the triumphs.

A FINAL NOTE

We are blessed, or cursed, as the Chinese see it, of living "in interesting times." Change and possibilities, variety and options, expansion and increase—these times are not only interesting, but *remarkable.* It is the career choice you make that will determine how your future will shape up, and how remarkable it can be.

The world is in flux, changing all the time. In one way, things will never be the way they were—but that's okay: They can be better. The best that we can give to ourselves is our strength, flexibility, and the understanding that we are going to change. You will have many chances to do many things in this life and be all the things you want to be.

It's my great hope that this book has been of help in steering you onto a clear road ahead, vision unobstructed, and that your journey will be a great adventure.

APPENDIX

PUTTING THE ANATOMY OF CHANGE TO WORK

The following exercises are an outgrowth of the ideas presented in this book. They are used as part of a workshop given as a companion to this book. For more information on *Shifting Gears* workshops, contact Carole Hyatt, 7 West 81 Street, New York, NY 10024

1. The purpose of this time line is to help you clarify what ideas, values, and interests are important to you for the rest of your work life.

A) Please fill in the dates:

CAREER TIME LINE

Year started work	***Current year***	***Last year you plan to work***

B) Draw a connecting line from the current year to the last year you plan to work. Drawing this "basket of time" will give you a visual sense of the time you have left to make improvements in your work life. The fewer years you have allocated to work, the smaller your basket of time will be, so get motivated to change! The greater sense of urgency you will have to change.

C) Ask yourself the following questions:
—With the work life I have left, what would I like to accomplish?
Be as specific or general as you would like.
—What kinds of satisfaction do I want from my work?
—What new skills do I want to learn or incorporate in my work?
—What other of my interests do I want to incorporate into my work life?
—What problems would I like to be able to solve as part of my work?
—What kind of work team do I want to be a part of? How do I want to interact with work colleagues and peers?
—What work-related mission do I envision? Do I want to be part of a goal in a local, U.S., or global community?
—Where would I like my retirement notice to appear and what would I like it to say?

2. What values are most important to you? What values do you want to be part of your next career? Choose and rank five values/items in terms of importance to you—5 being highest, 1 being lowest.

__ Money
__ Flexible schedule
__ Job security/stability
__ Finding a mate
__ Stimulation/learning
__ Relocation
__ Respect from colleagues
__ Autonomy/starting own business
__ Job advancement
__ Opportunity to build credentials
__ Other(s)

3. List the talents, skills, interests, and/or hobbies you would like to incorporate into your next career. (You will have thought of some in Question 1.)

4. The following categories are designed so that you can identify your comfort level in your work. Your style may change over time—you may also find you identify with more than one category. Mark down your M.O. based on descriptions from Chapter 2:

__ Lifer
__ Builder
__ Synthesizer
__ Reinventor

5. Using the previous four exercises, you are now ready to develop a set of guidelines that you wish to follow in your next career. Guidelines are formed by incorporating your needs, values, skills, likes and dislikes, and M.O. into set descriptions. For example, here are two of my guidelines: "I never want to run a company again. I need projects with definite beginnings, middles, and ends; that have flexible hours; stimulation and learning; respect from colleagues; and that bring in enough money to maintain my current lifestyle." And "These projects must incorporate my communication skills, love of travel, and 'build' (my M.O.) on what I already know, as well as 'synthesize' with new titles and responsibilities."
List five guidelines:

6. Using the guidelines you have created, you can now collect job/career titles. To do this, tell or write down your guidelines for friends, colleagues, experts, and family members so they can tell you what occupations/job titles they think match your guidelines. Do not eliminate any suggestions at this stage. Write down each job title on a slip of paper and keep them in a box. Once you have at least 30 title possibilities, choose five that appeal to you the most and write them down. You will have a focused set of directions/opportunities to explore.
Note: The more specific you have been in answering the above questions, the better job-title handle you will now achieve. So if you still feel vague about responses to previous questions, take the time now to hone in—and solidify—them, before approaching individuals for their responses to your guidelines.
(Minimum of) five next career/job titles:

7. Using your selected job titles, gather marketplace and trend information regarding the careers/fields reflected by these job titles: list pertinent information you find (this question refers to Chapters 1, 7, and 8).

8. Now take this information one step further and combine your job/career title with marketplace information, to come up with *adaptive career options*. For example: job/career title (seminar leader) + marketplace information (the need for advancement for women in the Pacific Rim) = *adaptive action*: Using American women as role models, give seminars in the Pacific Rim about women's roles, and subsequently create a new market niche. To achieve this goal, I will need to find a communications partner (part of the adaptive action). List adaptive actions you can explore (this question refers to Chapter 8).

9. You already have people in your life who can act as your advisors in choosing a new career path. Assign them now to help you and keep them in mind (this exercise refers to Chapters 7 and 8).

10. Your contacts are not just in your personal sphere: Reach out for specific names of experts, professionals, associations, clubs, counselors, courses, etc., and list them (this exercise refers to Chapters 7 and 8).

11. What specific tasks do you want to accomplish in the given amount of time(s) listed below, in terms of exploring the career options/paths you have now identified?

Time Table (Example)

3 months	*6 months*	*1 year*	*3 years*

12. If you really want to live by the aspects of work and the guidelines you have outlined, then make yourself accountable to another person by signing a contract, stating your intention to complete the preceding exercises. Make sure to choose a partner who will keep you accountable and not let you break the agreement.

Devise a schedule of check-in dates to discuss progress with your partner. You may need to check in as often as every day, or as seldom as every month.

Check-in dates:

INDEX

accomplishments, clarifying of, 190–191
Adaire, Jennifer, 228–30
adaptive action, 154–57, 158
  personality or personal history and, 155–56
  skills and competencies in, 154–55, 157
  use of, 156–57
addictions, 127–30
Alcoholics Anonymous, 179
alcoholism, 127–30, 179
ambiguity, tolerance for, 234
American Management Association, 24
Amos, Wally, 63–66
Anselmo, Anne, 98–99
arrogance, 92–95
Asher, Millie, 189–91
Ashley, Barbara, 162–64, 174
attitudes:
  about work, changes in, 26, 30–33
  adaptive action and, 157
  see also self-defeating attitudes

Baker, Norman and Mary Ann, 174–178
banking, 138
Barber, Ben, 40–41
Barkley, Nella, 84, 85
Barton, Celia, 123–24, 125
Bazelmans, Genevieve, 126–27
behavior, adaptive action and, 157
belief systems, 254–55
  consistency and, 97–98
  test of, as trigger, 90, 97–100, 105
Bellamy, Carol, 70–71, 76, 77
Berman, Norman, 40
blaming, 151–52
Block, Lois, 228
Boland, Rev. Jack, 179–80
Bolles, Richard Nelson, 194, 213
Bostwick, Burdette, 201
Bosworth, Phyllis, 71–74, 77, 215

Bowles, Stan, 34–35
Brenner, Don, 135–36
"bridge" jobs, 66–67
Bright, Anne, 138
Browne, Terri, 141–42
Buddha, 19–20
Builders, 56–62, 78, 256
  Lifers vs., 56, 57, 62
  profile of, 62
Bureau of Labor Statistics, 22, 35, 36
Burke, Edmund, 13
burning one's bridges, 120
burnout, 138
Burzynski, Stanislaw, 101–2
Bush, George, 215
business schools, 40

Cabrera, James C., 189
Cardin, Rick, 239, 240–41
career changes:
  doubts and fears in, 14–15
  options in, 26, 33–41
  reasons for, 12
  statistics on, 22–23
  summary of key points in, 256–58
  see also specific topics
career counseling, 192–96
  approaches in, 193–94
  building self-concept in, 194–96
  function of, 193
  self-assessment techniques in, 196, 197, 199–200
career path, defining of, 18, 187–210
  career investigation and, 188, 191–96
  outplacement services and, 188–91
  "safety net" auditions and, 188, 207–10
  self-assessment techniques and, 188, 196–200
  support groups and, 188, 204–7
  twenty-page résumés and, 188, 200–4
careers:
  conflicts between personal life and, 110, 141–43
  investigation of, 188, 191–96
  jobs vs., 46–47
  personal life affected by choice of, 90–91
  progression of, 31–32
career time line, 259–63
Carter, Jimmy, 215
Carter, Ron, 138
celebrity, 136
change, 18, 145–58, 256
  adaptive action as key to, 154–57, 158
  anatomy of, 17–19
  defining emotional line around, 146–48
  fear of, 153–54
  inevitability of, 19–20
  instincts about, 147–48
  most common obstacles to, 148–154
  as slowly revolving spiral, 18–19
chemistry problems, terminations and, 93
childhood refrains, reliving of, 110, 112–19
  key event from past and, 113–15
  meaning of, 118–19
  sense of obligation and, 115–16
  an unrealistic fear that event will recur, 116–18
Chrysler, Walter, 159
CMRA's (Convenience Mail Receiving Agencies), 239
commitment, 214, 217, 233
  change in attitudes about, 31
communications, 26, 27–29, 35
competencies, 157
  skills vs., 154–55
confidence, 194–95, 214
conformity, 31
confrontation, avoiding of, 149
confusion, 108
consistency, belief systems and, 97–98
consultants, 32
contacts, of entrepreneurs, 234
Cook, Pat, 123, 140
counseling, *see* career counseling
Craig, Van, 67–68, 69–70
creating openings, 216, 226–27

credentials, 255
  lack of, 212
  overemphasis on, 110, 133–37
criticism, sensitivity to, 152
Crystal, John, 194

Davis, Adelle, 101
decisions:
  either/or, 153, 161
  "have to," 150
  multiple choices and, 150–51
denial, 108–9, 138–39, 195
desperation, as trigger, 179
"Dictionary of Occupational Titles, The," 200
downsizing, 24
downtrends, getting stuck in, 18, 106–44
  career—personal life conflicts and, 110, 141–43
  credentials and, 110, 133–37
  emotions and, 106–9
  "if only" refrains and, 110–12
  most common reactions to, 108–9
  reality checks and, 109
  reliving childhood refrains and, 110, 112–19
  risk avoidance and, 110, 130–33
  self-defeating attitudes and, 110, 119–30
  staying on and, 110, 137–41
dreams:
  "someday . . .," 161, 174–78
  "what if," 110–11
drive, of entrepreneurs, 233
Drucker, Peter, 174
drug addiction, 127–30
duty, false sense of, 115–16

education, 38–41, 192, 229
either/or dilemmas, 153, 161
emotions:
  getting stuck in downtrends and, 106–9
  in response to change, 146–48
Employment Management Association, 24
empty promises, 95
energy, of entrepreneurs, 233
Entrepreneur, 234
entrepreneurs, 63, 231–53
  categories of, 235
  characteristics of, 209–10
  circumstantial, 231–32, 233
  courses and expertise sources for, 232
  failure rate of, 239
  franchisers, 235, 237–42
  increase in number of, 24
  initiators, 235, 248–51
  marketplace understanding needed by, 234
  married partners as, 235, 246–48
  niche markets for, 232–33
  partners as, 235, 242–46
  planners, 235–37
  qualities needed by, 233–34
  "safety net" auditions and, 188, 207–10
  sideline, 235, 251–53
Esserman, June, 15
ethics, conflicts of, 98–100
evolution, 147–48
excellence, perfectionism vs., 125
excuses, 148, 152
expectations, 150, 152
experiental learning, 38–39
explorers, 175–78
"extender" jobs, 33, 35–36
extremes, thinking in, 120

failure, 240, 250
  fear of, 123–25
fait accompli approach, 216, 219–20
false hope, 149
false pride, 120
fantasies, of revenge, 121–23
fatalism, 120
fate, *see* twists of fate
Fayne, Robert, 235–37
fear, 152
  of change, 153–54
  of failure, 123–25
  getting stuck in downtrends and, 108
  of making wrong choice, 150

of rejection, 224–26
as response to trigger, 84–85
that event from past will recur, 116–18
feedback, 234
feelings:
imparting disproportionate importance to, 120
see also emotions
Feldenkrais, Moshe, 167
Feria, Dan, 95
Ferraro, Geraldine, 91–92
firings, *see* terminations
Flores, Fernando, 169
Forbes, 29, 153, 242
Ford, Henry, 52
foreign culture, influences of, 26–27
franchising, 235, 237–42
drawbacks of, 238–39
main selling points of, 238
originating ideas for, 239–41
two types of people attracted to, 238
Friedan, Betty, 101, 141
Fuller, R. Buckminster, 100–101
future:
getting stuck in, 110–11
uncertainty of, 13–14

generalists, 253
George, Sherri, 110–11
Gibraltar Transmission Corporation, 240, 241
globalization of business, 26–27
goals, 47, 197, 203
"someday . . ." dreams and, 161, 174–78
support groups and, 204–7
Goldwyn, Sam, 158
Goodman, Brenda, 80
Gottlieb, Linda, 41–43
Grant, Rosalind, 95–96
Green, Robert L., 220–22, 224
Greenspon, William, 74–76
Greer, Germaine, 101
Gschwandtner, Laura and Gerhard, 246–48
guidelines, structure vs., 15–16

Hafner, Dorothy, 151
Halpern, Vic, 138–40
Harding, Marjorie, 87–88
Harrigan, Betty Lehan, 142–43
Harris, T. George, 170, 172–74
Hartley, Mariette, 222–24
Harvard University Business School, 233
"have to" decisions, 150
"having it all," 142
Heard, George, 193
helping others, 161, 178–86
Heyerdahl, Thor, 175–76
Holland Vocational Guidance test, 199–200
home businesses, 34, 38
hope, false, 149
Howell, Francesca, 204–7
Hyatt, Gordon, 217–18

ideals, adjusting to marketplace truths, 216, 222–24
"if only" refrains, 110–12
illness, as trigger, 82–83
impasses, 96–97
"imposter syndrome," 195
information, adaptive action and, 157
information technology, 26, 27–29
initiative, taking of, 216–19
initiators (entrepreneurs), 235, 248–251
interpersonal problems, 121, 125–127
terminations and, 93
interviews:
standard questions in, 214
training for, 215–16
intrapreneuring, 24, 34, 36–38
"It Doesn't Feel Right" Syndrome, 120

Japan, 26–27
Jenner, Bruce, 170–72
Jerris, Linda, 135, 137–38
jobs, careers vs., 46–47
Johnson, Samuel, 210
Jones, Christopher, 184–86

Kagan, Diane, 156
Kahn, Herman, 23
Kalin, Dr., 136
Kanter, Rosabeth Moss, 207
Keller, Helen, 9
Kelley, Nick, 57–59, 62
Kelly, Jean, 24
Kievman, Beverly, 131
Kiser, Virginia, 180–82
Kloss, Jethro, 101
Koch, Gail, 251–53
Kraselsky, Bruce, 24–25, 40
Kroc, Ray, 239
Kron, Joan, 256
Krulewitch, Deborah, 66–67, 68, 69
Kuhn, Daniel, 113, 118, 119

Langley, John, 201–2, 203
Larson, Scott, 86–87
Lawson, Bob, 87
layoffs, 24, 29
Lee, Michael, 182–84
letters, in selling oneself, 227
"life line," 199
Lifers, 48–56, 63, 77–78, 178, 256
  Builders vs., 56, 57, 62
  in changing companies, 50–52
  innovative, 53–56
  profile of, 55–56
  second careers of, 164–67
loss:
  blaming as response to, 151–52
  common reactions to, 95
  fear of, 148
  impasses and, 96–97
  numbness as response to, 108–9
  as trigger, 31, 90–97, 100–101, 105
loyalty, 31, 255
  conflicting ethics and, 98–99
Luce, Henry, 173
Lukins, Sheila, 243–46

McDonald's, 239
"Mainstream," 199
marketplace, 18, 25–45, 234
  adjusting ideals to truths of, 216, 222–24
  and changing attitudes about work, 26, 30–33
  foreign influences and, 26–27
  need for information about, 157
  options in, 26, 33–41
  restructuring and, 26, 29–30
  staying in tune with, 44–45
  success stories about know-how in, 41–44
  technology and, 26, 27–29
married partners, 235, 246–48
Marsh, Dan, 155
Mason, Jackie, 155–56
Mastin, Phil, 121–23
middle managers, 23, 31–32, 33
mission, pursuit of, 90, 100–105
mistakes, acknowledging of, 151–52
money, as measure of success, 233
Money, 238
Moore, Lynn, 142
Morin, William J., 93, 189
motivation, 31, 32–33, 203, 204
  lack of, 120
  triggers and, 82–84
multiple choices, 150–51
Myers-Briggs test, 199

Naisbitt, John, 202
National Business Employment Weekly, 192
networking, 51, 192
"new age" approaches, 32–33, 196
Newbourg, Margaret, 207–10, 233
niche markets, 232–33
"no," crisis of, 149–50
Nobel, Alfred, 86
numbness, sense of, 108–9

Obadia, Yvette, 92, 118
objections of potential employers, overcoming of, 218
obligation, sense of, 115–16
O! Deli Corporation, 239, 240–41
opportunities, seizing of, 216, 227–228, 233
outplacement services, 188–91

packaging oneself, 216–30
  adjusting ideals to marketplace truths in, 216, 222–24
  creating openings in, 216, 226–27
  fait accompli approach in, 216, 219–20
  playing wild card in, 216, 228–30
  putting spin on rejection in, 216, 224–26
  seizing opportunities in, 216, 227–228
  skill transfer and "seesaw" salary in, 216, 220–22
  taking initiative in, 216–19
Pak-Mail Inc., 239
partners, 235, 242–46
  choosing of, 242, 245
  married couples as, 235, 246–48
  successful, qualities of, 245–46
part-time businesses, 207–10
past:
  recreating key events from, 113–115
  reliving childhood refrains from, 110, 112–19
  yearning for, 111
paternalism, 140
path of least resistance, 150
Patton, Charlotte, 204–7
perfectionism, 121, 123–25, 142
Perls, Fritz, 96, 166–67
persistence, 214, 233–34
personability, 125–27
personal fulfillment, 23
personal history, adaptive action and, 155–56
personality, adaptive action and, 155–56
personal life, conflicts between career and, 110, 141–43
Peters, Harry, 132
Peters, Tom, 32, 85
Pinchot, Gifford, III, 36, 37
planners (entrepreneurs), 235–37
Pointer, Rob, 128–29
Polaroid Company, 32–33
"poor me" syndrome, 152–53, 161, 179
Porot, Daniel, 214
powerlessness, sense of, 109
presentation skills, 215–16
Previn, Dory, 113–15, 118, 181
pride, false, 120
"prisoner syndrome," 153–54
problem-solving ability, 233–34

Rabke, Barbara, 50–52, 55
Rand, Boris, 88
Rand Corporation, 22
reality, perception of, 107
reality checks, 109
  for career—personal life conflicts, 143
  for concern about credentials, 137
  for interpersonal problems, 127
  for living in wrong time frame, 111–12
  for past events running parts of one's life, 119
  for perfectionism, 125
  for revenge fantasies, 123
  for risk avoidance, 133
  for sensation seeking, 129–30
  for staying on, 140–41
Reinventors, 70–77, 78, 167, 256
  cycle of Synthesizer and, 162–64
  profile of, 76–77
  twists of fate and, 168–69
rejection, putting spin on, 216, 224–226
relocation, 34–35, 192
research:
  in defining of career path, 191–96
  on target company or industry, 204, 215
resources, of entrepreneurs, 234
restructuring, 23, 26, 29–30, 32, 35
résumés, 212
  terminations and, 201–2
  twenty-page, 188, 200–204
revenge fantasies, 121–23
revision, blaming vs., 152
Riley, Jack, 84
risk, 47, 56, 63, 69–70, 203–4, 233, 257
  avoidance of, 110, 130–33

Rivoli, Mario, 225
Rodale, J. I., 101
Rogers, Betsy Barlow, 167–69
Rose, Leslie, 133, 194–95, 256
Rosen, Jon, 215–16
Rosso, Julee, 243–46
Roth, Allie, 199–200
Rubenfeld, Ilana, 164–67
Ryder, Frank, 220

"safety net" auditions, 188, 207–10
salary, "seesaw," 216, 220–22
Sanfellipo, Joe, 239–41
Santini, Al and Alice, 115–18
Sartre, Jean-Paul, 178
saturation point, 87–88
school, going back to, 38–41, 192, 229
Schultz, Steve, 99–100
Schwartz, Bob, 52–55
security, 31, 55
"seesaw" salary, 216, 220–22
seizing opportunities to prove oneself, 216, 227–28, 233
self-acceptance, 186
self-assessment techniques, 188, 194, 196–200
  "life line," 199
  questions answered in, 197–98
  in selling oneself, 213–14
  tests, 196–97, 199–200
self-belief, 230
self-concepts, building of, 194–96
self-confidence, 204, 233
  support groups and, 204–7
self-defeating attitudes, 110, 119–30
  interpersonal problems and, 121, 125–27
  perfectionism, 121, 123–25
  revenge fantasies, 121–23
  sensation seeking, 121, 127–30
self-discovery, 159–86
  call of talent and, 161, 169–74
  "someday . . ." dreams and, 161, 174–78
  spirituality and, 161, 178–86
  twists of fate and, 161–69
self-esteem, 179
  job loss and, 108
  perfectionism and, 125
  rejection and, 224–26
self-help groups, 192
self-pity, 152–53
self-talk, 148
selling oneself, 18, 211–30
  adjusting ideals to marketplace truths in, 216, 222–24
  creating openings, 216, 226–27
  fait accompli approach in, 216, 219–20
  "handicaps" and, 212–13
  interview training and, 215–16
  inventive measures needed in, 213
  packaging oneself in, 216–30
  playing wild card in, 216, 228–30
  putting spin on rejection in, 216, 224–26
  seizing opportunities to prove oneself in, 216, 227–28
  self-assessment and research needed in, 213–15
  skill transfer and "seesaw" salary in, 216, 220–22
  taking initiative in, 216–19
sensation seeking, 121, 127–30
service jobs, 33, 35–36
Shalala, Donna, 39–40
Shaw, George Bernard, 105, 264
Shifting Gears workshops, 259
sideline entrepreneurs, 235, 251–53
Silicon Valley, 34
Silver Palate, 243–46
skills, 63, 69, 157, 192, 253
  assessment of, 108, 196–97, 198
  competencies vs., 154–55
  presentation, 215–16
  selling oneself and, 214
  specialization vs. diversification and, 202
  transferring of, at lower salary, 216, 220–22
Small Business Administration, 232
small businesses, 33, 34–35
Smith, Laurie Sanders, 204–7

Snyder, Wendy, 131–32
Sokolin, Gloria, 83
"someday . . ." dreams, 161, 174–78
spirituality, 161, 178–86
staying on, 110, 137–41
Stevenson, John, 92–95
Stewart, Mimi, 204–7
strategies, 203
stress, critical mass of, 87–88
structure, guidelines vs., 15–16
success, 136, 250
  money as measure of, 233
support, need for, 257–58
support groups, 188, 204–7, 250
Switzer, Katherine, 102–4
Synthesizers, 62–70, 77, 78, 167, 178, 184, 256
  cycle of Reinventor and, 162–64
  profile of, 69–70

talent, call of, 161, 169–74
technology, 26, 27–29, 35, 143, 154
terminations:
  chemistry problems and, 93
  outplacement services and, 188–91
  résumés and, 201–2
  self-esteem and, 108
Terry, Susan, 248–51
tests, self-assessment, 196–97, 199–200
therapy, "demons" from past and, 113, 118–19
time, mistaken concepts of, 110–12
time frames, realistic, 203
Toffler, Alvin, 38
triggers, 18, 79–105, 257
  description of, 79–80
  desperation as, 179
  feelings from childhood and, 112
  function of, 79
  incidents as, 80–81
  internal vs. external pushes as, 85–86
  loss as, 90–97, 100–101, 105
  most likely areas in life for, 89–105
  nonevents as, 85, 86–89
  pursuit of mission as, 90, 100–105
  responses to 81–85
  tests of belief systems as, 90, 97–100, 105
Trombetta, Le, 101–2
Trump, Donald, 29
twenty-page résumés, 188, 200–204
twists of fate, 161–69
  Lifers and, 164–67
  Reinventors and, 168–69
  Synthesizer/Reinventor/Synthesizer cycle and, 162–64
values, 22, 30
  see also belief systems
Verity, C. William, 29
Vreeland, Diana, 211–12

Walters, H. Bud, 49–50, 55, 167, 213
want ads, 192
Watts, Alan, 187
Weiner, Edith, 28, 32
Wesselman, Tom, 59–62
Westin, Av, 37
"what if" dreams, 110–11
"wild card" approach, 216, 228–30
women, career—personal life conflicts and, 141–43
Woodfin, Judy, 83
work:
  beliefs about worth of, 254–55
  as job vs. career, 46–47
workaholics, 128–29
work style, 18, 46–78, 256
  see also Builder; Lifers; Reinventors; Synthesizers
work week, shortening of, 25
World Future Society, 25, 35

Xerox Corporation, 36, 214

Yarosh, David, 85

Zackary, Chuck, 226–27
Zelig, 148
Zen philosophy, 223
Zuker, Elaina, 31

Carole Hyatt is a market and social behavior researcher, best-selling author, and worldwide lecturer. To date she has had seven different career titles in her "layered" worklife. Her longest stretch (eighteen years) was as president of Hyatt-Esserman Research Associates. The firm worked with Fortune 500 companies, government agencies, and philanthropic organizations. Her books, *The Women's Selling Game, Women and Work, When Smart People Fail* and *Shifting Gears,* are based on case studies of prominent and typical Americans.

Carole is on the worldwide speakers circuit and has spoken in forty states, Europe, Latin America, and Asia. The Carole Hyatt Success centers in Tokyo are entering their third year. Her television appearances include those on *Oprah Winfrey,* the *Today* show, *Good Morning America*, and *Sally Jesse Raphael.*

Carole lives in New York City with her husband, Gordon Hyatt. Their daughter, Ariel, is a college student.